MEMOIRS

"A Wonderful One Way Journey That Ends In Death"

K. V. CRANE

ISBN: 1499578679
ISBN 13: 9781499578676
Library of Congress Control Number: 2014909141
CreateSpace Independent Publishing Platform, North Charleston, South Carolina

Acknowledgments

For the task of converting my voice-recorded dictation to a first draft and the provision of preliminary editing, I owe much to Mathew Liston. For the extensive research documenting the Crane family origins from 1630, I owe much to Dr. Robert Kellogg Crane (1919–2010), chairman of the physiology department, Rutgers University Medical School, New Jersey.

I also owe much to the many books I frequently pull from my shelf that remind me of my past, clarify the present, and enlighten my future.

For their understanding and patience while assisting me as a story-teller, I owe much to my wife, my friends, my colleagues, and, especially, Joann Lake of Columbia-Greene Community College and the technical team at Amazon's CreateSpace.com.

Contents

"Destined to meet"

HAPPY SCHOOL DAYS
1941

PREFACE

The force and effects of the products of time are strange.

Hence, is there a heaven or hell?
Hence, where is heaven, and where is hell?
Hence, where are our deceased fathers, mothers, brothers, and sisters?

The answer, of course, is in one's *consciousness.* A consciousness ravaged by time, smoothed, mellowed, and invigorated by choices. Earthlings have experienced greater change in the past hundred years than in all prior recorded history, and our choices have multiplied. From cradle to grave, life is a supreme vocation of choices—choices that are strongly influenced by environment and heredity as the products of time bear down upon us.

Consider the life-altering choices spawned by a mere sample of the products of time.

Weapons, oil, religion, liquor, economics, horse travel, wars, electricity, refrigeration, atomic energy, people on the moon, computer chips, and, of course, psychotropic drugs—such products often provoke a volume of vignettes. For example:

A time to be born
A time to plant
A time to pluck
A time to die

—Ecclesiastes 3:1–2 (KJV)

I did not comprehend my parents' complexities, brought on by the products of their time (1898–1965).

Neither did I comprehend the complexities brought on by the products of my time (1933–?).

But the force and effect of the products of time are profoundly unique. Consider a mere sample of the products of my early time after the Great Depression: poverty, alcoholism, radio, nature's bounty, guns, war, and new religions. Blended, they formed the unpolished parameters of my happy days as a youngster. I embraced God and often would sing with him.

Soon, my teenage years brought new products of time: television, hypocrisy, delusion, sex, radar, mountains to climb, peer pressure. What to be? Can life be more than a boring cycle without God? I matured. My mind cleared, enthusiasm abounded as opportunity after opportunity bore down upon me. I could not escape the challenges, knowing that nothing is a problem and everything is a challenge. Successful endeavor became my primary reward, but the money too was nice, and I had fun. I met the challenges. I made the choices, and I take full responsibility for the successes and failures in my life without God's help or blame. And through it all, I continued to sing, but not as loud.

Suddenly, without warning, appeared a membership in AARP. I am a senior citizen. The products of my time have multiplied and have enhanced my life; consider a mere sample: personal computers, cell phones, texting, Kindles, credit cards, and, of course, psychotropic drugs.

With mild trepidation, I now understand my life is unique; every life is unique. Consequently, each generation is different and should expunge the oft-touted admonishments of parents to their offspring and embrace the force and effect of the products of their time, their choices, their lives, and their stories.

Inevitably, time forced me past senior citizenship into retirement and old age. The products of this time are fewer: arthritis, shortness of breath, fading eyesight, cataract surgery, cerebral infarction, quad bypass surgery, painkillers, and, of course, a mild groan with each attempt to stand. But now my stories take on a broader view of the meaning of life. It need not be a search for the Holy Grail of life—happiness—but merely the recognition of life stored in one's consciousness. I explain it in my stories. It's philosophical, perhaps, but people throughout the world have inspired debate and controversy on the provocative subject of happiness. And the debate worked for me, as offered in unedited correspondence included in the appendix.

Solomon, son of David, King of Jerusalem, teacher, explained his error: "What's there to show for a lifetime of working your fingers to the bone? One generation passes, and another one comes." Solomon continues: "Everything under the sun is vanity." And, "Life is a vapor that is not permanent." Theologians claim that Solomon, having been led astray by his great wealth, wisdom, and women, probably died a disillusioned and discouraged old man. But in the end, he got it right. Check it out in Ecclesiastes 2:11: "Life is vain, pointless." And: "There was no profit under the sun unless it is tied to the glory of God." Those are Solomon's unique stories, spawned by the products of his time. My stories are different and are not completely tied to the glory of God. My stories are tied to people, extraordinary people, incredible people, people who honored my requests for help even when offered little hope for reward. I am eternally grateful—yes, "humbled" But when my time comes, who will know if I got it right? My near-death story, "The Power of Prayer vs. 'Up Yours, Nurse Ratched,'"provides a hint. Yet I am happy and do not fear another judgment day.

In the end, time is even more than its products. It captures the pre-existing, life ever after, and is all-powerful, because nothing can stand against time, not mountains, not armies. Give anything enough time, and eventually everything is taken care of. All pain is gone, all hardship is eased, and all loss is absorbed. As you ponder this autobiography, you will conclude that my life was uniquely designed for me by the products of time, environment, heredity, and perhaps divine intervention. All have blended with my past, present, and future, as yours will be blended with your future. The past cannot be altered. The present is what I am. I accept my perceived future as a challenge, knowing the end is not far off. But why accept it? It is not how many years one has lived, but how one has lived the many years.

Stories, stories, stories—everyone has a story to tell. But why tell it? Why write it? Why read it?

Why? Because so many people have asked me to tell the stories time after time and have urged me to include them in my memoirs. Some people judge the stories too incredible and say that they can't be true. Others judge the stories too credible and that they must be true. In fact, they are true, except for the inaccuracies of age-impaired memories sprinkled with embellishment to improve readability.

The stories are an amalgamation of extraordinary events that constitute my life, a life filled with problems enthusiastically embraced as challenges that compelled life-altering choices that led me in new directions. From cradle to grave, all people make the same journey but choose different paths and encounter roadblocks, detours, peaks and valleys, fair weather and storms. Choices, choices, choices. Life is a supreme vocation of choices.

Although these stories are nonfiction, names have been changed to avoid a breach of confidentiality with my friends, clients, and colleagues as our lives crossed paths, merged, and faded into new directions. This method enables me to remain true to what I have lived without identifying the cast of characters who unknowingly have so profoundly influenced me to discover and embrace the Holy Grail of life: happiness.

While working on these stories, I relied on personal diary notes and on my memory, a memory damaged by a severe stroke ten years ago, now fading and playing funny tricks. Some things I remember clearly, as if they had happened a week ago, but others, are fragmented and foggy. After all, more than eighty-two years has placed me here. In everyday life, narrative and dialogue are our main means of communication. Therefore, I have reconstructed the narratives and dialogue formulating the alchemy of my life as though you were here listening to my voice recordings, now transcribed.

My stories are about:

A boy, age four, who smoked cigarettes with his father.

A boy, ages eight to sixteen, who lived alone in a chicken coop.

A teenager who quit school and headed to Alaska with his traps, guns, and a dog, became a farmhand in the Catskill Mountains of New York, and at age sixteen fell in love with the farmer's daughter, age fifteen.

An adolescent who graduated high school in three years and then served in the Marine Corps.

A destitute young man, age twenty-one, who married the farmer's daughter and matriculated at Pace College, New York City, under the GI Bill.

The stories continue with love as we strived together for sixty-five years, uninterrupted. I was a public accountant, tax expert licensed by the IRS, titled "Enrolled Agent," and my clientele was made up of lawyers, doctors, CEOs, and dairy farmers; the amalgamation perpetuated happiness. The final story, the epilogue, plans a happy death for this octogenarian multimillionaire as I build my own coffin.

And through it all, you will hear me sing,

"Lucky, lucky, lucky me, I'm a lucky son of a gun
I work eight hours; I sleep eight hours. That leaves eight hours for fun."

I. Childhood

A Smoking Camel

This day is *my* day, a special day and mine only. I know it's true—at least, that's what Mom and Dad told me last night as they tucked me into bed. The year is 1937—I think—which makes it my fourth birthday. But how can I be certain of this date? I can accurately date this memory by examining precise images etched in a child's mind and revisiting the evidence that created those images: our home, now remodeled; the narrow, tree-lined dirt road, now widened and paved; and the one-room shack where my friend Moses lived on the sloped way down to the old mill pond. All are still there, except Moses and his shack.

I never knew why he failed to call me by name. He always referred to me as "young man." One morning, I recall him yelling, "Young man, will you come sit a spell?" I rushed to the table and chairs at the corner of his narrow porch. As he poured Cambert's tea (one quick dip of a used tea bag into hot water; add a dash of milk and sugar), he warned, "Now, be careful, young man, when you sasser'n blow your tea."

He seemed to worry about me at all times. Mr. Moses helped with chores on small farms in the area. He was a friendly old man, and I know everyone liked my friend Mr. Moses, including the shack owner, who named his favorite colt "Nigger." But a few weeks later, Dad explained that Mr. Moses had gone away forever, and the owner was going to burn down his shack.

The remaining evidence, located ten miles north of Princeton, New Jersey, now bears the historical marker *Circa 1820*. The site exemplifies a patch of early colonial rural life with well-preserved original structures, including a triple-arch stone bridge crossing a small trout stream. A dam backs the water under the bridge, forming a large pond that flumes power over a paddle wheel that turns three huge grinding stones. The bridge, gristmill, and three homes are collectively known as Bridge Point (zip code 08558).

Our home, like all the others there, is old and cold.

An enclosed, winding staircase from the living room leads up to a narrow hallway, and a string of eerie bedrooms followed by another winding staircase that exits down to the kitchen at the opposite end of the house. I loved that old house, with its strange smells, creepy sounds, and dark cubbyholes to explore. Precocious and high-spirited, I concluded, "This is *my* day, and I'm going to do what I want, *my* way. I'm now a man!"

I eased out of bed at the sight of a sharp beam of sunlight dancing through a large tear in the tattered window shade. *Great, I thought, there is sufficient light to see if anyone else is awake.* I paused at each bedroom door as I tiptoed toward the staircase down to the living room. All was quiet, so I leaned back in Dad's recliner, snatched a Camel from the opened pack nearby, and lit my first-ever cigarette. *Life is great! I'm now a man.*

I heard boards creaking and assumed it was someone using the staircase to the kitchen on their way to perk the morning coffee. No worries; the kitchen is on the far-east end of the house. I visualized the familiar coffee-making ritual: first, start a wood fire in the stove, and then fill the coffee pot with water from the squeaky, old hand pump. *Lots of time to spare,* I thought, so I leaned back, drew hard on the cigarette, and filled my lungs as grown-ups do. I tried to make smoke rings while exhaling, but no rings formed, only balls of wet smoke that randomly filled the air with each uncontrolled cough. "Yes, sir," I sputtered. "I'm a man."

In my euphoria, I failed to listen for the routine squeaky sound of the hand pump. Nobody was in the kitchen; in fact, the creaky sounds had come from the staircase next to Dad's recliner. Suddenly, out of nowhere, Dad was at my side. Calmly, he said, "Good morning, son.

Happy birthday!" Vainly, I tried to hide my cigarette. "Time really flies. You're now four years old. Mind if I join you?" I quickly moved to my little chair alongside his recliner as he commented, "Sure looks like a nice day coming up. Do you mind if I have a cigarette with you?" His warm, relaxed voice invited me into his world and instantly evaporated my stored fear of punishment. My dad loves me. Yup, I'm now a man!

"Son, we've had several days of rain on and off, but this looks like a perfect day coming up. What do you say we drop off some corn at the mill, and while they grind it, we can fish from the bridge for a few nice brook trout?"

"That's a great idea, Dad. That way, when Mom gets up, we can have trout and cornmeal for breakfast. If we're lucky, maybe we'll catch enough fish for everybody, so bring extra corn just in case. Dad, this is the best birthday I've ever had!"

"That's great, son, but first I have to have a cup of coffee."

As we entered the kitchen, the fire was roaring hot, and the coffeepot on top was about to boil over. Apparently, whoever had provided this courtesy had gone back to bed. "Ah," Dad exclaimed, "I love to start the morning with a cup of fresh-perked coffee and a cigarette. How about you? You want a cup of coffee?"

Wow, my first cup of coffee! Clear and crisp, I replied, "Sure!"

Dad poured two cups of coffee and roughly shoved me out of his personal chair at the head of the table. "You're growing up, son, but you're not ready to sit in *my* chair. Besides, it takes longer to get food at this end of the table." The tinge of hurt feeling from his put-down disappeared when he said, "How about a cigarette with your coffee?"

Back in my comfort zone now, I sat tall and said, "Sure!"

My Dad was amazing. He was right-handed but lifted the cup with his left hand while his right hand precisely moved the pack of cigarettes to extract one at a time. I accepted the first one; he then served himself. We firmed up one end of each cigarette by lightly tapping it on the tabletop. Dad preferred book matches instead of wooden stick matches, for good reason. He opened a book of matches with his thumb and two fingers. Holding the open pack with his thumb and index finger, he raised a single match with his first finger and closed the pack under the match, thus heeding the warning: Close Cover Before Striking. With the book safely cradled in his hand and his first finger under the vertical match, his thumb curved the match over his finger down to the scratch-pad. With smooth precision and unfailing effort, his thumb forced the match across the scratchpad, causing a flash of fire and smoke to magically appear in his hand. He lit our cigarettes, mine first, then leaned back in his chair and commented, "Isn't this great?"

We talked man talk, drank coffee, and chain-smoked cigarettes for what seemed an hour or more. (Actually, in retrospect, I believe it was less than thirty minutes.) My throat and lips now registered an ache high on the pain scale, caused by my feeble attempt to keep up with Pop. As saliva gathered in my mouth, I fought back the gnawing urge to spit. I carefully balanced a half-smoked Camel on the ashtray while attempting one more sip of unsweetened black coffee. My laughing and smiling ceased as I mustered the effort (from where, I don't know) to suppress the urge to gag or explosively barf.

"Are you OK, big boy?"

Like a man, I replied, "Yeah, I'm OK, just a little tired. I got up real early because it's my birthday."

He smiled and remarked, "I understand. Well, grab the bag of corn, and let's go fishing."

Now on the brink of disaster, I blurted out, "Dad, I have to go to the outhouse. You go ahead. I'll meet you at the bridge in a few minutes."

"OK, but don't take too long. You know the trout bite best early in the morning."

He disappeared out of sight as I leaped from the back porch and trotted over the single-board path to the outhouse seventy-five feet from the kitchen. As I ran along the path, water and mud squirted out from under the eight-inch-wide boards. Almost there!

Without warning, I was crippled by peristaltic spasms forcing every drop of unsweetened black coffee, now laden with nicotine and stomach acid, to spew forth. Finally, I caught my breath, unlocked the backhouse door, and teetered on the east hole of a two-hole wooden outhouse. Hour after hour, I defecated in one hole while throwing up in the other without moving from the seat. Everything swirled in a dizzy pattern as I drifted in and out of a foggy realm. My head slumped forward into my hands, supported by stubby elbows propped on bony knees. My dizzy mind registered fear of the oft-repeated warning: "Your feet can't reach the floor, so always lean forward and hold on. Otherwise, you might fall through the hole into the pit." Spears of cold air and bright sunlight knifed through hairline cracks to dance in weird angles on the opposite wall. I'm weak. I'm exhausted. I'm puked out. I'm sick, sick, sick!

The slow rhythm of footsteps on spongy boards, followed by a knock on the door, snapped me back to reality. "Ken, are you OK?"

"I'm OK."

"What's the matter?"

"I'm tired. I got up too early."

"Well, it's your birthday, so we have a lot to do. Sorry you didn't join me at the bridge. The trout were really biting this morning."

He clasped my shoulders to guide my weak, feeble legs in the required straight line back to the kitchen porch. I stopped abruptly to regain balance on the narrow boards, tipping and jerking from his weight behind me. My tear-filled eyes could not focus on the treacherous board path ahead of us, and my feet could not find a safe path back to the porch.

"Hurry up, son! Breakfast is ready."

The cool air laden with a sickening, pungent aroma settled over us as we approached the old house. Still guiding me with one hand, Dad exclaimed, "Ah, my favorite breakfast: cornmeal and fish cooked in hog fat! After we eat, let's have coffee and cigarettes while your sisters clear the table."

The smell of breakfast fish, the aroma of unsweetened black coffee, and the thought of smoking cigarettes overwhelmed my stomach.

I stood tall, cried uncontrollably, and screamed, "I don't want any fish, and I'm not going to smoke a Camel!" Impulsively, I ran up the winding staircase, leaped into bed, and buried my head in shame. It's my birthday, but I'm *not* a man!

Shakespeare Is Drunk

I pushed hard against the headwind that extended my trip by half an hour. My brother Ed—eighteen months younger—used me as a windbreak, enabling him, with great effort, to keep close behind. We flipped our junky bikes on the ground and cautiously walked toward the excitement. People were yelling and bright lights were changing colors in the early evening. The strange, loud sounds of hammers, bells, and rifle shots mixed with nifty music blended into a cacophony we had never heard before.

It is August 1942. I am eight years old. I have learned the value of nonverbal expressions. Perhaps a wounded-puppy look while fumbling for a coin would allow our admission to the Belle Mead Firemen's Fair free of charge.

This was our first fair. The attendant stamped an ink mark on our wrists and pointed. "Your father is over there, by the nail-driving stand." Each year, the local fire company sponsored a small county fair to support the war effort. A Ferris wheel and a musical carousel were the main rides. Hawkers announced their small exhibits and games of chance for people of all ages strolling around carrying trinkets, dolls, and stuffed animals.

"Popcorn, popcorn—get your buttered popcorn."

"Hot dogs, hamburgers, try our sausage and peppers!"

The smells, the lights, the sounds, were exhilarating. Ed darted here and there. "Ken, look at that! Let's do this! Let's check things out!"

I grabbed his arm. "No. Mom said I have to stay with Pop. There he is, at the nail-driving game."

The challenge was to drive a nail head-deep into the pine beam in four strokes or less. What a spectacle! Pop randomly swung the hammer but couldn't hit the nail on the head. He was drunk.

Following his heart attack at Bridge Point four years ago, doctors had prescribed two shots of whiskey, morning and evening. I was constantly reminded, "Always stay with your father in case something happens." That responsibility became increasingly difficult—and often impossible—as he fell deeply in love with his medicine. He was now a full-blown alcoholic, the local drunk with ten children, scorned by local poor people, admired by all who understood his brilliant, drunken mind, hated by churchgoers, and loved by me. My schoolmates and their parents paused briefly, jeering and laughing at the spectacle. I watched from a distance, embarrassed, ashamed, and totally disgusted.

At that moment, Dad turned and addressed the sparse crowd: "The whole world is a stage, and we are but actors playing out our assigned roles. This is a tale filled with sound and fury, signifying nothing. But I blame none of you for *my* problems caused by the war, the Depression, my heart attack, Prohibition, no food, no gas, no money, and no friends. You see, folks, as Mr. Shakespeare wrote, 'The fault lies not in the stars, dear Brutus, but in ourselves.' So go on and laugh; I know the fault is all mine. But what about *your* faults? Joe said he chopped a tree down, and Jim helped him chop it up. Joe's house burned down, and Jim claimed Joe's house burned up. Schoolteacher Bergen said she met my 'ants.' I asked her which ones, the red ones or the black ones, or the gray-haired ones, each with two legs? 'Irregardless, Mr. Crane. You know what I mean.' 'Yes, I do. But, Schoolteacher Bergen, don't you get it?'"

His inebriated mind exposed a large hippocampus filled with trivia mixed with intriguing facts—facts he thought might neutralize the disdain for him. "Ladies and gentlemen, you are benefactors of my ancestors. Laugh all you want! I'm the black sheep of the family, but the name Crane is solid in the history of this great country. Have you forgotten? Crane was one of the original settlers of Elizabeth and one of the colonists who planted the first English settlement in what is your state, the state of New Jersey. He was there in the year 1665 and took an oath of allegiance toward King Charles the Second on February nineteenth of that year. Recorded deeds in Trenton are proof that what I say is true. King Charles deeded land in and around Elizabeth, New Jersey, to John Crane, Daniel Crane, Jeremiah Crane, Ezariah Crane, and Jasper Crane.

"In the year 1776, Stephen Crane was a leading patriot of New Jersey during the Revolution, the sheriff of Essex County under George the Third, and judge of the Court of Common Pleas during the agitation concerning the Stamp Act. He was elected a member of the First Continental Congress, which met in 1774. The engraving, *The First Prayer in Congress,* displays his portrait. This engraving is at Carpenters' Hall in Philadelphia. He was also a member of the New Jersey legislature and senate. Have you forgotten Crane was a member of the First Continental Congress that appointed the intellectuals to write our Declaration of Independence in the year 1776? He was the first trustee of the First Presbyterian Church in Elizabeth and mayor of the borough. You are here, folks, because of my family!

"Crane met his death on June seventh, 1780. British troops under Colonel Knyphausen landed from Staten Island with the purpose of destroying the American Army at Morristown and capturing General Washington. Their route lay through Elizabeth, Springfield, and Short Hills. However, they only reached the bridge over the Rahway River. The Jersey Militia drove them back to a small farm, where they stayed long enough to sack the church and burn every building in the town except two before retreating to Elizabeth. On June twenty-third, another attempt was made by the British, now under General Clinton, to reach Morristown by the same route as before. Along the road leading to Springfield, Stephen Crane was taken prisoner. The soldiers vented their hatred of this patriot, labeled a 'notorious rebel' by brutally carving him with their bayonets, causing wounds from which, one week later, he died. His tombstone bears the date July first, 1780.

"Have I mentioned the story of his son, Jonathan? He suffered like his father at the hand of the Hessians and died, also, as a result. And what about Joseph Crane? He was sheriff of the county, also a judge, and lived in Elizabeth, New Jersey. Believe these stories. Jonathan Crane was killed by Hessian soldiers. The story was printed in the Newark *Sunday Globe* newspaper on April twentieth, 1930, the year of the hundred-and-fiftieth anniversary of the Battle of Springfield.

"I may be the black sheep, but the Crane family has provided you with a string of ministers, lawyers, brave settlers, and the Declaration of Independence for this great country. Did you laugh at Jonathan Crane, who gave his life while brilliantly leading the British away from Washington's troops at Morristown on their way to Trenton? And people throughout the world know my uncle Stephen, author of *Maggie, The Open Boat*, and *The Red Badge of Courage*, to name a few."

Sometimes his hands, on extended arms, waved in convincing gesticulations to emphasize salient points of his presentation. This could go on for an hour. "I am merely the one bad apple in the bountiful harvest, so live on, you good, righteous people!" Ed seemed to enjoy the attention and moved closer to Pop.

I loathed such scenes and stayed in the bushes along the unlit, darkened perimeter, out of sight of my friends and schoolmates. Condescendingly, Pop closed his toothless gums tightly against each other. His lips puckered forward as he positioned himself in a defiant stance and admonished the dwindling group of onlookers. "I am what I am because that's what I am. So says Popeye the Sailor Man. So says me." When someone lingered, he added, "You don't like that? Then take this!" His tongue darted through bulging lips into his left nostril and quickly retracted, only to be slipped into the other nostril. My young mind could not comprehend his disdain for those people he had filled with disgust. Time after time, I also escaped, filled with disgust.

Throughout my life, simple, current happenings often triggered flashbacks to my youth, a time when my impressionable young mind was challenged by deep emotional paradoxes highlighted daily by this brilliant, disgusting alcoholic, my Dad.

Such a flashback occurred recently, a week after Christmas…

Burn, Baby, Burn!

Ken Jr. dragged the Christmas tree from the huge living room at 375 Fingar Road in Hudson, New York, also known as B-Jack Farms. He jammed the tree trunk deep into fourteen inches of snow slightly softened by the afternoon sun this cold, cloudy day in January 2008. Smiling, he remarked, "Have you ever seen a Christmas tree burn?"

In a flash, I mentally checked the conditions. No wind, no loose clothing, a safe distance from the house, a water hose available. I knew exactly what would happen. The yellow flame from a butane grill lighter started the fire. The tree nearly exploded. Fierce flames shot through the seven-foot tree with such force that it momentarily created its own wind. A tornado of burning pine needles rose thirty feet straight up, pushed over the edge of the heat funnel, only to flutter back and form a ring of gray dust on the snow. In the center remained a blackened tree trunk with bristly branches stripped of life. The flame was gone. The cold air snuffed out lingering sparks. A few wisps of smoke signaled the end, all within fifteen seconds. The suddenness, the fierceness, and the finality triggered a flashback to my boyhood days when Christmas trees were burned annually.

Ed entered my hiding place in a bush at the county fair.

"Don is here to take Pop home. Maybe we can win a prize in the talent show."

"OK, it's worth a try. And then we have to go home."

We signed in and immediately went onstage. A weak floodlight blurred our view of the judges and the small group of onlookers near the stage. The stage was a five-by-ten-foot portable wooden platform borrowed from alongside the highway. Each morning, farmers removed forty-quart milk cans from their coolers and placed them on this elevated platform at the roadside. A scheduled flatbed milk truck loaded with farm-numbered cans stopped each morning to exchange empties for full cans to be delivered to the local creamery.

Ed followed me onstage. We looked skyward to allow our voices to reach the microphone lowered to the first notch. The group snickered as I cleared my throat. It sounded strange over the loudspeaker, and I wondered, *Is that really me?*

We began to sing, "We've been working on the railroad, all the livelong day. We've been working on the railroad, just to pass the time away. Can't you hear the whistle blowing…?"—Ed chimed in with the "Whoo-whoo!" of the train whistle—"Rise up so early in the morn, can't you hear the whistle blowing (Whoo! Whoo!) Dinah, won't you blow your horn. All together now! Dinah won't you blow, Dinah won't you blow, Dinah won't you blow your ho-o-orn. Dinah won't you blow, Dinah won't you blow, Dinah won't you blow your horn. Second verse! Someone's in the kitchen with Dinah, someone's in the kitchen I kno-o-ow. Someone's in the kitchen with Di…naaah…strummin' on the old banjo."

The mixed group of onlookers clapped a generous applause. We bowed to the right, we bowed to the left, and then we bowed to the center. Ed whispered, "They like us. I wonder what the prize is." Ed wiped his hands on his dirty bib overalls. I readjusted the kneesocks along the elastic bottoms of my tattered, winged knickers. I wondered what had taken place onstage prior to our act while I was hiding in the bushes. We stood tall and proud as the contestants returned to the platform. They had nice clothes and polished shoes. Their hair was combed. Their families clapped and cheered wildly as the speaker summarized the talent show.

I slithered to the edge of the platform with Ed in tow. I jumped from the side into the shadows, pulling him along. He protested, "Stop it! Stop it, Ken. Maybe we will win."

"Don't be stupid, Ed. Those are the goody-goodies around here. We are the dirtbags. Let's go. We have to get home." From a distance I heard, "And the winners are…" We came in last.

The wind at our back easily pedaled us home. Blood was oozing from Mom's right eyebrow. Pop had slugged her. I rushed to her. "Are you OK, Mom?"

"Yes, I'm OK. Don't create a problem. You go to bed and forget this ever happened."

Reluctantly, I obeyed. Snuggled between soft blankets, I gazed through fluttering maple leaves at the panoply of stars and dreamed about far-off places, especially Alaska. I liked sleeping outdoors because it created fanciful thoughts of the future, not nightmares of the past. The experience delivered a peaceful realm of dreams that filled my young mind with positive clichés: *Accentuate the positive, eliminate the negative, and don't mess with Mr. In-Between. My glass is half full, not half empty. Life is not filled with problems; it's filled with challenges.* At least, that's what my alcoholic Dad told me. But I believed him; I loved him.

Weeks rushed by, unremarkably. I awoke at daybreak, as usual. A light snow had fallen during the night. Frost was all about. Soon, I would move into the brooding coop (a small, one-room building where we raised baby chicks) and build a fire in the potbelly stove. Elsie, our Guernsey cow, mooed for attention. Her schedule was strict: One, give me a scoop of grain. Two, milk me. Three, feed me grass or hay. Wag, our black Labrador retriever, followed me everywhere. But this morning, she was very slow as we responded to Elsie's demands. While milking the cow, I talked to Wag as she pumped out eighteen puppies. It was very cold in the barn, so we moved them into the brooding coop.

A severe sinus condition, coupled with unidentified allergies, kept me out of the house except when fighting for food. Dr. Hewstead, our traveling country doctor, told me to take an aspirin a day, sleep outside, and keep my nostril tissues soft with a liberal coat of "bag balm." We applied OC grease on Elsie's udder and teats because if they became chapped and sore, she would kick at the milker. The OC grease worked fine on her teats, and it worked fine in my nose.

Every hour of every day was slotted with a planned objective to fill my mind and soul with joy and satisfaction. It did, thanks to Dad.

"Plan your work, then work your plan, son." And work my plan I did: rise at 5:00 a.m. to milk Elsie, feed the chickens, and feed the dogs. Wash up, if possible—one bathroom, eight siblings! Argue, push, and shove for food (usually bread and milk, or an egg, or cornmeal). Dress for school (shoes, one of two shirts, and one of two pairs of bloomer knickers). Be home by three o'clock. Do chores. Shoot birds and wild game with my .22 rifle for much-needed food. I seldom completed school homework; it interfered with my joy of living off the land. A bachelor boy with his dog, in his own home, I gravitated toward a diet of stews, cooked in one kettle on a potbellied stove in the brooder coop.

I loathed the turmoil at the big house, where a pride of lions and a pack of male hyenas maneuvered for bits of food. Mom rushed back and forth from the stove to the table, carrying bowls filled with anything edible. Alcoholic Pop jabbed any elbow on the table with an eating fork. Seventy-year-old Aunt Annie stood guard with a heavy yardstick or a light frying pan, ready to smack anyone allowing their urge to eat to become too rough. The rules were simple: *No elbows on the table. Bring the food to your mouth, not your mouth to the food. Keep your mouth closed with food in it. No talking. And "no dod-darn chee-heeing!" You are at this table to eat and for no other reason. Show me your plate and always ask permission to be excused from the table. Anything left on your plate will be your next meal until it's eaten. And last, only God can help you if I hear a fart.*

Sibling rivalry urged us to instigate someone into trouble. This was not *Little House on the Prairie* or *The Waltons* with John-Boy. It was more like *Candid Camera* or *America's Funniest Home Videos*. Practical jokes became a must in my life.

Pop handed me the saw as I crawled under the best cedar tree in the woods. If there was no abandoned bird's nest inside, I secured one from the box in my brooder coop. Christmastime was especially exciting: wondering, anticipating, hoping…but always disappointing. Mom played Christmas carols on the old upright piano. We gathered together to sing traditional songs. We prepared piles of molasses popcorn balls. Everyone was happy and cheerful—no arguing, no bickering. Everyone rushed to help each other. Respect filled the air (except for Pop).

Mom kindly, but sternly, insisted, "Christmas is more about the birth of Jesus, not the joy of receiving presents."

By this time, I knew exactly what was coming and what I would get for Christmas. "Let's all sing 'Joy to the World.'" I loved this time of year. For one week prior to Christmas, I crawled in bed with my brothers, usually two or more per bed. Don read us stories about Uncle Wiggily, Brer Rabbit, and Little Black Sambo, and of the experiences of Henny Penny in the story "Chicken Little."

With lights out, deep sleep ensued. Living outdoors sharpens otherwise dull senses. Consequently, when sleeping indoors, even barely audible creaking sounds excited my Pavlovian response. Fully alert, I instinctively reached for my .22 rifle left in the brooder coop. Was someone playing a practical joke to make me think it was Santa Claus? I checked each person in the four bedrooms. All were sound asleep. It was 2:00 a.m. Silently, I eased down the twelve steps to the dining room. Quiet as a shadow, the cougar in me stalked the prey in our living room.

Suddenly, there was a flash of light. I leaped at the person and drove him to the floor. The lighted match flew up and away from the Christmas tree. Pop was crying. I had seen Christmas trees burn outside, but never in a home. His inebriated mind unloaded the torment layered thick around his heart. Barren self-esteem and deep depression exposed this dangerous drunk. He babbled, "I'm a complete failure. There are no presents. I have no money. We shouldn't have a Christmas tree. There's not going to be a Christmas."

I sat down beside him and placed my hand on his arm. "Sure there is, Dad. Christmas is all about Jesus's birthday, not about money or presents. You're not a failure; you just had too much to drink. Besides, we have birthday parties for everyone, so why not have one for Jesus? Birthdays come and go, and we want you at the parties as usual."

He sat up. "There shouldn't be a Christmas party. There is no Father God, so how could he have a son? Jesus was simply another Jew convincing his followers to believe a bunch of mysterious tales. That's why I tried to burn the tree. Christmas shouldn't exist, and we shouldn't either."

"But, Dad, what about us? Don't you care about us?"

"You know I do, son. I care about the whole family. I don't want to talk about this anymore."

Experience had taught me to tread lightly when dealing with a drunk. In this home, care was used in place of love. "You're right, Dad, but I know you'll feel different about it tomorrow. Come on, let's go to bed. I'll help you upstairs. Besides, we need you to fork elbows off of the dinner table." We quietly wobbled to the upstairs hallway and paused briefly.

"I'm sorry, son. I do care about all of you. I didn't mean anything I said back there. Please forget it. Let's keep it our secret and not tell anyone about it." I promised not to tell.

Several days later, a whiff of citrus drifted into the bedroom, overriding the urine stench in my bed. Wood in the old basement furnace burned to ashes every two hours, leaving the entire house ice-cold by morning. Often, we wrapped heated bricks in towels and placed them under the covers close to our feet. We fell asleep comfortably, but by morning, we were chilled to the bone. Every night, Ed's urine set my circadian clock for early morning. Don generally slept late and occasionally also wet the bed. The pee spread over the rubber mat under the sheet to my side of the bed. There was no escape. I tightened the covers around my neck to filter the air delivered to allergenic sinuses until they demanded relief. No problem, just a challenge.

I greeted every day very early in the morning, establishing a valuable, lifelong habit. A glance at the kneesocks pinned to the mantel confirmed the gift of a tangerine in the toe of each stocking—rare treats indeed: a blessing. We were so lucky! But the house was freezing. The broken stairs creaked their warning as I descended to the basement to tend the furnace. Intently, I navigated a dimly lit path across the dirt floor. Scrap paper and twigs kindled a small flame that quickly ignited large chunks of wood into a blazing fire. The three-foot, cast-iron doughnut top of the old furnace became cherry red within thirty minutes. The heat traveled through a four-foot square grate in the floor.

Carbide lights had been replaced by electricity, controlled in each room by a wall switch or a pull chain. The Christmas tree lights flashed bright colors as the plug made contact in the receptacle. In the glow, I caressed the wrappings of each present, hoping to guess the surprise hiding within. I counted the gifts from Santa Claus to others while searching in vain for my present. Prospecting ended abruptly at the sound of hushed footsteps moving toward the kitchen. Let the party begin!

Pop slid the coffeepot to the cool side of the stove and warned, "Don't leave the damn coffeepot unattended when the stove is so hot! How much wood did you put in the damn thing anyway? The coffeepot is about to boil over. Now I have to let it stop perking before I can even pour a cup of coffee. You know I need the first cup of coffee immediately after I wake up."

"Sorry, Dad, the house was so cold I filled the stove with extra wood to warm it up faster."

"Well, next time, don't load it up like that, and keep an eye on the coffeepot."

"Dad, I never put my eye on the coffeepot."

"You're a young man now, and you know what I mean, so don't sass me. Let's have a cup of coffee and smoke a Camel."

"No way, I don't like coffee, and I hate cigarettes."

An army of footsteps on pine-board floors rumbled overhead as door latches clicked open and closed. Our one toilet flushed incessantly to accommodate so many people as the household came alive. Dad finished three coffees with his cigarettes. Everyone gathered in the living room before breakfast, unwilling to delay their surprise gifts.

I knew last night before singing "Joy to the World" that it would not happen. Pop announced name after name. Finally, I heard, "To Ken, from Aunt Josie. To Ken, from Santa."

Everyone received several useful gifts. Socks, a belt, a shirt, underclothes…except me! Each Christmas, I was truly excited. Each Christmas, I was truly disappointed. The same letdown, year after year: a used deck of playing cards from Aunt Josie and an IOU from Santa Claus.

My young mind understood. Christmas is all about Jesus, not about money or gifts. But that did not explain the painful "Why me?" artfully concealed behind smiles and contagious excitement. Mixed feelings of resentment, envy, and happiness lured a prodigal boy, already launching practical jokes, to expand such tendencies.

Brother Dick, age four, excitedly ripped the paper from a present as big as him. He swayed back and forth, hugging it as he often was hugged, but not me. Soft, black-and-white flannel cloth filled with stuffing created a lovable young panda bear. Small, black ears flopped with every movement as clear button eyes rolled gently in the center of his mask. Perfectly formed lips exposed a red cloth tongue. Exhibits at the Belle Mead Fair displayed such prizes. In the excitement, I reached for the panda. Dick turned away, squeezing tightly, warning, "It's mine! Don't touch it!" In a flash of devilishness, I sucker-punched the panda squarely on the nose, fiercely launching it across the room toward Ed. Ed jumped up and gave it a swift kick that drove its contorted body up, up, up, and away, back into Dick's hands. We laughed as Dick cried.

Conflicting thoughts filled my dreams. The brooder coop was warm, but by morning, it would be freezing. Wag and her puppies kept my feet warm. I was happy to awake dry and urine-free. The stoked fire in the potbellied stove radiated warmth throughout my brooder coop but could not soothe my hurt. I placed the "IOU a pair of socks" in the box with the prior unkept promises.

That night, Wag listened intently to my dissertation while her puppies nursed an assigned nipple. Wag tipped her head from side to side, sympathizing agreement with every spoken word, as I unloaded my burdens on the subjects of Christmas, Jesus, presents, the Golden Rule, love, and the absence of love. Her motherly touch and gentle understanding lulled me to sleep, risking a chance to dream—*"Perchance a chance to dream a scheme."*

I awoke at dawn, fully invigorated, but I did not sing. I was consumed with a purpose that would not let me sing until a good deed was done as scripted in my dreams. The big house was cold and quiet. I started a small fire in the kitchen stove and a big fire in the furnace. On the way to the bathroom, my sinuses torqued my face. The stench of Ed's urine (and probably Don's too) prompted a mischievous mind into action. The cast-iron furnace top at the foot of the stairwell was cherry-red hot, just right to melt crayons dropped on top. Putrid fumes quickly rose up the stairwell into the bedrooms as I blended copious squirts of pee with the smoldering crayons. Outrageous moans and groans of disgust from the bedrooms signaled my success. Satisfied, I locked the kitchen door on my way out, singing my way back to my brooder coop. My friend Wag was at the door, waiting for my report. She was very pleased; we were happy again.

Ed and I harassed, teased, and tormented Dick relentlessly. Surgery after surgery reconstructed a cleft palate, leaving him with a typical hare-lip, scarred by the operation that detached it from his nose. His damaged lips sounded *p*'s as *m*'s. As a result, when teased, he could only "munch" us. We never hit each other, but teasing and practical jokes became our daily entertainment. Pop was drunk most of the time. Mom's time was consumed with efforts merely to exist. Dick received love. We received care. There was little discipline except at the dinner table. Two precocious boys were out of control and had a kid brother to pick on. What could be better?

We lured Dick to use secret messages over our telephone made with two buttons, a long string, and two tin cans. A clear voice could only be heard through a tight, straight line, forcing the snug buttons to vibrate against the bottom of each can. Communicating through a garden hose was much better. Sound travels through the hose down, up, and around corners to the listener's ear.

Dick always horned in on our games, but this time, we were ready. He yanked the hose from me and warned, "Mom said let me play too."

I quickly retrieved the hose and said, "OK, but wait your turn." Ed was high above in the haymow; I was far below in the barn. "The Germans are counterattacking through the woods behind the barn. We are forward observers reporting their activity directly to General Patton." I handed Dick the telephone.

Duty, excitement, and drama compelled him to inform the general of the tanks and the number of enemy foot soldiers rapidly closing in on us.

Dick's report was brief but exact. Excitedly, he reported, "We can't hold out much longer, sir. What are your orders?"

Loud and clear, General Patton said, "Don't say a word. Keep the receiver to your ear. I have a long message for you."

He paused for the message.

When it came, he threw the garden hose aside and grabbed his ear, screaming, "I'm telling Mom!" He ran from the barn, crying. Ed and I laughed uncontrollably as water through the hose flushed out Ed's urine.

Three days later, I was sent to live and work on the neighbor's farm a mile away: the Jelliffs. Room and board, plus twenty-five cents per week, was my pay.

It was then that Frank Sinatra stunted my growth.

Frank Sinatra
Stunted My Growth

Life with the Jelliffs was simple: eat, work, sleep, school. That's it. No playing, no practical jokes, up at four thirty in the morning, hand-milk cows until my arms ached, usually two and a half hours, and then eat breakfast at seven. Next, wash, change into school clothes, usually bloomer-winged knickers, and at seven thirty, help place our day's production of milk cooled in forty-quart cans on the roadside platform. The school bus stopped for me minutes later.

Back home from school at three thirty. Change clothes. Feed chickens. Collect eggs from the nests. Grain the cows. Shovel manure from the gutters. Milk the cows by hand. Feed the calves. Spread hay in the mangers. Turn off the lights in the barn.

Eat dinner at six thirty. Help in the kitchen until we settled in the living room to hear the war news reports. Gabriel Heater would announce, "Good evening, folks, I have good news tonight." He delivered positive reports, even when our troops were forced to retreat. Pop said, "A cup half full is better than a cup half empty."

At seven thirty, sweep loose hay back into the mangers. Turn night-lights on in the chicken houses. Electric lights encourage hens to feed intermittently at night instead of sleeping on the job. An egg per day per chicken is the targeted production, but it cannot be sustained without adequate lighting during the night.

The chicken house was ninety feet long, divided into three sections, with chicken wire stretched from ceiling to floor, wall to wall. The levered switches of the fuse box clicked loudly, closing the circuit that lighted a dim bulb hanging in each pen. In a flash, a hailstorm of rats leaped from the feed trough, racing in all directions to escape. Noisy chickens fluttered from the roost, dodging rats as they hopped onto the narrow perches attached to each feeding trough. An army of rodents invaded the area every night. We shot them, trapped them, and caught them, but each week, there were more and more rats.

Mr. Jelliff turned off the radio as I entered the living room. He sternly engaged the same nightly interrogation, a quick checklist of the "did yous?" Including, "Did you turn on the lights in the chicken house?" My answers were always yeses.

"How many rats did you see?"

"I saw hundreds and hundreds, maybe even a thousand."

"I don't think there were *that* many. But one is too many. They're eating us out of house and home. The chicken feed is costing me more than I get for the eggs. We're becoming overrun with rats. Maybe I'll have to sell the chickens. I don't know what else to do."

Sleep usually came easily after twelve to fourteen hours of scheduled activity, seven days a week. But tonight, my troubled mind was filled with empathy for Mr. Jelliff struggling to solve the rat problem. A problem? No way! It's not a problem, just a challenge. At least, that's what Pop always said whenever he heard the word *problem*.

Morning chores finished. Breakfast as usual: one egg, a slice of jellied toast, and cornmeal moistened with a measured amount of milk (never enough). Mrs. Jelliff, a tall, thin lady wearing a long, flowered, old dress partly covered by a clean but well-worn waist apron, scurried about the kitchen. Frank Sinatra's singing stopped her routine every morning, leaving me an overcooked egg, no milk for the cornmeal, or no cornmeal for the milk. My allotted time was short; often my breakfast was, too, all because of Frank Sinatra.

Days passed quickly. Rats multiplied weekly, creating an irresistible challenge. Pop said, "Plan your work, then work your plan."

The plan: Use a brace and bit to drill a pencil hole through the wall on each side of every escape opening. Inside the chicken coop, place a brick four inches in front of each rat hole. Attach bale wire around the ends of each brick. Push the other end of each wire outside through the drilled hole. Drive a stake in the ground by each wire. Allow several days for the rats to acclimate to escaping over the obstacles.

I kept the plan a secret. My empathy would be satisfied when Mr. and Mrs. Jelliff praised me for doing them a big favor. Now to work the plan.

I placed the last of three heavy five-gallon pails on the ground-level porch. I heard Mr. Jelliff in the kitchen as he reached for a lantern, angrily repeating, "What can be keeping that boy?"

I stepped inside, too excited to speak rationally. I failed to notice the blood. My hair, my face, my shirt, my shoes, all soaked with blood.

"My God, boy, what happened?"

Excitedly out of control, waving my arms, I blurted out, "I killed all the rats! Look, I have fifteen gallons of dead rats!"

"My God, boy, how did you do this?"

"I just worked my plan. I eased around the chicken coop, quietly pulling wires. Bricks moved over the holes, blocking all the exits. I checked each wire, making sure each red brick inside the coop was pulled over the escape hole and each wire firmly secured to a stake. I grabbed my club, flicked on the lights, and started swinging. Rats flew in every direction as I killed them on the floor, in the air, and on the mesh wire separating the pens. Each pen was the same: scared rats mixed with terrified chickens as if raided by a den of foxes. I hit a rat and two chickens with one swing. The two chickens are OK, but the last rat died instantly as it tried in vain to move the anchored brick preventing its escape. Bulging eyes popped out when I smashed its head against the brick. They won't eat any more of your chicken feed! Now you won't have to sell the chickens."

Mr. Jelliff made no comment. Mrs. Jelliff warmly instructed, "It's getting late. Wash up and go to bed. Put your bloody clothes in a pail of cold water."

The tired, proud boy dropped into deep sleep, satisfied with his success at meeting the challenge. Thank-you, praise, and, reward would be mine the next day. The dirty rats were dead!

Mrs. Jelliff hurried my breakfast as she hummed strange songs. She served me a perfect sunny-side-up egg on toast. She picked up a bowl of cereal, commenting, "I fixed oatmeal instead of cornmeal."

Great! I thought. *Maybe it's one of my rewards.*

Then it happened again. "Clang, clang, clang went the trolley, Ding, ding, ding went the bell, Zing, zing, zing went my heartstrings. From the moment I saw you, I fell." Her arms flew up across her chest. She swooned. "I just *love* that man!" My breakfast hit the counter, then the floor, sending oatmeal and glass shards in all directions. Once again, I had half a breakfast because of Frank Sinatra. I wanted to smash the radio. I wished bad things for him.

I was about to deliver the milk cans to the platform and then catch the school bus. Mr. Jelliff stormed into the kitchen in a rage. He bellowed, "You're not going to school today! You're going to remove those bricks and wires and plug up all those holes you drilled in my chicken house. When you finish that, get those dead rats off of my porch, and see to it they're buried deep in the ground so nothing digs them up. You scared the hell out of my chickens, so now I have only half as many eggs. You'll get no pay until the chickens are back to normal." Fear washed away my pride, my satisfaction, and my success as I put fifty cents on the counter, my wages for two weeks.

His rage always included "keep your mouth shut" and "do what you're told." I did, but his twenty-year-old son did not. Whenever he visited to help gather hay or corn, they wound up in a violent fistfight. The son beat the hell out of his father.

Begrudgingly, I carried out his orders: Pull out the anchors. Remove the bricks with wires attached. Putty the holes closed. Bury the rats. But all the while, evil thoughts consumed my mind. I wished the rats would come alive; I'd lock them in the chicken house. I'll kill a chicken or two each night for the rats. I'll replace good light bulbs with bad ones.

Nasty Mr. Jelliff continued during lunch with all the "did-yous." All my answers were yeses. I said nothing else as he raged on. "Don't do anything around here without my permission. Don't try to think; you'll just get in trouble. I'll do the thinking, and you do what you're told, nothing more, and nothing less. Is that clear? I said, is that clear?"

"Yes." Disappointed, hurt, and seething with anger, I finished afternoon chores, milked cows, and ate my dinner in silence.

Nasty Man continued: "I hope you learned your lesson today. I can't afford people like you on my farm. You'll have to work harder. Go sweep in the hay and turn on the lights in the chicken houses."

My mind raced as I slowly walked the lane past the chicken houses to the barn. Revenge was my purpose: Drop the lantern in the hay. Dump water in his gas tank. Burn Mr. Nasty's toolshed. Turn his dog loose with the chickens.

The *click, click, click* of the switches lighted each section of the chicken house. My Sunday school teacher appeared in the dim light at the far end, pointing her finger at me. Sternly, she warned, "Vengeance is mine, sayeth the Lord. Always remember, no good deed goes uncriticized."

I answered the vision, "I hate Mr. Nasty! Twenty-five cents a week is not enough. I'm overworked and underpaid. I go to school hungry, and now I hate Frank Sinatra with his 'clang, clang, clang' trolley!"

I walked the long lane to the house. Lights faded as I continued on for a mile. I could make it without them. I missed my brothers and my sisters. I missed Mom and I missed Dad, even if he was a drunk. I was homesick. My dog rubbed against me, circling and wagging her tail excitedly. I closed the door on the brooder coop. I'll have a full breakfast tomorrow! Good-bye, Mr. Nasty. Good-bye, Frank Sinatra!

My Brooder Coop

The Big House

II. Teen Years

I Want to Be a
Taxidermist and Farmer

Elsie, our orange-and-white Guernsey cow, nudged her baby along as she followed me to a patch of fresh spring grass. Every aspect of the outdoors began to mold the self-reliant, independent traits that were to determine my future: sleeping outdoors, the universe above, a cacophony of night sounds in spring, the excitement of thunder and lightning in summer, and the stark silence of winter filled the voids of my soul.

Elsie pressed her lips against the ground to capture every fragrant spear of new spring grass while making guttural sounds instructing her baby to stay close by. During these formative years (from six to twelve), the intrigue of nature, the fascination of all things real or imagined, impressed me to greet each day before sunrise with unnatural euphoria. At sunrise, the birds and I started each day with a song. John Gambling's radio program became my favorite as he sang, "Pack up your troubles in your old kit bag and smile, smile, smile. What's the use of worrying? It never was worthwhile. *Soooo*...pack up your troubles in your old kit bag and smile, smile, smile."

Ha, ha. No more Frank Sinatra! The bigger the problem, the more difficult the solution; the greater my satisfaction would be. Strangely, what others call hard work became my passion and obsession, a lifelong search for new challenges. How else can one explain the impassioned desire of a ten-year-old boy to kill hundreds of rats with a club and then proudly display their bloody carcasses in three five-gallon pails?

These years are filled with "Ken-undrums" only to be chastised by the beneficiaries.

Bolt, Wag's puppy, born in the barn two years earlier, scoured the area in front of me, searching for the scent of any creature worth shooting. We were inseparable. Instinctively, he stayed within range as would any well-trained Labrador retriever, ready to pounce on the downed prey.

Suddenly, two armed men leaped from a jeep, shouting threatening orders. I often hunted rabbits hiding in the short, thick grasses along a high, barbed-wire fence with an overhang curved three feet toward the enclosure. "Drop your weapon now!" shouted the men, while both aimed their pistols at me.

Strangely, I was not scared or intimidated. In fact, this was not the first time; neither would it be the last such incident. I was legally hunting on my Sunday school teacher's farm, with her permission, in violation of nothing. Regardless, I eased the gun to the ground, yet taunted the aggressors, as usual. I often studied life in this area half a mile from my brooder coop. I seldom returned without a good supply of food, thanks to Bolt. Short grass, tall grass, thick brush, and then tall trees buffered an isolated security fence surrounding a military supply depot and a German prisoner-of-war camp. Deer, rabbits, pheasants, squirrels, woodcocks, and such inhabited the area. It was well protected with floodlights on manned guard towers at appropriate intervals and patrol vehicles traveling the fence line 24/7.

A tree stand for hunting allowed a clear view of prisoners two hundred yards inside the fence. While waiting for a squirrel or other edible creature to come into range, my mind raced to comprehend the dichotomies of war. I was surrounded by nature at its finest. The prisoners were laughing, playing games, all having fun. Dad hated Germans. Germans hated Jews. Japs hated Americans. But why should we kill each other? The answer came quickly when a fox passing by carrying a rabbit in his mouth dropped dead with my bullet through its heart. We are part of nature. We are animals.

The pot of rabbit stew simmered on the wood-burning stove as I skinned the fox, including its face, legs, and feet. It would be packed in salt, the first step to preserve the hide for mounting. I scraped the skull clean of flesh, removed the brain and eyeballs, and then packed the parts with salt. I had decided to become a taxidermist. Lessons from the Northwestern School of Taxidermy in Omaha, Nebraska, filled the mailbox each month. Detailed lessons inspired me to dissect every dead creature available: pheasants, deer heads, household birds, and cats. I had refused to stuff my neighbor's dog, but I did agree to mount his trophy black bear. My days in grade school were filled with hard work on the farm: hunting, fishing, delivering newspapers on bicycle, fending for myself outdoors and in the brooder coop. I loved it all. Nothing was a problem. Everything was a challenge—except for school. School was a big problem. School interfered with my lifestyle, but not my education, simply because it was sheer torment to spend days in a classroom instead of the great outdoors. Besides a healthy diet of fish and game, I earned more money fur trapping than the combined activities of my classmates.

This was not the frontier. Hillsborough is merely fifteen miles north of Princeton, New Jersey, and thirty-five miles west of New York City. Regardless, the rural farming area had an abundance of muskrats, raccoons, weasels, foxes, skunks, and occasionally a mink or two. Muskrats were especially plentiful in the many brooks and streams and became my major source of income during winter. My circadian clock forced me out of bed well before dawn, knowing full well that after sunrise, a muskrat will chew off his leg to escape, leaving his bloody foot in the jaw trap. I did not allow this to happen.

By spring, the large mason jar, carefully hidden at all times, was nearly full of money. The Northwestern School of Taxidermy required prepayment for all supplies ordered by mail. The list of supplies grew longer and longer as salted carcasses accumulated throughout the winter and muskrat revenue filled the jar to pay for the supplies. The list included scalpels, brain spoons, an assortment of glass eyes, arsenic in five-pound bags, other preservatives of all sorts; paints for lips, inner ears, and mouth; wrappings and paste to make mannequins; needles and cord to shape and stitch the hides, to name a few. But the list never exceeded the money in the jar.

I anxiously checked the mailbox week after week, but still no supplies arrived. I prepared a business letter to the school requesting an immediate explanation for the delay. As I reached the mailbox this time, a chill flooded my mind. Mom had not been available to fill out the postal money order as before to pay the monthly cost of my correspondence lessons. I remembered putting the supply list in the stamped envelope while Pop and the clerk counted the money from the jar, mostly change and one-dollar bills. Pop had said, "Ken, go shut off the truck and wait there. I'll be right out after we finish counting." He was sober, not a whiff of alcohol on his breath. But my mind flashed the thought, *No, no way! He wouldn't have—*

I confronted Pop. He was drunk. With tear-filled eyes, he babbled pathetic, impassioned pleas. "I'm sorry, son. Please forgive me. Please, please forgive me, son. I'm so sorry."

I know he meant every word from the bottom of his heart. I believed him. I forgave him by the example offered by our church minister time and time again. Pop confessed his sins, swore an oath to God never to corrupt his soul with alcohol again. "The Pledge" seldom lasted six days; then the addiction overwhelmed his body and soul once again, year after year. Where was God?

The birds, black bear, and the neighbor's cat packed in salt slowly decayed, along with a host of other critters I had intended to stuff and mount. I placed the stench-laden body parts deep in a common grave, along with my dreams to become a taxidermist.

• • •

By 1941, shortly after the United States entered World War II, basic items could no longer be purchased without government ration coupons: gasoline, sugar, and meat (except chicken), to name a few. Each week, the entire family processed 150 to 200 broilers (young chickens at one and a half to two pounds at dressed weight) to fill orders for the employees at the government depot and prisoner-of-war camp. We never deviated from Pop's strict assembly-line orders. Dick and Ed caught chickens and stretched their necks between two nails on a stump. I lopped off the heads in rapid succession with single swings of the hatchet. Their mindless bodies flip-flopped around on the lawn "like headless chickens." Occasionally, the bloody scene was quite comical. Don, Irene, and the others selected a motionless body to be scalded in one of the metal tubs of water boiling over an open fire.

Pop staggered back and forth, warning, "Keep things moving. Hold one leg of the chicken and use the stick to keep the bird underwater while you pump it up and down for ten seconds. Toss the steaming bird in a pile to cool for the pluckers."

Plucking feathers is a time-consuming process; all hands joined in whenever possible. Mom and Aunt Annie singed hair from the birds over an open, flat flame, gutted them, and placed the end products in a paper bag supplied by the customer with his or her name on it. Customers lined up every Friday and Saturday, week after week. Pop took their money in his left hand before releasing the brown bag from his right. Each person handed him another bag with a name on it and a chicken order for the next week.

We never saw the money, but baby chicks were delivered each week. The feed bill was paid each week, and Pop stayed drunk 24/7. Everyone was happy but loathed alcohol, including Pop.

Pop castrated Elsie's six-month old baby that later developed into prime beef on the dinner table. My young mind registered the perplexing dichotomy: Why do we raise animals and name them, but then eat them? Elsie's mournful calls drove me in desperation to borrow against next year's muskrat money to buy a half-grown female calf for her. With chickens, ducks, cows, and dogs all around me and days filled with hunting, fishing, and gardening, it was easy to conclude that I wanted to be a farmer.

Seeds of Religion

Mrs. Pearson warned me of the dangerous Germans in prison behind the barbed-wire fence ajoining her ninety-eight-acre farm. She ended each Sunday school class with a prayer for our soldiers being killed or wounded in far-off places. She thanked God for sparing the life of my brother Doug, who was bayoneted during hand-to-hand combat in the Philippines on Guadalcanal. Doug, the family leader, was two years younger than our brother Howard, who was fighting in Okinawa. Mrs. Pearson convinced me beyond all doubts that prayers would save my brothers and kill our enemies. Every day, I studied the Bible, page by page. I memorized the titles of all the books of the Bible, Old and New Testament. I prayed for my brothers' salvation. I prayed to release my father from the devil's grip. I prayed for my mother and others around me. I never prayed for myself.

The standing congregation clapped vigorously in support of Mrs. Pearson's praise that placed me at the top of the class as a dedicated believer in God. Her vision was that I would become a man of the cloth, destined to carry on God's work, embellished and satiated with every word that reinforced my wish to succeed. I proudly accepted a new Bible with my name engraved in gold leaf on the cover.

Elsie gave birth each year. During her gestation, milk was plentiful for the family and last-born calf while Elsie grazed on summer grasses— but what about the long, cold winter? Don and I rented thirty acres from Mr. Jelliff to raise hay and grain to sustain her purpose through such times.

Farming is steeped in our culture through the grace of God by planting a seed through copulation, or in the ground by design, or in a spring blossom by pollination, all driven by a predetermined, primordial instinct for propagation.

Farming is a labor of love, celebrated each year on the third Thursday of November, Thanksgiving Day. (Thursday is "Thor's day"—he is the Viking god of thunder and lightning). It inspires all who contemplate the bountiful harvest from purposeful effort. It allows one to "reap the seeds one sows."

Our old Model B John Deere tractor popped several times as Dad laboriously cranked the heavy cast-iron flywheel. A two-quart tank supplied gasoline to be ignited by a spark from a magneto instead of a battery. The engine struggled and then fired on one cylinder. Soon it fired on both cylinders, and a hand valve switched the fuel from gasoline to a fifteen-gallon tank of diesel fuel. Steel wheels front and back provided unusual traction as the fist-size lugs dug deep on soft ground, but when on a hard surface such as stone or concrete, the tractor shook violently as it jumped up and down. Pop would say it was "like riding the handles of an industrial jackhammer." An iron pin through a clevis connected the twelve-inch, two-bottom plow to the drawbar of our tractor.

I slowly pushed the three-foot hand-clutch rod forward and headed toward the thirty acres to be tilled for planting. The unit easily traversed a shallow drainage ditch alongside Mrs. Pearson's half-mile-long driveway separating our property from my destination. A dead tree at the far side of the field became my target while the tractor strained against the load as the trip plow turned twelve-inch furrows of heavy sod.

Idle talk at church included speculation on who plowed the straightest furrow, who planted the straightest row of corn, and who raked the straightest row of hay. I wanted to be mentioned. Hour after hour, the tractor groaned on. Wisps of diesel smoke scented the warm spring air as furrows turned straight as an arrow. I sang Mrs. Pearson's favorite church songs the entire time, happy to be doing a man's job. *What a terrific day*, I mused. *The weather is perfect. No breakdowns, seed and fertilizer have been delivered. Weather permitting, Don and I will complete disking, harrowing, and planting in a couple of days.* I sang, "Oh, what a beautiful mornin', oh, what a beautiful day! I've got a wonderful feeling everything's going my way!"

Pop staggered toward me with a uniformed New Jersey state trooper. He quickly stepped between me and the trooper, who was trying to question me. "Have you been using this tractor?"

"Yes."

"Did you cross Mrs. Pearson's driveway twice today?"

"Of course. There's no other way to go back and forth to the field."

"Mrs. Pearson claims you're ruining her driveway with your lug-wheel tractor."

"I don't believe this. It's just an old, dirt driveway full of potholes. I kick up less dirt in a year than their horse and wagon does digging in each day."

"It doesn't matter," the officer sternly warned. "If you cross it again, you will be arrested for trespassing."

Pop was furious. I was stunned. I had no doubt that Mrs. Pearson, my stern, Bible-thumping Sunday school teacher, would have me arrested; therefore, I bounced along the highway fronting her long lane and continued my farming as planned, once again deeply believing I had done nothing wrong.

Conundrums began to threaten the strong religious teachings from the Bible, the church, and Mrs. Pearson as those teachings came in conflict with my experiences with Mr. Nasty—"Don't try to think, you'll just get into trouble. I'll do the thinking. You do what you're told, nothing more and nothing less. Now go bury those bloody rats deep."

Hypocrisy seemed to be everywhere. "Do unto others as you would have them do unto you." "Pray to God" to spare my brothers, but kill all Germans and their brothers. "Forgive us who trespass, as we would forgive those who trespass against us." "Love thy enemy and thy neighbor," even if it's your Sunday school teacher who wants the police to arrest you for crossing her potholed driveway.

The study of nature supplied answers to my circling mind that the study of religion did not. I no longer attended Sunday school and seldom attended church but continued to study the Bible. Understanding and songs replaced confusion and anger as the natural order of life offered endless explanations to otherwise complex feelings. I now had all the answers.

Eighth grade was boring except in springtime, when outdoor activities filled my day. School buses regularly transported my brothers and sisters to and from school, but I seldom complied. Instead, I walked miles of hedgerows toward the school, gathering tent-caterpillar egg pods attached to the twigs of wild chokecherry trees. Each spring, the board of education sponsored a contest, paying ten cents per hundred egg pods, as a means to control the defoliation of leafy trees. Chokecherry trees, the preferred host for the moth eggs that hatch into tent caterpillars, are easily located by following their unique scent, recognizable only by an experienced outdoorsman. Generally, I won the contest. Occasionally, I was late for class. The lesson: the early bird gets the worm; I got the money.

The egg count was verified by three students, each from a different class. Moon Mullins, the only black boy in our school, assisted with the count. Racism was in full force. Prejudice abounded. As nature took its course, Moon Mullins was heckled relentlessly. Consider that "birds of a feather flock together" but share the same airspace. Coyotes drive foxes from their marked territory to control their food supply. Red ants and black ants attack and kill each other if they attempt to cohabitate. I prayed my brothers would return safely from the war and that they would kill lots of Germans and their brothers. Mrs. Pearson's survey marked her territory (her driveway) as animals do, warning, "Stay off, or else!" I call it the "pissing dog syndrome." Mr. Jelliff and his rats, guards at the German prison camp, and my Sunday school teacher plotting to have me arrested exposed hypocrisies that created an amalgamation of emotions that could be understood only by a study of nature and animals. Moon Mullins, "the shine," my good friend, did not know he was an animal. My acceptance of human behavior, driven by nature's primordial animal instincts, caused me to be much smarter than my classmates. To prove it, just ask me!

Environment versus heredity versus the truant officer carried me through freshman year at Somerville High School. I loved learning but hated school. Mom prepared mush of oatmeal, cornmeal, or rice and scrambled eggs for breakfast, while we stuffed our school lunch bags with peanut butter sandwiches. Pop sipped a cup of coffee, added salt to three eggs cracked into a tall glass, and slurped them down. The sight and sound of that slime clearing the glass with two disgusting gulps, each filling his toothless mouth, signaled the end of his favorite breakfast.

Alcohol, cigarettes, and emphysema had disabled him. His coughing and wheezing inspired me to escape school classes. "Plan your work, and work your plan." The plan: exit the bus with lunch and books in hand, walk two miles to the south branch of the Raritan River, where a cache of supplies was hidden: fishing supplies, camp stove, rain gear, salt, and so on. Spend the day studying and completing homework assignments, eat lunch, clean fish, then walk back to school and board the bus to return home as usual. Each week, prepare a forged statement from Dad: *Please excuse my son Kenneth's absence from school on (date X). He suffers from a chronic, untreatable respiratory ailment. Signed, Howard K. Crane, father."* The note was handwritten and signed with a signature stamp I had purchased from an office-supply store.

I worked my plan brilliantly. On foul-weather days, I often blew my nose in class, rubbed my eyes, and fake-coughed to disrupt the class and annoy the teacher. Occasionally, I was asked to leave the room. My plan worked magnificently until that fateful day late in May, the school year nearly ended. A truant officer took me into custody and unceremoniously exposed my scheme. I mocked with pleasure the stupidity of being suspended from school for cutting classes. Regardless of the suspension, my passing grades for all subjects allowed me to be scheduled for sophomore classes. Classes started in September with a warning from the school: "Kenneth was absent from school fifty-three days during the last term of forty-three weeks. Excessive absences for any reason will cause a student to lose credits for each class not attended, as required by law."

I faked headaches, difficulty breathing, and stomachaches. I complained about people spying on me. "Stop bugging me! Just leave me alone!"

Pop grabbed a beer. There was no sermon about the value of education or my future. He simply read a notice from the school and then said, "Now what do you intend to do about this?"

With my mind racing, after a brief pause I replied, "I don't know."

Reluctantly, for six weeks, I faithfully attended sophomore classes. But shortly after October 8, 1949, at age sixteen, I quit high school. A yearning for hunting, trapping, fishing, farming, fighting for food, Batman and Robin, Superman, the Lone Ranger, Daniel Boone, Davy Crockett—and Sgt. Preston, the Canadian Royal Mounted Police officer, and his dog, King—blended the alchemy for my life. To be a mountain man on the frontier of Alaska was my dream.

After the war, in 1945, the Belle Mead Army Depot slowly became inactive. Caravans of trucks hauling war material and German prisoners no longer jammed the highways leading to and from ocean ports. Now, day after day, smoke billowed high in the sky as huge piles of war surplus burned to ashes.

Ed and I removed staples holding three strands of taut barbed wire to the post and temporarily kept them apart with a cord tied in a bow-knot. The prisoners were gone, guard towers were empty, and the fence patrol traveled the perimeter twice a day instead of continuously as before. The base commander's son, Ed's classmate, fed us details for the plan to rob the base supplies heaped two stories high for burning. New camping gear of all kinds, canteens, stoves, tents, canvasses, knives, cooking utensils, clothing, blankets, cots and bedding, leather and wool aviation jackets, webbed belts with brass buckles, shirts, trousers, coats and uniforms—everything I would need in Alaska, going up in smoke! This sight, juxtaposed with my needs, was unconscionable, unbearable.

Ed and I took it, load after load, into the woods to be hauled away later in Don's 1935 Chevy car or Pop's old Ford pickup truck.

At the sound of a patrol vehicle, we leaped through the barbed-wire fence and pulled the bowknot, allowing the wires to snap back into place undetected. The war ended, troops returned home, and family life returned to normal.

Doug married his California nurse, Erma, and returned home after two years in a military hospital. Shortly thereafter, he enrolled at Pace Institute, a business school located at Park Avenue in New York City. Howard decided to build homes to meet the huge demand for veterans' housing. Levittown, a huge postwar development plan for South Jersey, had just received final approval. I quit my full-time job at the feed mill at Howard's request to work full time building a house on a lot sub-divided from the homestead. We agreed that my wage would be paid in full when the house was sold. Alone in the brooder coop with a job next door, lots of fish and wild game, plus food from Mom's table and clothing from the army depot left me little need for money. Besides, the lump-sum payment from Howard would grubstake the trip to Alaska.

Construction at that time was labor intensive. Power tools were not yet available. Consequently, a year passed before the certificate of occupancy was issued allowing the house to be sold. The stage was set for my departure to Alaska. I intended to receive a government-sponsored quitclaim deed issued to qualified persons who homesteaded designated parcels of land for a minimum of three years. No money was required. I now had 150 jaw traps, a shotgun, and two rifles with ammunition, a loyal dog, and enough gear for extended life in the wilderness. All I needed now was the money and adequate transportation for the six-thousand-mile trip. Cash savings, back pay, and work along the way should cover the cost of this planned, twelve-month journey. Once there, I would have no need for money. I would be free. "The lust for money is the root of all evil." Here comes a bombshell.

When Howard sold the house, he bought a five-hundred-acre farm in the Catskill Mountains of New York, six hours north of Belle Mead,

New Jersey. There was no money left for Ken. Howard applied mild persuasion, urging me to work for him at his newly acquired dairy farm. My life changed dramatically, and once again I was a farmer.

Up at 4:30 a.m., stoke a fire for coffee, assemble two state-of-the-art surge milking machines, and carry forty-quart cans with strainer to the center aisle between two rows of cows. All milking equipment had to be scrubbed and sterilized after each use. I quickly rolled the upright, full cans of milk—weighing nearly a hundred pounds depending on the butterfat content—to the attached milk house and lifted them into a cold-water storage vat. Daily milk production is measured in pounds, not quarts. When shopping, notice the increasing price of milk labeled skim, 1 percent, 2 percent, and whole. The price of milk to the farmer is based on the butterfat content, which fluctuates from day to day and cow by cow, depending on her consumption of silage, grains, and hay. Twice daily, Howard pushed a wooden, three-wheeled feed cart along the mangers and scooped a predetermined amount of expensive, mineralized feed grain to each cow. Each portion dished out depended on her contribution to profit. The more butterfat content, the more each drop of milk weighs. The more pounds of milk sold, the more money earned each month. Accurate records are essential.

Besides milking cows twice each day, extensive hand labor included shoveling manure from the gutters, forking tons of green chop from the silos, removing tons of hay from the mow and distributing it to each cow, spreading manure on the fields as fertilizer, and grooming the cows and treating them for a host of ailments, injuries, and diseases. Country people often referred to as "dumb farmers" must possess a working knowledge of meteorology, chemistry, veterinary medicine, animal husbandry, mechanics, business law, carpentry, plumbing, AC and DC electricity, mathematics, fulcrum engineering, forestry, and more—a "Jack of all trades." A farmer must regard problems as challenges to be overcome by an endless labor of love. Boredom is impossible while accepting the challenges sixteen hours a day, seven days a week, every week of every year.

Finally, my insatiable desire for challenges was being challenged, but not sufficiently. Howard was overweight, undermotivated, and overworked. As with most farms, expenses often exceed income. Hence, the "three Ds": debt, disagreement, and divorce, in that order. Howard's wife, Chicky, preferred the city life and seldom visited the farm. She filed for divorce. Experiences in the brooder coop had prepared me well for the bachelor life ahead. Breakfast, lunch, and dinner were planned ahead, as were cleaning, laundry, and the rest. We kept the dishwasher Chicky had won on a TV show. Time became a premium. Still, with surplus wildlife in the area and two well-trained hunting dogs, bag limits were obtained in half the time as in New Jersey.

Around May 15 of each year, the dairy herd remains in pastures except for milking time twice a day. Barn chores are replaced with efforts to store next winter's fodder. Those efforts include spring planting of corn and soybeans, and harvesting a variety of hay, alfalfa, clover, timothy, trefoil, and grasses, all uniquely prepared for storage in a silo, grain bin, or hay mow. My songs filled the air as I met the challenges. I sang, "Whistle while you work, whistle while you work" and "Oh, what a beautiful mornin', oh, what a beautiful day! I've got a wonderful feeling everything's going my way!" I was aloof. "Mine eyes have seen the glory of the coming of the Lord."

In late September, heavy frost covered the lush pastures, causing the cows to remain in the stanchions longer each day. Indoor chores inevitably replaced the outdoor activity as frost, ice, and snow asserted their influence. I contemplated. I wondered. I pondered. How could I ever own a farm, home, or business, handicapped by ending my schooling at age sixteen? Prospecting was risky. Fur trapping was on the way out because of animal rights and the production of artificial furs. Working on this farm wouldn't do it. Conclusion: get an education.

Mr. Waterman, the high school principal, leaned back in his chair, placed his hands behind his head, and smiled sternly, insisting, "This won't work. You can't be serious. You expect to enroll in our high school four weeks after opening? You want to double your schedule after being out of school for a year and a half? I don't think so. When will you study? When will you do your homework? This won't work."

"Mr. Waterman, that's my problem. What do you have to lose by me trying? Besides, maybe I can find someone to help with the housework."

It became clear that my cocky, self-assured attitude sparked that parental guidance ploy: "All right; he has to be taught a lesson."

"Fair enough," he replied. "Consecutive classes will be scheduled all day as you requested, with no study halls or library time. You will have a twenty-minute, restricted lunch period. Excessive absences from class for any reason will cause you to fail that class for the semester. Familiarize yourself with our rules and report to your homeroom teacher, Miss Lockner, Monday morning at the scheduled time. We do not tolerate tardiness."

An unconvincing smile and a weak handshake confirmed his unspoken belief that within a month, once again I would drop out of school. Hard work and intensive study complemented my average scholastic abilities and created a false impression that I was a smart kid. The next nine months can be summarized in three words: work, work, work. Housework, farm work, schoolwork.

Barbara Lockner, a very attractive, very single, very pregnant homeroom teacher, encouraged other classmates to help me meet my student responsibilities. Our responsibilities included raising money for the junior prom, local charities, and for our future senior trip. It also included participating in fundraising drives, bake sales, and group carwash activities. But was I a sophomore or a junior student? A new or repeat activity was scheduled each month after the appointed chairman announced the success or mediocrity of each individual student's effort. Ashamed, I cringed, but I clapped along with others as names were read from a performance list to be posted on the bulletin board.

The following months had to be different. I stood before my classmates and calmly explained the details of my daily life. "And in conclusion, I will not attend the junior prom, go on the future senior trip, or seek benefits from your fund-raising activities. I hope you understand why I cannot be a part of this class in the same way all of you are."

Two days later, much to my surprise, Miss Lockner privately commented, "Ken, you seem to have it all over the other students."

"Thank you, but that's not true. It's just that I'm here for a different purpose."

It was rumored that we had the hots for each other, something I vehemently denied. Regardless, she invited me to attend a meeting that evening at Tom Murphy's home. I was further surprised by individual student offers to help me with laundry, housework, and specially prepared cakes and pies for the bake sales. I strictly limited the help, stating, "I really appreciate what all of you are doing for me, but I can't offer anything in return except a thank-you."

The next morning, Miss Lockner gave me a tardy excuse for my first-period class and stated, "We have to talk about last night."

"Miss Lockner, you asked me to follow you to Tom's home in my car with a couple of other students. It was snowing sideways with a thirty-mile-an-hour wind. Visibility was nearly zero, a whiteout, and your taillights were packed with snow, leaving a faint, red glow. I don't know why you were stopped in the middle of the road. You shouldn't have stopped there, and I shouldn't have hit you."

"The damage to my brother's car is a lot more than your damage, so I believe the fair thing to do is for each to pay our own repair costs." We shook hands to seal the agreement.

My first impression of this new Chevrolet convertible with smashed headlights, crushed fenders, grille, and hood belied the insurance adjuster's damage report. Howard calmed my worries. "It's not as bad as it looks, Ken. But you will have to pay the deductible of five hundred dollars."

"That's fine with me, but you know I don't have any money. You still owe me for a year's work building the New Jersey house, and I've received only a few dollars from the farm."

"That's true, but don't forget the cost of your room and board and the use of my new convertible. Besides, you know I would pay you if I had the money."

"Yes, I know that. By the way, will you have the money for my class ring?"

"We turn the cows out to pasture in May. Our grain bill will be down twelve hundred dollars. I'm sure we can spare eighteen dollars by June first for the ring."

The next day while rushing to class, I carelessly bumped into Ace Breen, the school bully, knocking his books to the floor. He squared off, danced up and down, and snarled, "You think you're hot shit!"

With hands raised in surrender, I insisted, "I'm not going to tangle ass here in the school, but we can have it out tonight at the soccer field."

Ace, the town lawyer's son, wanted to believe he was tops in all things—hence the name "Ace." A large group of students gathered behind the school just before dark. Ace, a senior classman, was the biggest guy in the school, with a demeanor equally intimidating. In less than a minute, he was on the ground, blood pouring from a broken nose, moaning in agony while holding his stomach. I stood by briefly and remarked, "From now on, just leave me alone."

That night, Howard received a threatening phone call from Attorney Breen accusing me of attacking his son. A lawsuit was to be filed. Ten days later, during a heated discussion—no, an argument—with my business law teacher, Stubby Ballard, a tall, lanky kid seated behind me, started burping. The teacher's explanation of a "holder in due course" was clearly wrong. Each time I offered proof of her error, Stubby burped. Everyone laughed. I ordered, "Don't do that again!" Stubby stood up. I immediately stood up and shoved him backward over the desk, warning him to stay down. In seconds, Mrs. Becker, a slim, old lady with glasses and squinty eyes, stepped between us and ordered me to the principal's office. I left the classroom as directed but instead went downtown to Lawyer Breen's office.

"I'm sorry, do you have an appointment?" the receptionist asked.

"No. I'm Ken Crane, and I have to speak with Mr. Breen as soon as possible."

A voice from another room called, "Oh, Mr. Crane. Step into my office."

"Mr. Breen, I'm not sorry for fighting with your son, Ace, but he had it coming and wouldn't stop bullying me."

"That's OK, Mr. Crane; I investigated the matter and concluded that Ace got what he deserved. Forget about it, but thanks for stopping in."

"It's not about Ace. I'm in trouble, and I need your help. I need a written definition of a 'holder in due course' to settle a dispute with my business law teacher."

He immediately dictated a letter: "A 'holder in due course' is an innocent, third-party holder of a valid, negotiable promissory note." He stressed the word *innocent* with a detailed explanation.

"Is that all, Mr. Crane?"

"No. I'm supposed to be at the principal's office at this very moment because of a dispute in my classroom. Mr. Waterman will suspend me from school unless he understands what happened." I explained the details.

"Well, Mr. Crane, it sounds to me you are at fault."

"It's Stubby Ballard's fault, because he wouldn't stop burping. The teacher didn't do anything about it. Your letter proves her mistake about the definition of a 'holder in due course.' She makes two mistakes and keeps her job. I shouldn't have pushed Stubby Ballard, but that's only one mistake. Mr. Waterman warned me about the rules before I started classes in October, but I don't want to be suspended from school for one mistake. Will you help me? I promise I'll pay you as soon as I get some money."

"Mr. Waterman is a fair man. I'll call him and try to help, but I'm not making any promises."

Stubby Ballard and I faced Mr. Waterman as our teacher looked on. I apologized to Mr. Waterman and my teacher and reluctantly shook hands with Stubby. I was relieved to hear a stern promise of suspension from school for the slightest infraction during the remaining four weeks of school, our probationary period.

Time passed quickly, uneventfully. Strangely, evening phone calls from California caused Howard to rush for the phone and settle into private conversations—sometimes once a week, then every evening, and occasionally, also during lunch hour. Cows were in the pasture. Howard smiled as he studied the milk check, commenting, "We did real good this month."

"Great, but don't forget, I'll be getting out of school in two weeks and will need the money by then to pay for my class ring."

"Ahh, that's right, but remind me again next week."

This was an exciting time: little or no homework and relaxed rules in the hallways as students exchanged yearbooks for a comment or signature across their pictures; a crescendo countdown to the end.

Miss Lockner held the box high. "Your rings are here." Everyone was anxious to examine the end product, an oblong, turquoise stone with a small, gold-leaf center mounted in place with a 14-karat gold base reading "19" on one side and "53" on the other. A joyous time indeed, as girls playfully toyed with gestures to place boys' rings on ribbons around their necks. As I tried to leave the room unnoticed, Miss Lockner handed me my ring. "Pay me when you can."

"Thank you, Miss Lockner, but I don't know when that may be. I cannot accept the ring." Embarrassed, ashamed, and heartbroken, once again I thanked Miss Lockner for all she had done for me during the school year.

That day, I had it out with Howard. He unloaded all his problems and apologized for being broke. After paying the $500 deductible for the car accident, he claimed there was no money left to spare. The last day of school, I paid the $18 and left the school with my report card and the class ring. I passed every subject—mostly Cs, a few Bs, and one or two poor but passing Ds.

Farming breeds a peculiar attitude. Next year will always be better. Howard admired my ring and marveled at my report card. "I didn't think you could do it. I guess your high score on the state Regents tests tipped the scale."

Relieved, I simply commented, "I don't know. Maybe I just got lucky."

Howard was deep in thought, very pensive. "I've been talking with Irma for several months. Doug divorced Irma over a year ago. Chicky has divorced me and isn't coming back to the farm. I have to go to California for Irma, and I'm wondering if you would run the farm for ten days. Irma has agreed to live here at the farm, and if all goes well, we'll get married in the fall. This year should be better for all of us."

Of course I accepted the challenge. Of course, at eighteen, I was a man. Of course, I now understood the hassle over the $18.

Ten days passed in one day. No problems. Milk production was up. The first cutting of hay was ready for the mow. Howard praised my efforts and applauded the results. Irma changed her mind and broke off relations with Howard. I was happy to hear about that. I liked sister-in-law Irma as Doug's wife but detested the thought of sister-in-law Irma Erma as Howard's wife.

A strict routine controlled our life to the exclusion of all else. Week after week, I thought of home and Pop's one-liners: "Plan your work, and work your plan," "Plan your life and live your plan." My plan was unchanged: get an education. Howard made no comment as I revealed my intentions: "I'll help you through the hay season, but when the mow is full, I'll be leaving for New Jersey."

August 15, we shook hands and shared warm, caring feelings as good friends often do. "Good luck, keep in touch, and thanks for everything, et cetera." Regardless, to desert my brother under these circumstances weighed heavily on my conscience and spawned Howard's resentment, which I was to endure for the rest of his life.

High School Yearbook 1953

Home Sweet Home at Age Eighteen

After several days of cleaning and making minor repairs, the brooder coop seemed like old home. I was happy to regain my independence, free of the imposed pressures of the past year and a half. Soothing rain on the roof lulled me back to Howard's farm. He was alone. My desertion, his depression, no wife, no girlfriend, no money, no Ken: for the first time, I realized a correct choice often hurts others, physically and mentally.

Unstructured activity for two weeks seemed like the summer vacation others talked about. I relaxed, fished the north branch of the Raritan River at my old spot, and explored the banks of Noel's Brook for muskrat dens. Fishing season was to end shortly. Hunting and trapping season would begin. I was an experienced farmer at age seventeen; good-paying work was available and as much as I chose. My senior year in high school was uneventful. I didn't cut classes. I studied hard; trapped muskrats; hunted pheasants, rabbits, and deer; and milked cows at Bogner's farm, a mile south of my brooder coop. Phase one of my plan was now complete. For many years, my former classmates questioned how I pulled it off—to be out of school for a year and a half, yet graduate from Somerville High School with my original class. This caused much suspicion. My grades were average or below. I wasn't a smart kid. I guess I just got lucky.

Quiet time by a stream, strolling through the woods observing nature, watching stars at night, perpetuated my dreams. *What shall I be?*

What shall I study? How will I pay for college? Little did I know, little did Doug know, he was strongly influencing my decisions, my life-altering choices.

Phase two of the plan: cause the government to pay my college tuition. Two years of military service could entitle me to four years of higher education. Family tradition favored the Marine Corps, but that required a minimum enlistment of three years. "Sorry, Mr. Recruiting Officer, that is not my plan. I'll join the army, navy, or another branch of the service."

He stopped me at the door. "I have an idea, but I've never tried this before. Everyone enrolled in the military reserves must be drafted to active duty for failure to attend training sessions. If you enlist in the Marine Corps reserves and fail to arrive for training, you will be drafted for active duty for two years."

Three months later, November 23, 1953, I reported to the Newark, New Jersey Armory for a physical exam, swearing an oath of allegiance, and a bus ride to boot camp at Parris Island, South Carolina.

The intensive, sometimes brutal training was not difficult for me due to my past lifestyle. Rural country boys endured boot camp much better than affluent city boys. Nearly half of the original recruits were mustered out of the platoon during boot camp training. Cigarette smokers experienced the most difficulties. Physical or mental reasons for discharge varied widely, but size or stature were not part of the decision. It shocked me.

Pete hollered from the second-story window of the base medical building. "Hey, Crane! I have to talk with you." He had been dropped from the platoon four weeks prior, along with several other recruits. As usual, no reason was given. He met me at the entrance, eyes flushed with tears. A hidden surge of sympathy and embarrassment stalled my gesture to shake hands. Crying, nearly out of control, he wrapped his arms around me and pouted, "I can't take this anymore."

Back home, he had been a big, tough guy, a team captain, a Somerville High football star, but here, he was a pathetic little man, broken in spirit, deeply ashamed, lonely, and homesick. That afternoon, he poured out his heart to me. As I left, he secured my promise not to disclose any of this back home. Once again, I failed to avoid his pleading embrace. He envied me, but I am a marine, and I don't hug human males.

Recruits from other units replaced those eliminated from our ranks. With bands playing the Marine Corps hymn, "Esprit de Corps," and "Semper Fidelis" swelled the chests of each marine as platoons marched in perfect harmony past the review stand. Suddenly, I understood the message from my great-uncle Stephen Crane, delivered to the world through his book *The Red Badge of Courage*. The American flag undulated gently, followed by inspiring parade flags identifying each battalion, company, and platoon. However, one flag electrified the very fiber of my bones.

The cadence ended when the sergeant shouted, "Pla—tooon—Halt! Lef-ta face. Or-der arms!" The entire platoon responded to the commands as one. "Present colors!" Our platoon leader marched forward. "Halt, left face!" Still at attention, he held our platoon flag high. We were the best at Parris Island for that training period.

Our company commander stood tall and proud, delivering a congratulatory message to the troops for their successful completion of boot camp. "You have earned the distinction to be part of the military elite. You are now marines. You are the base honor platoon."

An orderly marched forward to supply the awards. Our commander carefully pinned a medal alongside my Good Conduct ribbon. The medal is the size of a silver dollar but shinier. Two M1 rifles cross the hollow center and two sides of a wreath. The award distinguishes the relatively few marines who score above 220 out of a possible 250 points while firing from various distances up to five hundred yards. The qualifying weapon is a gas-operated, semiautomatic M1 rifle weighing 9.1 pounds. "Rapid fire" or "fire at will" is ordered by the range officer on the firing line. Loudspeakers blared: "A hundred yards, off hand, you have ten seconds to fire one full clip. Ready on the right, ready on the left, all ready on the firing line. Fire at will."

At other distances the commands varied slightly: "Ready on the right, ready on the left, all ready on the firing line. Get down there, get down there fast, get that first shot off." Each time, our platoon responded in an instant as the range officer lowered the start flag with a snap of his wrist.

Our commander continued: "Congratulations, Private Crane. This medal distinguishes you as an expert rifleman."

Rigid as a statue, I responded, "Sir, thank you, sir!" We exchanged perfect salutes.

Platoon after platoon marched to the music, as we did. Singled-out recruits like me were ordered front and center. Finally, the band stopped playing. The ceremony was over. Familiar commands filled the air: "Tench-*hut*! Right shoulder arms! Forr-ward, harch!" Heels clicked in rhythm to the cadence as we left the parade field, heading to our tent area. "Platooooon halt! Or-der arms! Pa-rade rest! At ease."

Our platoon sergeant continued: "Congratulations. You have endured some of the toughest training the military has to offer. You are not just marines. You are the best. You are an honor platoon. Never forget—once a marine, always a marine. You are to report to your company headquarters tomorrow at oh-eight-hundred for transfer orders. Semper Fi! Pla-toon dismissed!"

Excitement filled the air as footlockers emptied and duffel bags filled. A ten-day leave was scheduled before reporting for new duty. In full uniform, spit-shined shoes, a good behavior ribbon, and an Expert Rifleman's medal on my chest, I arrogantly, defiantly, proudly, independently, marched to our company headquarters. My mind strummed the guitar while I sang to my sweetheart as I did before enlisting in the Marine Corps:

"There's a star-spangled banner waving somewhere, in a distant land so many miles away. Only Uncle Sam's great heroes get to go there, and I hope I may get to go there too someday." ...as I did before enlisting in the *Marine Corps (a riff on "There's a Star-Spangled Banner*

Waving Somewhere," by Paul Roberts and Shelby Darnell, ©1942, Bob Miller, Inc.).

Robustly, I continued:
"I'll see Lincoln, Custer, Washington, and Perry, Nathan Hale, Cole, and Kelly too
There's a star-spangled banner waving somewhere and in that heaven there will be a place for me."
I am nineteen years old. I am a man. I am proud. I am a marine. I want my sweetheart to see my medal. I am conceited.

At company headquarters, we waited for the staccato command: "Next! Front and center." The master sergeant seated next to our company noncommissioned officer asked, "What is your name, rank, and serial number?"

"Sir, Private Crane, sir. Serial number one-four-two-three-one-eight-three, reporting as ordered, sir."

"At ease, Private. I see you have an Expert Rifleman's medal." The NCO stepped from behind his desk. "Keep up the good work, Private."

My chest expanded on every word until embarrassment and humility extinguished my moment of glory. I couldn't believe the fruit salad of ribbons, medals, and clusters on his chest—Iwo Jima, Guadalcanal, Normandy, a Bronze Star with a cluster, a Purple Heart, and many more symbols of bravery I did not recognize. Here was a real man, a real marine—certainly, not me. My uniform fit loosely now as shame and humility shrank my stature. When we shook hands, I eked out the words, "Sir, thank you, sir."

My family and friends are mostly in Hillsborough, New Jersey, but my girlfriend lived in Stamford, New York, six hours away. Overwhelming primordial urges compelled me to continue bonding with my high school sweetheart. The extra travel time caused my ten-day leave pass to expire as if it were for one day. When that day arrived, I checked in at Camp Lejeune, North Carolina, and discovered my next challenge. Each student marine is granted a choice of next duty station depending on scholastic position in the graduating class. Number one choice the Brooklyn Navy Yard. I scored second highest and chose the next best duty station: Quantico, Virginia, thirty miles south of Washington, DC.

The Korean War ended but fifteen hundred marines stationed at Quantico still had to be paid cash wages, bimonthly. For the next two years, maintaining individual payroll records, counting cash in small bills to be secured in each payroll officer's floor safe, was my job; that is what I did. During those years, as planned, I migrated north and south whenever authorized, including weekends, allowing time, distance, and circumstances to properly test our love for each other and fuel the desire to bond in holy matrimony. Also, my plan for government-paid college tuition forced me from the bars and fellow marines, back to the barracks to improve my chance of passing a college entrance exam.

My plan continued: in three months, I would be honorably discharged from military service. At age twenty-one, I embraced the ultimate challenge and married my high school sweetheart, age twenty. The ceremony took place five miles from Howard's farm, at the Methodist Church in Prattsville, New York, on August 6, 1955. But I often wondered: *Are we legally married?*

Wedding Day
August 6, 1955

III. My New World of Business and Organized Agriculture

The Star Breeding Farm
(Yes, Stars Are Born)

We were married August 6, 1955. I was honorably discharged from the United States Marine Corps on November 23 and started as a freshman at Pace College in New York City on January 5, 1956. This was all according to a plan dreamed with my sixteen-year-old high school sweetheart on October 8, 1950, my seventeenth birthday. With a wife, a home (albeit a chicken house half remodeled), and college tuition to be paid under the GI Bill, the challenge was obvious. Our plan was crystal clear. I'd work at Bogner's dairy farm a mile south, trap muskrats, and hunt wild game in my spare time. In the spring, Alice would tend the garden and raise broiler chickens. We bought three hundred throwaway rooster chicks at one cent each, knowing from Dad's experience raising broilers that there would be a high mortality rate. But we lost only five chicks and sold the rest for cash sufficient to pay the entire feed bill. The planning left us with 150 chickens for the freezer, free of charge; wild game meat; and garden vegetables galore. We summarized future plans as a crisp, gentle breeze fluttered the autumn leaves where I had slept years ago before frost had urged me into the brooder coop for the winter. Alice posed question after question. All the questions were "what-ifs" and "how-will-we's."

I admired the brooder coop a grape arbor away and consoled her. "I can't answer all of your questions. And of course it will be a challenge. But there's no reason why we can't do it. Let's write up our plan. Hunting season has started, and trapping season opens next week. Besides, what can we lose by trying?"

Soon, our freezer was full of venison, rabbits, squirrels, pheasants, squabs, frog legs, fish, and many other creatures that, if mentioned, might offend a normal person. Money was seriously budgeted, allowing few purchases other than condiments. Occasionally, I brought home flowers from a City Hall Park vendor to lighten Alice's burden as she toiled—fall, winter, spring, and summer, season after season. Déjà vu—nothing is a problem, just a challenge. Wrong! Money was a problem, a huge problem. Bare necessities were a luxury. Under the GI Bill, the cost of tuition and books was paid to me monthly, but little or no money was allotted for subsistence.

Our monthly income was budgeted as follows:
1. Car expense from the chicken house to the Somerville, New Jersey train station eight miles away.
2. A commuter-train ticket from Somerville to Hoboken, New Jersey.
3. Ferry expense to cross the Hudson River and arrive at Canal Street, New York City.
4. Subsistence necessities: salt, pepper, bread, etc.

Thus, a country boy entered a different world. With briefcase in hand, he boldly walked several blocks to and from the high-rise college directly across from City Hall Park, often catching the last ferry at night, crossing from New York City to Hoboken, New Jersey. The daily trip each way allowed desperately needed study time but was grossly inadequate. Homework was completed helter-skelter as financial pressures forced priorities to consume the time scheduled for education. Consequently, I was placed on scholastic probation. A daughter born on February 6, 1958, was not part of our plan. Conclusion: Alice would have to feed the rats.

Several international drug companies, including Merck, Warner-Lambert, and Johnson & Johnson, had recently established research laboratories in our area. While I searched for employment, my farming experience urged attention toward the laboratory animals. After a quick market research and a few phone calls, our rat business started with a hundred females and twenty males.

As supervisor of the Diehl Manufacturing Company's audit group, I was granted permission to confiscate hundreds of obsolete bolt boxes for my personal use. The boxes were nine by fifteen inches and five inches high, with metal-reinforced corners. Each could be a perfect rat nest. We fashioned lids out of wood and mesh wire that allowed the rats to consume food placed in a *V* shape of wire on the lid. The Belle Mead Inn, alcoholic Pop's watering hole, provided an endless supply of empty beer bottles. Once filled with water, a curved glass tube corked into each bottle, hooked and placed upside down with the tube through the wire, allowed each rat to lap water anytime, a drop at a time. Our initial venture capital of approximately $118 included costs for 120 rats, corks, and glass tubes. The Belle Mead Farmers' Coal and Feed Mill, my employer at age sixteen, allowed me a thirty-day charge account for rat food. Thus, Star Breeding Farm commenced business.

Rats are extremely prolific, a lesson learned by all who invest time and money in a rodent breeding facility. Males will breed any female in estrus at any time. Gestation normally lasts nineteen to twenty-one days, producing a litter of ten to eighteen pups. The lactation period seldom exceeds three weeks, and unlike most mammals, the mother will conceive again before weaning her offspring. Pups must be isolated at age three weeks, or interbreeding mutation may occur, destroying a healthy genetic base.

Within forty-three days, we turned a profit, tripled the number of breeding female rats, and improved the genetic base by trading newborn males for unrelated males. Advance orders for AZ rats put our rat factory on overtime. These rats, aged two to three weeks, were sold for pregnancy testing. We had little knowledge of the rodent business, but money was pouring in. Weekly profits often exceeded $100. Soon, our rat production demanded more and more habitat. Bolt boxes, wire lids, and water supply had to be fabricated, labeled, and shelved quickly. Within two months, we housed over two thousand rats in nesting boxes stacked eight feet high, row after row.

Consider the following calculations: Rats' lactation period is twenty-one days; each female averages eight offspring (half of them female). Thus, the first lactation produced eight hundred pups. Second lactation is at forty-two days. For a hundred females plus the four hundred from the first lactation—five hundred females—each with an average of eight pups, we have four thousand pups. At the third lactation, the geometric progression from the original one hundred females plus four hundred from the first litter and two thousand females from the next twenty-five hundred breeding females. And so on. The geometric progression for sixty-three days of rat production, starting with a hundred females, gives 24,800 pups (less mortalities and nonbreeders).

In light of such facts, production must be strictly controlled. Our inventory was limited to what would fill commitments and advance orders. We accepted large, out-of-state orders to be picked up at our farm in three to four weeks. At the same time, we processed short-term, small orders of fifty to a hundred rats, to be delivered locally. Business was booming, and there was no end in sight. The phone rang. "Hello? Yes. This is Star Breeding Farm. No, I'm sorry. We don't deliver out of state. Yes, of course. We will be happy to accept your order, provided we receive full payment before you pick up. What is the name of your company?"

"We are a laboratory animal broker located in Connecticut. We serve companies throughout the East Coast and parts of Canada. We are looking for a long-term contract to supply our clients with pathogen-free rats. Are you interested?"

"Yes, sir, very much so. How many rats are we talking about?"

"Right now the numbers range between five hundred and eight hundred rats per week. Companies all over the world are investing heavily in medical research, posing a strong demand for laboratory animals, especially pathogen-free rats. Will you be able to fill such orders?"

My mind raced for an answer. Although I didn't know what a pathogen-free rat was, I declared, "Absolutely. When would you like to start?"

"Our driver and lab technician can be at your farm on Saturday. We need to inspect your facilities, and if satisfactory, we will buy five hundred rats and take them with us."

Elated, I slowly cradled the phone and tiptoed to the tune, "Happy days are here at last!"

Days later, the driver and a gray-haired passenger stepped from the middle-aged hearse now backed up to our barn. "Mr. Crane, I presume?"

"Yes, sir. How are you?"

"Fine. I'm Dr. Benson. We're here to inspect your operation. Our agent tells me you can provide a weekly supply of pathogen-free rats."

"Yes, sir, I believe we can."

"Well, let's take a look. Where are your breeding facilities?"

I opened the barn door and remarked, "Right here. You're welcome to look around."

The doctor stepped inside without comment. I recognized his expression: *You can't be serious!* He walked along the rows of bolt boxes, peering into one now and then. Authoritatively, he remarked, "Mr. Crane, are these your 'pathogen-free' rats?"

Ignorant of the meaning, I nervously replied, "I think so, don't you?"

Without replying, he returned to the hearse and handed me a pamphlet that outlined strict standards for breeding pathogen-free laboratory animals. Then he added, "I'm sorry, Mr. Crane, but your facilities do not meet our minimum standards. If you improve your operation, I am certain we can do business."

He sensed my disappointment, my embarrassment. I appreciated his sympathy, his travel expense from Connecticut, and his wasted time. My premature excitement while singing, "Happy days are here at last!" had instantly vanished with the word *pathogen*, leaving in its place the word *ignorance*.

I examined the contents of the breeding box at which he had asked, "Is this what you call a 'pathogen-free' rat?" Much to my surprise, some of the litters of white rats were not the intended white. Some had gray ears and spotted bodies like Dalmatians. Some were pure white or solid gray; some were a collage of black, gray, and white. Obviously, those pups had been sired by a wild rat. But how did that happen? Copulation must have been through the small, mesh wire fabricated onto the bolt box lid. Regardless, I now knew these were not pathogen-free rats— germ free!

The next day, Sunday, I answered the phone. "Mr. Crane"?

"Yes, sir."

"This is Dr. Benson. Did you study the paperwork I gave you?"

"I didn't study it, but I understand the requirements. I don't have enough money to support my family, so to invest in a business at this time is out of the question."

"Well, that's why I'm calling you. Would you be interested in a business arrangement to help us obtain a steady supply of pathogen-free laboratory animals? I was impressed with your ingenuity and enthusiasm. I discussed the matter with my colleagues, and they have authorized me to offer the following proposal: if we finance the construction of a controlled-environment facility on your property, will you agree to accept full responsibility for the operation? Of course, our lawyers will have to work out the details."

In fact, I had studied the pamphlet in detail. To market pathogen-free animals, they must be born and raised in a highly controlled environment. That included a concrete building, air-purification systems, restricted entry by authorized personnel only, and a specialized diet. The goal, of course, is to raise the animals under sterile conditions.

"Dr. Benson, I sincerely appreciate your offer. But I cannot take advantage of this tremendous opportunity at this time. My overall family situation simply cannot include more complications or responsibilities. I'm sure things will improve in the near future, and if your offer is still available, I definitely will go forward on your terms. This could be a fantastic business."

"Thank you, Mr. Crane, it's been a pleasure speaking with you. Good luck, and from time to time, let me know about your progress."

I was about to end our conversation when Dr. Benson said, "By the way, I chuckle whenever I see your business card. 'Star Breeding Farm'—how did you come up with that?"

"Well, Dr. Benson, I thought of Serutan—you know, that fiber-type laxative product widely promoted on radio and television?. The commercial always ended with a catchy statement: 'Remember, Serutan spelled backward is *nature's*.'" I wanted purchasing agents to remember our business card and telephone number. At the top of the business card, domed like a rainbow, it read, "Star Breeding Farm." At the bottom of the card, forming the base of the rainbow, it said, "Remember, Star spelled backward is Rats."

That afternoon, Alice quickly lifted and closed the lid on a fifty-gallon, heavy-duty cardboard barrel. With the help of several people, the barrel soon contained our entire rat population. They died quickly from a continuous flow of carbon monoxide piped from our pickup truck. There was barely a sound or movement each time Alice lifted the lid, dumped in rats, then instantly closed it, time after time. The barrel was nearly full. Thus ended the lives of five thousand rats. Thus ended Star Breeding Farm, but it was not forgotten. Remember—Star spelled backward is Rats.

I Want to Be an Accountant

Arthur Andersen and Company, one of the "Big 8" accounting firms in the United States, established an internal audit group for Diehl Manufacturing Company, a subsidiary of Singer Sewing Machine Company, located in Manville, New Jersey. After one month on the job, I accepted a supervisory position for an internal audit group of accountants, a private office, and a personal secretary. It was a humbling experience at age twenty-five to lead a staff of professionals more experienced and much older than me. Some were twice my age. For the first time, I felt the pleasure of respect and appreciation without the negatives often attached to kudos. Apparently, my self-reliant past had filled me with confidence, and an "I can do anything" attitude masked my apprehension and fear of not meeting the expectations of the executives who had put me in this position. A year passed, filled with compliments that warmed my heart.

The company paid for special night classes at Pace College in New York City, and I was encouraged above all else to become a "company man," including eliminating my activity as a public accountant income tax consultant. Much to my surprise, I was offered a high-paying position at company headquarters in New York City. "The chance of a lifetime," I was told. "A path to the top has been cleared for you."

I was elated by the news. Our money troubles would be over. No more electric or telephone shutoff notices. No more bill collectors at the door. And perhaps, yes, perhaps, I would be able to buy a present now and then for my wife. Rumors of an executive shake-up in the home office were bandied about during the week and caused me to reply, "This is a great opportunity, but I want to talk it over with my wife. I have to think about this."

"What is there to think about? No one in our company has been promoted like this, and we want you in the assistant controller's office immediately."

The harbingers of this great promotion, now shocked in utter disbelief at my casual response, politely demanded an answer by 4:00 p.m. the next day.

Excitement filled the air as Alice rushed food to the dinner table, remarking, "This is what we've been waiting for. But is it what *you* want?"

After much talk, a couple of drinks, and a sleepless night filled with anticipation, my self-assured personality again took charge. The next morning, I submitted my resignation to leave the company in favor of my independence as a public accountant. A brief discussion prompted the question, "What on earth caused you to make such a foolish decision?"

"It was not easy at first, but I realized you made the decision for me. I was told a path to the top has been cleared just for me. I would be filling the position held by a fifty-five-year-old man, cleared out of the path after years of loyal service to the company. How am I to accept such treatment when it's my turn to be cleared out?"

Again, a brief discussion ensued. "This rarely happens, and only when it is in the best interest of the company. Do you want more time to reconsider your decision?"

Confidently, I replied, "Gentlemen, you have honored me in ways beyond my wildest dreams. I don't know how to express greater appreciation for what has been done for me, except to say thank you. My decision came through from self-evaluation. I will not allow any person, business, or situation to sink their claws in my ass and control my destiny. I have no idea where this choice of independence will lead me, but my perverse desire to triumph over adversity is fueled by my nonpurchasable attributes. I'm not the man for the job. I will not surrender my independence. Thank you for the opportunity."

"Financially poor" was not an accurate description of our plight. Destitute was more accurate. As such, any gain, ever so small, was very satisfying. Bart Bennuto, a young attorney who had recently passed the bar exam, sat quietly in the adjoining barber chair. Small talk concluded an arrangement to lease space next door and share the reception area and adjoining, one-room office. The arrangement was simple. When he had clients, I would disappear. When I had a client, he would disappear. Confidentiality would be maintained at all costs. The barber, Doug DeSicco, chimed in, "That's a great idea. I'll have my lawyer and accountant right next door. What could be better than that?"

A handshake sealed the deal. Thus began a chain of unique experiences beyond imagination and often unbelievable. It was a proud moment to see my name on the door in bold, black letters outlined in gold leaf: Kenneth V. Crane, Public Accountant. The picture window prominently displayed Bartholomeo A. Bennuto, Attorney-At-Law.

• • •

Months later, a particular day became long and arduous. "Mr. Z," a middle-aged man, was visibly shaken. His bookkeeper and accountant had not yet surrendered the trucking company records to the IRS when I was retained to defend against serious charges collectively referred to as "tax evasion." An analysis of the issues clearly indicated the records had been falsified, leaving no chance to claim otherwise. Within minutes, Mr. Z said, "I know I'm in serious trouble. That's why I'm here. I want you to take care of this for me, no matter what it costs." He tossed an envelope on my desk. "Here's a little 'grease' for the agent. He'll go along with everything."

I saw dim lights in the kitchen as I walked from the detached garage to the big house, our home. While warming my dinner, Alice broke the silence with, "How was your day?"

"My day was OK. Are the girls in bed?"

"Of course. You look troubled; what's the matter?"

"I'm dealing with a very nasty IRS case. The client gave me this envelope. He will pay my fee, plus this amount as a bonus after the case is settled." On the envelope is written: *$4,000.* This was a huge amount of money in 1962.

"What are you going to do?"

"I don't know. We need the money so bad. I haven't paid my full share of office expense for nearly five months. We have shutoff notices for the gas, telephone, and electric here at home. Also, our heating fuel bill is due in less than two weeks. We sure need the money. How do you feel about it?"

"We've been through far worse financial troubles than now, so don't do this on *my* account. It's your decision, so don't ask me to decide your rights and wrongs."

As I drove to the office in the morning, I reflected on my job as a plumber's helper at age twelve, working for Mr. Noel, who tried to pay me wages he thought I was worth. I refused to accept anything exceeding my considered worth and immediately handed back half of the money paid. My alcoholic father praised me for that gesture. A flashback reminded me of his words, "Never accept anything you alone, in all honesty, cannot justify the entitlement to. Otherwise, someone will get their claws in your ass."

"Good morning, Mr. Crane. Mr. Z wants to meet with you this morning. Also, his IRS agent is scheduled for one o'clock."

"Darlene, this is going to be a very difficult day. I don't want any interruptions, and hold all of my phone calls."

I sat quietly at my desk, still pondering the situation. Unlike priests or attorneys-at-law, accountants can legally be forced to violate most assumptions of confidentiality with their clients. Accountants' work papers, schedules, and records of all sorts can be subpoenaed for examination by IRS agents. Accountants can legally be compelled to testify against their clients and reveal damaging statements that would otherwise be concealed in accordance with privilege laws granted to other professionals.

I advised Mr. Z to retain attorney Bart Bennuto, who would then hire me to handle the entire matter, thus sheltering him under the attorney-client confidentiality laws. Most of the information, other than the trucking company records, would be considered privileged. As such, it could not be forced into evidence.

Mr. Z listened intently as I handed him the envelope of money, and he immediately shoved the unopened envelope containing $4,000 into his pocket. "I still want you to handle the entire matter, because I know you'll do your very best for me. I just hope I'm not arrested and put in jail."

He explained, "When you returned the four thousand dollars, I was surprised, especially since the envelope had not been opened. Bribes, kickbacks, and fixes, often disguised as gratuities, are taken for granted in my business. It is referred to as 'grease.' I've forgotten the joy and satisfaction, the valuable self-esteem, the good feeling that is absorbed by simply doing the right thing. Thank you. I want to come clean so I don't have to worry about this anymore. It's been driving me crazy. I want you to handle the entire case, without a lawyer. Please settle everything with the IRS as you see fit, regardless of the consequences."

Later, a big, burly, well-dressed man in his forties handed me his credentials and announced, "My name is Mr. Blattsburg from the Internal Revenue Service. I'm here to examine the records of XYZ Trucking Company, together with the individual tax returns of the owner shareholders. I will need source documents substantiating all relevant issues. Are you prepared to begin?"

Mr. Blattsburg's appearance was as intimidating as a court-martial ruling being announced to all marines. Those start with the caption, "Case Number such-and-such; the *United States of America v. Private Little*." Visualize "The *United States Vs. Mr. Z*."

I submitted the required power of attorney executed by Mr. Z authorizing me to act on his behalf. Mr. Blattsburg and I settled around a conference table piled high with records. With a sigh, I commented, "It appears this is going to be a detailed audit over a long period of time."

"Not necessarily," Mr. Blattsburg responded. "It all depends on Mr. Z's submissions. We have to tidy up certain details required to clear the audit through our internal review section. Do you have an offer in compromise?" His demeanor, expression, and open hand on the conference table indicated a need for grease. It provided a perfect opportunity to redirect the course of events.

I proceeded with confidence and conviction. "My client has asked me to settle all issues with the IRS in a manner consistent with his responsibilities according to the law. Each issue, therefore, must rise or fall on its own merits. Since we have not examined the issues, obviously I cannot make an offer in compromise at this time. Any action we take must conform to his desire to 'do the right thing, whatever it costs.' I realize audits of this magnitude often take a year or more to resolve. Regardless, I would like to begin right now."

"Mr. Crane, are you sure that's what your client wants to do?"

"Yes, I'm sure."

"Mr. Crane, you are not an attorney. You're not a CPA. You're an enrolled agent. I want to discuss this personally with Mr. Z."

"I'm sorry, Mr. Blattsburg. I cannot—"

Darlene interrupted, "Mr. Morgan is on the phone and insists you speak with him right now."

"Darlene, did you understand me? I said hold all my calls."

"Yes, but he demanded to speak with you anyway."

"Tell Mr. Morgan I'm in the middle of a meeting with an IRS agent and cannot speak with him now. I'll call him right after the meeting."

"I'm sorry for the interruption; perhaps it was fortuitous."

I continued: "Mr. Blattsburg, we are required to abide by the well-established procedural rules setting forth our authority to make demands on each other while carrying out our respective duties and responsibilities. Mr. Z has appointed me his attorney-in-fact, granting me the authority to act in his best interest as if he were here himself. If you attempt to speak with Mr. Z without me present, he will demand a lawyer and proceed with the audit as summarized in Circular 230, published by our Internal Revenue Service. I would like to proceed with this audit with your assurance that together, we will attempt to cause these defendants to pay their just taxes, interest, and penalties. Do I have your assurance?"

Minutes passed without comment. Papers and files were shifted without purpose. Mr. Blattsburg, now expressionless, simply stated, "I will be here at your office, Monday morning at nine."

Darlene warned me to call Mr. Morgan, stating, "He was really nasty to me and said, 'You tell Crane when I call, he is to take my call *no matter what*. He'd better realize who's putting butter on his bread.'"

"Hello, this is Mr. Crane. May I speak with Mr. Morgan ?"

"One moment, please."

An angry voice responded, "Listen, Crane—"

I interrupted, "No, *you* listen, Morgan . Did you tell my secretary...?" I read back his message.

"You're damn right I did. And you'd better listen and understand—"

"No. *You* listen. *You* understand. I lived without butter on my bread before I met you, and I'll live without butter on my bread after I don't know you, so as of right now, *you* go to hell!"

A month prior to this obnoxious encounter with Mr. Morgan, Bart Bennuto had informed me of his plans to start a law practice in Somerville, seven miles north of our present office. Therefore, he would rarely use this small office, and I would have to absorb most of his share of its expenses.

His partner, Richard Clampton, summarized the new arrangement: "The law firm Clampton-Bennuto will continue to pay part of this office expense for one year as a trial run." Bart'sname was to remain on the front window, and we would continue paying part of Darlene Duffy's salary as receptionist. She was to schedule Bart'sappointments through the Somerville office; I was to pay for her bookkeeping and secretarial time. Rich suggested we diligently refer clients to each other. Also, to ease my financial plight, his firm would pay me a flat, monthly professional fee to service their accounting and tax reporting obligations.

"How do you feel about the deal, Ken?"

"I think it's more than fair, but I'm not sure I can hold up my part of the bargain."

"Bart and I understand that. We know you will do your very best, and that's good enough for us. Our office is at Thirty-Two Division Street in Somerville, over the post office. It will be ready in three or four weeks, so stop by next month and check us out."

Crowded on the small, street-level side door was printed "Law Offices, 2nd Floor." Upstairs, prominently displayed at the entrance, was "Clampton, Bennuto, and Morgan, Attorneys at Law."

Thus began thirty-five years of dealings with lawyers, including twenty years of contentious, life-changing episodes with Bob Morgan — episodes that are unbelievable, but all true. He characterized me as a wasp: "You never know when Crane will sting."

Own Land, Son—They Ain't Making No More of It

We reached for the side railing that wasn't there when a step cracked under our light weight as we eased onto the side porch. The roof was leaking and about to collapse against rotted corner posts, and glass windows randomly broken or frameless. I banged the sticky kitchen door closed. Marveling at the oft-parroted sales pitch, "This place has character and old charm."

"My God, what have we done?" exclaimed Alice. "Look at all these problems. We've just traded a nice house for this?"

The full range of my character became exposed like a snapshot of our past: the wrestling matches with my brothers, high school completed in three years, Marine Corps training, never give up, and the blind determination to overcome difficulties now became firmly secured in my personality by the endless clichés and snappy comments of my father: "How do you move a stone church? One stone at a time. How do you climb a mountain? One step at a time." The story of Henny Penny, "Chicken Little," etched feelings in the very fiber of my bones: a belief that if you want something done, you should do it yourself, and don't wait for help promised by well-intentioned others.

My unabashed optimism versus Alice's negativity exemplifies the saying: "Love attracts opposites." We seldom argue, but our relationship has been sorely tested by my glass being half-full while hers is half-empty, an itch I've scratched for sixty plus five years, unsuccessfully.

Excitedly, I chimed, "You don't understand. This is a *house*, but we can make it our *home*. I'll fix the steps and porch right away. We can remodel the kitchen, take down the stovepipe, and replace the wood-burner with a gas range and oven; we can move the wall sink and tear out the old pantry. We'll have a countertop, a dishwasher, and a picture window over here. I'll install a crank-out Andersen window over a new sink. I'll Sheetrock the wainscoting, and you can paint the whole kitchen any color you want. These are not problems, they're challenges."

"Oh, really? And when do you think all this will be done? You don't have the time. I don't have the know-how, and we don't have enough money to pay the first mortgage, let alone the second. You're always looking for miracles."

"Maybe so, but miracles happen at once. The impossible takes *me* a little longer. As my dad would say, 'plan your work, and work your plan.' These are not problems; they're challenges. So let's work together as partners and make it a fun project."

"Some fun," she replied. "This is one partner who's not going to use that outhouse with knotholes through the sides."

"Fair enough, so put that at the top of the list, and I'll plug the holes first thing tomorrow."

She smiled and lamented, "Well, it's better than we're used to," as she added it to the "do-it-first list" along with countless other tasks. As we developed the "work your plan" detail, the list grew exponentially as the proverbial "light at the end of the tunnel" faded into darkness.

Optimism and blind enthusiasm energized the bulb in the mind of this father of one that transferred the light from the end of the tunnel directly to the opening. But the dark abyss beyond scared the hell out of his pregnant wife. Regardless, as usual, we acknowledged the problem, accepted the challenge, and began to climb the mountain, one step at a time. "Wow, our first real estate deal: the homestead."

• • •

"Honey, wake up! Wake up!" With calm desperation, she insisted, "Please hurry! I'm not sure how much longer I can hold out!"

I secured two housecoats and a blanket as we methodically eased our way to the car. I pressed hard on a chrome button that excited the exhausted battery in the old thing. It struggled to accomplish its intended purpose that frigid, dark morning, January 7, 1960. Agonizingly slow, the engine caught a rhythm and gave me a tinge of relief that disappeared when the gas gauge failed to move from the big *E*. The situation in this rural area eliminated all options except one: divine intervention. If one night's supply of oil lasted eight nights to give us the menorah, surely, fumes in an empty gas tank will last eight miles to the hospital to give us a baby.

Afraid and teary-eyed, she blurted out, "How could you do this?" followed by a scathing review of my obsession for challenges.

The boa constrictor in my stomach tightened its hold on the small intestines and lower vital organs as I gently placed my hand on her thigh and quietly pleaded, "Relax, calm down, everything will be OK. I've done this many times, and I know exactly how far we can drive on an empty tank."

At last, a step into heaven. Life is great. Driving our exceptionally warm junk car with a full tank of gas, and my head filled with pride and my heart filled with love, I admired my head majorette, my junior prom queen, the mother of our pudgy, pink baby with a full head of brown hair with silver tips.

I carefully lifted the soft, thin blanket to expose her squinty, blue eyes. Overwhelmed with pride, I knew the doctor was right when he whispered, "You have the most beautiful baby I've ever seen." (Clearly, he was less sincere to the other fathers in the waiting room.)

Unlike the thirty-five-minute race to the hospital, I extended the trip home to preserve this dream. Euphoria floated gentle, aloof feelings from our hearts to our minds to our lips as we eased our way home. I gently touched the baby and said, "Honey, she'll never be a problem, just a challenge."

Mother and baby settled in the rocking chair as I hurried to our roadside mailbox, still hoping for a reprieve.

I Want to Be a Landlord

Burdens of landlords are generally self-evident, causing lease agreements to stipulate consequential damages for seemingly endless anticipated or potential acts of landlords and tenants.

That is why I have been told so many times, "To be a landlord, you must be nuts." As with most opinions, there is an element of truth there. Regardless, at age twenty-five, I planned to acquire rental real estate based on the idea that no matter where I was or what I was doing, there would be monthly cash income, large or small, as profit or simply a means to juggle finances. Naively, we became landlords. Happily, we remained somewhat nuts.

Landlords, not slumlords, often percolate a brew of mixed feelings. Here are a few to test your mettle. Each is true.

Tenant #1: Never Rent to Friends or Family

My mind raced for solutions to the many challenges I had accepted—perhaps more than I should have. A fist full of mail and the familiar voice of a Good Time Charlie in our living room nudged heaven from my realm to be abruptly replaced with harsh realities on earth. My newly wedded brother, Ed, a year and a half younger, sat comfortably on our tattered sofa, supported by a pyramid of *Life* magazines on one end and a cinder block at the other. His desperate plea to rent our apartment had seemed like a good idea three months ago.

Ed and June had no place to live and no money for rent. We had no money for a babysitter and no money for help at my office. The solution was obvious: Ed and June would lease the apartment. June could cross through the laundry room to become our babysitter from nine to five while Alice resumed as receptionist and secretary at my office. The triangle money would cover the monthly second-mortgage payment.

The high and noble ethical standards infused into my soul at Pace College forced my young, high mind to explain: "We have to maintain a paper trail. Alice will give June a check each week for the babysitting job, and you give her a check each month for the rent." Relief and happy resolve filled the air as we shook hands on the deal, but I felt a chill as my father's voice came from the clouds: "Son, never rent to friends or family."

I continued to open the mail as Ed detailed the critical need for more time to pay the back rent. His bonus commissions from Prudential Insurance Company would be here in a couple of weeks; always the same promises, seldom kept. June entered the living room, picked up scattered toys, and removed my necktie from the curved feet on a plaque of a trophy deer head mounted over the fireplace.

Her perpetually happy, bubbly personality belied the uncompromisingly self-serving interpretations stored behind an attractive face, between cute ears, on each side of a box of rocks. All enjoyed each other's humor. I liked her, and we generally laughed together over unthinkable observations and comments pouring through her naive, seventeen-year-old lips. I clearly heard her daily admonishments: "Don't hang your ties on the deer feet. Take your shoes off in the kitchen, not the living room. Don't leave your shirt on the armchair."

Her penetrating voice halted intermittently like the piercing skip of chalk on a blackboard. The shrill sound fired through my earplugs, hastily inserted at the sight of her. She laughed at my clownish conduct and accepted my purse-lipped expressions for what they were: self-preservation. Even our dog howled in pain at the sound of her voice. The Good Time Charlie stopped laughing and joking as he read "Final Notice: delinquent mortgage payments. Foreclosure proceedings will be initiated unless payment is received in seven days."

"What are you going to do?" he asked.

I sat down and calmly said, "I'm sorry, Ed. You have to pay the rent or move. I have no choice. Besides, Alice paid June each week for baby-sitting, so what happened to the money? We had an agreement."

Overweight June sat next to Ed, nervously balancing on the tattered, unstable sofa. Like a military first sergeant, she took charge of the situation. "Wait just a minute. I'm not moving. Ed shook hands on the deal; I didn't. I earned the babysitting money, and it's mine. Ed owes the rent, not me. Besides, I used the money to make weekly payments on a new sofa."

Ed slowly glanced right, then left, as he stood and silently offered a handshake. No one in the room could avoid the unpolished stones randomly fired from the box of rocks between June's ears.

I remained seated and said, "I'm sorry, bro." I handed him the eviction notice. With heavy heart and troubled mind, my anguish could have been avoided if only I had followed my father's advice: "Never rent to family."

Tenant #2: A Fishy Deal

Ed and June moved out as his good friends, Bucky and Betty, moved in. Bucky used a cash settlement to pay security and six months' rent in advance. I cut him a break, signed a rent receipt, and settled the delinquent mortgage payments. Everything was fine until Bucky landed in jail for stealing trout from the New Jersey state fish hatchery. His plan: stash trout inside a pair of exceptionally large bib overalls worn over his tall, thin frame. A leather thong around his neck secured a fishing reel under the bib. With one foot at the pool's edge, he quickly hooked large breeder trout that filled the left leg, the belly, and the right leg of the overalls. Slightly overloaded, he retied the cord around his right ankle and donned an oversized raincoat. His slow, old-man gait belied his twenty-two-year-old face shaded by a tall collar. Everything had been according to plan, he explained. In the gate, catch the trout, and back to the old pickup truck, all in less than thirty minutes. As he reached for the door handle, a stern voice from behind had cautioned, "Just a minute, sir!" He fake-jerked muscle spasms to disguise the flips of the last dying fish, unsuccessfully, and was immediately hauled off to jail. Exit Tenant Number Two.

Ed and June snagged a bargain for a small house on two acres five miles from us. The little stone house in the mountains was surrounded by fruit trees, berry bushes, nut trees, and grandfather oaks securely rooted among rare bluestone boulders. Minnesota Mining and Manufacturing Corp., better known as 3M, quarried and processed the rock into granular for various applications, including grit for asphalt roofing shingles.

Poison ivy tugged at the rotting framework of an old chicken house with an attached garage. It also entered every room of the house through fractures in the walls caused by weekly blasting at the 3M quarry. The place had been abandoned but still had great potential. The house could become a home.

We enjoyed cookouts together, occasionally shared home-cooked dinners, and often hunted wild game or caught exotic, local food such as suckers, snapping turtles, catfish, eels, and, especially, frogs. These were happy times. Ed and June did not hold a grudge or harbor animosity toward me—I guess.

Two years later, I vividly recalled that fateful day when Brother Good Time Charlie and his wife had no money or a place to live. Still, I evicted them. I also recalled Tenant Number Two, Ed's best friend, Bucky. While he was in jail, his wife had no money, so I evicted her. Now, Ed wanted me to rent the apartment to his insurance client and friends, Bill and Marian Brian.

Tenant #3: Rub-a-Dub-Dub, an Elephant in the Tub

Bill, a slight man of a hundred pounds, a janitor, and Marian, a five-hundred-pound behemoth, settled in the apartment with their cocker spaniel. Their kind, endearing ways created the bond of an extended family. Although the rent was never late, I sensed difficulties on the horizon. I had learned the lesson "never rent to family," but subdued, latent apprehension also surfaced at the thought of "never rent to friends."

Marian often settled in a chair with our baby in her arms while Alice politely guarded against sudden infant death. Sweet Marian was so fat that the baby's cries faded as it carelessly slipped between two gigantic, blubbery mountains with nipples on each apex. Jovial, good-natured Marian accepted the jovial nickname "Mother Jugs" as I cautioned, "Let the baby breathe. We don't have a snorkel!" Our children grew as Marian fattened up.

Marian filled her days eating and doing meticulous housekeeping while Bill planted exotic flowers in multiple patches throughout the backyard. Special care produced a garden of long-stemmed gladiolas, nodding flowers more brilliant than a sky full of rainbows. Tammy, our six-year-old daughter, enjoyed Cambert's tea in the afternoon with Uncle Bill and Aunt Marian. Four-year-old Debbie and two-year-old Ken practiced sibling rivalry.

Years later, Bill charged through the connecting laundry room into our kitchen, frantically pleading, "Mr. Crane, I need your help, I need your help right away!"

"What's wrong, Bill? What's the matter?"

Hysterical and out of breath, he gave no reply except "Please hurry." As we entered the bedroom, he blurted out, "Marian is stuck in the bathtub."

What a sight. No metaphor is adequate to capture the scene. Huge rolls of fat pressed against the high sides of this old-fashioned, porcelain and cast-iron, colonial bathtub with tiger paws. It held her like a beached whale. Strong arms could not extricate that massive ass. Perhaps she would float up as the tub filled with water.

Marian wiggled and squirmed as she tried to rise up, while Bill slid his hands and arms along the tub's sides to loosen its grip on the blubber. It didn't help. When he withdrew his arms, water gushed into the void and over the sides of the tub. Perhaps a bar from the windowsill to the appropriate rung of a stepladder would suffice. Bill lifted from behind while she tried to chin herself. It didn't work. Partially raised, she slid back, pinching Bill against the wall. Conclusion: a hundred pounds of bones cannot lift five hundred pounds of blubber!

The final attempt: as water drained, Bill towel-dried her back and arms. Marian inched forward until her knees touched her ears. She pulled hard on the overhead bar. She groaned against the suction holding her like cranberries in an open can. Cranberry sauce must be pushed out from the bottom. With my help from behind and Bill lifting piles of flesh up and away from the tub sides, she began to rise, but only as high as permitted by my lift from under her armpits. No place to stand, with my back against the wall, my curled toes took hold deep in folds of flesh. In a flash, I straight-armed her as my feet walked down her back, pushing her up. As the full moon rose and became wider than the tub, I thought of my religion and the twenty-third Psalm: "Yea, though I walk through the valley of the shadow of death, I fear no evil." I thought of my wedding: "...let no one put asunder."

Now erect, Marian briefly stood motionless to regain strength; I thought of death: one slip, and I was a dead man. Endless kudos came my way as she cautiously stepped from the tub to a floor mat. Silently, I absorbed her accolades and saw a part of her inner being hidden within her bulk. She was a kind, wonderful person.

Bill grabbed a clean towel and continued drying the thirty-three-year-old elephant as she slowly pirouetted. I sheepishly squeezed by to silently slither away. Still naked, she turned frontal and said, "Mr. Crane, thank you." To this day, the experience still haunts my mind with surprise, amazement, and endless admiration. Except for the huge jugs, everything was concealed behind mounds of bulging fat. Regardless, during the ordeal, she stood before me naked, unembarrassed, and utterly without shame.

But why would anyone wash an elephant in a cereal bowl?

Guess Who's Coming to Dinner?

We speculated about the strange visitors behind locked doors. Their laughing, joking, and unintelligible sounds continued for days, sometimes a week or more. The situation was not objectionable, but indeed puzzling. Bill avoided us whenever those people arrived. He must have sensed my curiosity piquing, causing him to invite me to meet them. Always polite, but extremely timid, Bill remarked, "Mr. Crane, when you have time, I would like you to meet my relatives."

"I have time now. Besides, I'm anxious to meet your friends."

A voice responded to a tap on the locked kitchen door adjoining our laundry room. "Is that you, Uncle Bill?"

"Yes, and Mr. Crane, our landlord."

His niece, Dottie, led us past a sofa bed and chair narrowing the path through the dining room to the living room, where two people sat watching television. The gentleman rose for the introduction, but I abashedly declined to shake hands.

Bill's brother-in-law was a man six feet tall. A bubble of leathery skin with two holes served as a nose (I guess). When he spoke, his shallow cheeks tugged his fat lips and exposed a double row of undersized teeth in the center of his mouth; also, he had three eyes. In a clear, deep voice, he said, "Hello, I am Jerry. Relax; I don't eat people!" This time, I shook hands, but I didn't know which eye to look at!

He eased head hair over his brow and sightless eye in the center of his forehead. I looked away. His voice was manly, articulation perfect, and his demeanor was above reproach. He gestured. "May I present my wife, Martha?"

As he spoke, I stepped to the front of a high-backed chair to address the lady. There sat a five-foot-two, reddish-pink human with her feet submerged in a bucket of warm water. The sight of her was shocking, the scene surreal: no eyebrows or eyelashes. No visible hair except small patches of fuzz on her scalp. A thin, loose muumuu ended embarrassingly short of her knees. Large scales of dried skin littered the carpet and chair.

Through dry, swollen lips came a crisp, warm greeting. "I'm pleased to meet you."

I couldn't bear to look at her, and I sure as hell wouldn't touch her for a handshake. I reluctantly said, "Hello."

Unbelievable, perhaps, but here they were in my house, a three-eyed monster with his wife, the fish lady—Marian's sister and brother-in-law.

Bill broke the silence. "Jerry and Martha are temporarily out of work and want to stay here to help care for Marian, if it's OK with you."

I maneuvered for an escape route and stated, "I have to check with Alice, so I'll get back to you tomorrow."

Bill chattered bits of information as we wove our way back to the kitchen. "I promise you, they won't cause any trouble. Marian is barely able to walk until she loses some weight. They can help us until the circus opens again further south, probably two or three weeks. They have very little money and no place to stay. We can pay a little more rent to help cover additional expenses."

"That's not the problem, Bill. I don't know how the rest of my family will handle this."

Fifty years later, I am still amazed at how well they accepted, without reservation, the two circus freaks next door. Three-eyes gave Ken Jr. an Indian turquoise medallion to hang around his neck with a leather thong. He entertained our children by squeezing clay into perfect forms of little bears, bulls, and elephants to dry in the sun. He became their friend. Debbie and Ken continued to rival over the generous supply of intriguing colored-glass marbles. Tammy often visited these tenants, but I demanded she shower immediately afterward. I really hated those fish scales! At last, spring came. Our friends left. They returned many times, until…

A Tractor Tire in the Bedroom

Bill rushed through the connecting laundry room into our kitchen and calmly explained, "Mr. Crane, I'm sorry, but we need your help."

The Pavlov dog in my mind warned, "Oh no, not again! Not the tub!" We stopped in the bedroom, where Marian had fallen and couldn't get up. She rested comfortably under a sheet, her head pressed deep in a fluffy pillow.

Elementary education forced the conclusion: we cannot put her back in bed. Dad's solution: "Plan your work, and work your plan." Dismantle the bed. Clear the area and roll her onto the springless mattress positioned on the floor. This time, I encouraged Bill to take the lower end.

The sheet slipped, tangled, and ripped apart under the strain. Marian groaned and flung it aside. Smiling, the adult manatee said, "All right, boys, now go to work!" With her effort and our great help, she rolled over the flattened edge of the mattress onto the legless bed. Completely exhausted, with an airy sigh, Marian smiled and said, "Thank you, thank you."

Greatly relieved that no harm had come to our friend, I humorously replied, "It's always a pleasure to see you. I know you're falling for me." Kind humor was OK, but Marian's obesity invited serious consequences, as you are about to learn.

Shocked awake by sirens and flashing cherries, I leaped from bed and descended the long staircase on my way to Bill's apartment. Police and EMS workers busily cleared a path from the front door through the living room and dining room to the bedroom. One glance at Marian on the floor prompted a snappy order from the supervisor: "That won't work, get it out of here!" An aide collapsed the scissor-legged gurney and quickly returned with a flat bed board. Aides politely kept her covered as they gently rolled, lifted, and tucked to cocoon Marian and bind her to the board with countless wide straps. Her width far exceeded the board's.

Six men, two at each side and one at each end, lifted and quickly set her down. She could not fit through the doorway; neither could a truck tire pass through in that manner. The boss snapped to action with a rectangular throw rug. "Tip her sideways on the rug and slide her out." She easily slid through the doorway, flat out through the wide path of furniture, tipped up through the front door, flat out to the ambulance parked against the porch steps. "Her weight is choking the life out of her," remarked an assistant.

Bill was sad, solemn, and pensive. The cocker spaniel was lonely, whiny, and annoying.

Three days later, doctors removed sixty-five pounds of fat from Marian's waist. Her condition was serious but stable. Her enlarged heart was unable to adequately supply oxygenated blood to all parts. Another operation was recommended to remove large amounts of fat.

After intensive care, recovery, and weeks of rehab, laughing, joking, happy Marian announced, "I'm coming home the day after tomorrow." The next day, she died.

Bill was shocked speechless, and his lack of emotion troubled me. He carried the dog at all times but didn't tend his gardens. He refused our invitations to dinner. There was no religion in his life.

He made funeral arrangements with grace and dignity. A profusion of flowers around the casket (special order) scented the room where few people sat. Bill sat alone in the front row until we joined him. A short service ended with a eulogy offered by the funeral director. Bill leaned toward me and asked, "Mr. Crane, will you be a pallbearer?"

Ruptured L-4 and L-5 caused my back to scream, "No!" but my heart fired a shot to my brain that ordered my lips to say, "Yes, of course." Incredibly, it all went well...until I made a fatal mistake.

Can a Broken Heart Kill?

As usual, I momentarily sat on the edge of the bed, enthusiastically prioritizing my "work your plan" commitments. My circadian clock, set years ago by gathering trapped muskrats before dawn, hand-milking cows before school, and working for three hours before breakfast, forced me wide awake. I prefer to wake up naturally rather than be forced awake by bells, alarms, bugles, or as in the Marine Corps, reveille...reveille... reveille!

I love the early morning. I would sing songs as the sun rose while nature encouraged all things to propagate. I would try to play with Alice. I hummed love songs like "You are my sunshine, my only sunshine," or "Oh, what a beautiful mornin', oh, what a beautiful day. I've got a wonderful feeling everything's going my way." A nudge coaxed her to play. "OK, hon, it's your turn. Guess that tune. Come on, hon, guess that tune!"

As usual, she groaned, "It's five a.m. Leave me alone!"

Teasingly, me: "I want you to enjoy the morning."

Sternly, her: "You enjoy it your way, and let me enjoy it my way." She always buried her head under a pillow and growled a stern warning. "Leave me alone."

That's another itch I've scratched for fifty-eight plus five years, unsuccessfully.

Suddenly, mornings are different. I no longer sing. Every day, five consecutive days after the funeral, hostile thoughts fill my mind as sleepless nights and overworked days take their toll. In my weakened state, I fear jeopardizing an alleged fraud case initiated by the IRS referred to me by a local law firm. That damn cocker spaniel howls mournfully, night after night. This is not a challenge; it's a damn big problem!

I muddled away most of the day at the office and arrived at the country club to burn off anxiety. My anger struck the sweet spot on every stroke to the fourth hole of the front nine. I lightened up with gratitude for a great day, anticipating an impressive score of ninety—exceptional for me! My beloved one iron, the only driver I could control, clicked another great tee shot two hundred yards in the center of the fairway. Ego-induced admiration and conceit forced me to sing, "Oh, what a beautiful mornin', oh, what a beautiful day," as I eased the electric cart along the path dividing the front nine from the back nine.

Before I could complete the second stanza, "I've got a wonderful feeling everything's going my way," three tall, well-dressed men in plain clothes blocked the path. One stood directly in front with both hands raised in an "I give up" stance. The other two, one to my right and one to my left, posed in a shootout stance with one hand inside his jacket. The man flashed a badge of some sort and then barked, "We are Secret Service on official business. Turn around and leave, *now!*"

Instantly, my adrenaline-driven anger and hostility resurfaced. Guards at the German prisoner-of-war camp are ordering me to drop my weapon. I am twelve years old. My misplaced anger prompted a careless, high-risk retort. "Screw you guys, get out of my way!"

One stepped alongside, his hand still in the covered armpit. He firmly stated, "Mr. Donovan is on the course. No one is allowed to pass by."

Hostility and disdain made me stupid. "So what? I don't know who he is, and I don't give a damn. I don't care if God himself is behind you. I'm a member of this club, and I'm playing through."

Two men pressed against the cart. One moved threateningly close and warned, "For the last time, I'm not asking. I'm ordering you to leave *now!*"

Once again, my alligator mouth put my canary ass in danger, but this time the canary dominated. "I'm sorry, gentlemen; lately my mind has been elsewhere. You're only doing your job. I'll wait in the clubhouse and finish my game later."

I'm not a drinking man, but a tall scotch and water helped arrange my questions to the club starter. "Who the hell is Ray Donovan? Why was I thrown off the course? I have a special membership, authorized personally by Mr. Schiavone, the club owner."

"Yes, I know. I'm sorry, Mr. Crane. Mr. Donovan is secretary of labor, appointed by President Reagan. He is the subject of a congressional investigation involving government contracts and organized crime. The Secret Service is here to deal with continuous death threats against him." He continued: "I closed the front nine on the red course, but somehow, you slipped by. I caught serious hell from both sides—Mr. Schiavone and the Secret Service. I'm glad it's all behind us. I've posted a guard at the tee-off until Mr. Donovan completes his round. Have another drink on me."

I preferred a soft drink, but accepted another stiff scotch and water after informing Alice I'd be home around eight o'clock. A light dinner and mellow wine defused my anxiety as I resolved minor business problems at a client's restaurant. Totally exhausted and emotionally drained, I was greeted by Alice with a hug and a kiss. I tossed my jacket on the armchair and flipped my necktie over the deer foot.

Then it started. That damn cocker spaniel was at it again! No yelping, no whining, no barking, just those incessant, mournful howls. The sound stretched long and hard and then faded off, like a lonely wolf searching for a mate, hour after hour.

I yelled at Alice, "That's it! I've had it! I can't take any more of this. Get Bill over here right now."

Pathetic Bill sat quietly as I paced back and forth near him, gesturing an emotional diatribe fueled by fury: overworked, the impending IRS audit, and especially the sleepless nights had numbed my brain. "This has to stop! Do you understand? The dog has to go, or you have to move."

My pitiful attack drove Bill to unspeakable anguish. Head lowered, eyes flooded, through quivering lips he sobbed, "I'm sorry, Mr. Crane. I got rid of the dog after Marian died. I'm all alone now, and I loved Marian so much, I can't stop crying. The noise is me."

Lord knows I tried, but nothing could lift his burden. The damage had been done. I suffered every day until, according to his doctor, asbestosis and mesothelioma silenced him forever. But surely, he died of a broken heart.

The lessons learned here helped us greatly to avoid tenancy problems from then to current time We gifted the New Jersey properties to Ken Jr. and encouraged him to deal with the rental problems his way but also to heed my Dad's advice: "Never rent to friends or family."

As husband and wife for nearly sixty years, we maintain our home, five rentals, and three hundred acres of farmland at B-Jack Farms, Hudson, New York. But I must confess, for reasons I fully accept, including growing old, that the daily challenges are slowly, inexorably, becoming problems. And occasionally, I agree with the ridicule. "To be a landlord, you must be nuts."

The Rise of Partnerships

As I contemplated my future, my thoughts drifted back in time, from the big house to sleeping on the lawn, to the brooder coop, to Howard's farm, back to the brooder coop, then to a partly remodeled chicken house, and now back to the big house, but this time with a wife a two-year-old daughter andTammy, our firstborn. Good things were happening in quick succession.

A vision to meet the public's essential business needs caused Bart Bennuto and me to invite Frank Gross, a middle-aged man and chief of our local volunteer firefighter company, to serve the public through Hillsboro Realty and Insurance Company. A roadside sign listed: Law Office, Public Accountant, Real Estate, and Insurance. A small, inside directory indicated each separate office. Canons of professional conduct clearly set forth ethical standards that could have raised a concern that our close business connections might have been violations. In fact, not only must violation be avoided, but even the *appearance* of impropriety. Accordingly, separate ownership of each office was required.

"Good morning, Frank. How are you?"

"Not so good. They can't seem to find out what's wrong with me. A few more tests next week should provide some answers."

"Well let's hope so. By the way, I received verification from the state and IRS that you are now authorized to open for business. We need office space. How are you making out with that ranch house across the highway?"

"Great! You are absolutely right. It will go up for sheriff's sale next month. But where the hell are we going to get the money? We don't even know what the sale price will be."

"I don't know either. But let's think positive and agree on the amount we are willing to pay. Then we'll obtain commitments for that amount. I understand the full sale price must be paid to the sheriff within fifteen days of the sale. The minimum bid will be twelve thousand, the amount to clear the mortgage. We will also have to pay any delinquent real estate taxes. But what is the fair market value of a two-bedroom ranch house on two acres along US Highway Route 206?"

Frank reviewed comparable properties in the area and suggested we limit our bid to $20,000, even though the property was worth at least $25,000. The challenge, of course, was to secure adequate financing on short notice. As I entered a branch of State Bank of Raritan Valley eight miles from our office, Mr. Benson abruptly stepped from his private office and greeted me with a handshake and kind words. "It's good to see you, Mr. Crane. How are you? How are Mrs. Crane and the children?"

"We have two children, but everyone is fine, thank you. How are things with you?"

Mr. Benson, a silver-haired, dignified executive, had formerly been my boss as CEO of Diehl Manufacturing Company. He remembered Alice as the pretty company mail girl working there during my two years in the United States Marine Corps. "It's great to see you. What brings you to our bank?"

"Well, I have a financial situation developing, and I thought perhaps someone here could help me." At that time, I didn't know that Mr. Benson was also chairman of the bank's board of directors.

"Please step into my office, and let's discuss the matter." After reviewing events from my time at Diehl Manufacturing Company to the present, he remarked, "You did an excellent job with our internal audit group, and I'm confident you will succeed with your endeavors, regardless of the difficulties you undoubtedly will encounter. I will recommend to the loan committee to preapprove a mortgage for twenty thousand dollars, provided the fair market value of the security property exceeds twenty-four five."

Five days later, a bank loan officer informed me of the preapproval for a first mortgage not to exceed $20,000. "Prerequisites for the closing will be mailed to you in a few days. By the way, Mr. Benson asked me to deliver the good news and his message: 'Good luck at the sale.'"

What a great day!

We were blessed with extremely miserable weather—so miserable, in fact, that the sale might have been adjourned. Frigid wind, sleet, and snow pelted the windshield as I cautiously drove to the county courthouse at Somerville. I arrived just in time to hear the sheriff read a standard auction procedure and advise everyone that the sale was final to the highest bidder. He continued, for the record, that a deposit of 10 percent of the sale price had to be paid to the court immediately after the sale and that the balance was to be paid to the sheriff within fifteen days. The sheriff identified the property to be sold by address, lot, and block number and immediately began the sale. "This sale is started with an opening bid of eleven thousand four hundred. It is the minimum sale price set by the mortgagee. Are there any other bids?"

A well-dressed stranger said, "Yes, eleven thousand five hundred."

I quickly responded, "Eleven thousand six."

The formality continued.

"Going once, going twice, going three times...are there any other bids?" A brief pause ended abruptly with a loud thud of the gavel. "*Sold* for eleven thousand six hundred dollars. Please pay the clerk one thousand, one hundred and sixty dollars."

A wind-driven blast of sleet and snow nearly ripped the papers from my grip as I headed into the teeth of the storm. But the warmth of sun in my heart urged me to skip through the sleet and the snow to the tune of "Zip-a-dee-doo-dah, zip-a-dee-ay; my, oh, my, what a wonderful day. Plenty of sunshine heading my way. Zip-a-dee-doo-dah, zip-a-dee-ay!"

Widespread public advertising had sparked considerable interest in this choice highway property. But can you believe it? Only one other bidder had shown up for the sale. We had acquired the property for half its value. What a bargain!

The storm raged on as I returned to my office. Most businesses had closed, even though it was only 11:30 a.m. Ecstatic over our good luck, I phoned Mr. Benson, only to learn he had closed the bank for the day and would be on vacation for three weeks. But the sheriff had to be paid before then. The next day, a loan officer assured me that my loan request has been expedited and said not to worry about it. Still, I couldn't quell the feeling something was wrong. Nervously, I asked the sheriff to accommodate an emergency situation if the funds were not available precisely on the fifteenth day after the sale.

"Under certain circumstances, we can extend the payment for a short period of time, provided there are no objections filed with our office by then. Otherwise, we will have to sell the property to the next highest bidder, and you may lose your ten percent deposit."

Still concerned and apprehensive, time passed agonizingly slowly. Secretary Darlene finally announced, "Mr. Crane, you have a call from the sheriff's office on line one."

"Hello?"

"Mr. Crane, I have bad news. An objection has been filed. You have to pay the balance by eleven o'clock tomorrow. Otherwise, I am required to accept payment from the next highest bidder and retain your deposit."

"How the hell did this happen? It's after four o'clock and you're telling me I have to deliver ten thousand four hundred dollars to your office tomorrow morning by eleven? I don't believe it."

"But I'm notifying you immediately, according to the law."

"Well, who filed the objection?"

"That's privileged information, and I'm not allowed to disclose the name. I'm sorry, Mr. Crane, but good luck."

Minutes later, a bank clerk delivered the news. "Your mortgage application has been denied."

Momentarily stunned, I thought, "This is not a challenge; this is a *damn big problem!*" Miracles happen at once, but the impossible takes me a little longer. The scramble began.

The Hobart Farm account had $700 set aside to pay bills. For now, I'd forget the bills. I'd delay payment of $650 on the first, second, and third home mortgages. I met the local branch manager of the First National Bank of Central Jersey at his office late at night to process an unsecured loan for $3,000, his discretionary loan limit. A summary of the good news: farm account $700, delayed mortgage payments $650, First National Bank loan $3,000, food money $50. The good news was, I raised $4,400. The bad news: it was 11:00 p.m. and I was still $6,000 short.

The primary objection to my request for loans from friends and family was the short notice and urgency. Alcoholic Pop's unpaid debts in the area, coupled with a list of his bad checks not yet redeemed, instilled widespread apprehension in the community concerning the entire Crane family. Exaggerated gossip, such as "like father, like son," "an apple doesn't fall far from the tree," or "be careful, they can't be trusted," exacerbated the issue. My personal and business relationships had been plagued by such unfair aspersions since my days in grade school wearing knickers, week after week.

My mind continued racing throughout a sleepless night. Now 6:00 a.m. The thought struck me as I leaped from bed: *I still have five hours to raise the $6,000. I'll liquidate my accounts receivable by urging all clients to pay their bills.* Fortunately, most clients paid my bills as the service was rendered; therefore, my accounts receivable seldom exceeded $1,500. Call after call, hour after hour, the same response: "Sorry, we need more time. You should have called sooner."

Reality set in. My persistence faded. In forty-five minutes, we would lose a terrific real estate deal and forfeit our deposit money.

"Mr. Crane, John Paniteri is on the phone. He says it's a personal matter."

John owned and operated a gas station with a small car wash and auto repair shop. He had been a friend and good client for less than a year. He owed me no money. "Hi, Ken. I've been trying to call you all morning, but your line has been busy. I heard you have a financial problem and need some help."

"You heard right, John. I have to pay the sheriff ten thousand four hundred dollars by eleven today, otherwise the ax will fall."

"That's what I heard. But I put together six thousand four hundred. That's all I have."

"How much?"

"Six thousand four hundred."

I could hardly believe the confirmation. "That will do, John. But how soon can I get the money?"

"I can meet you in about twenty minutes at the corner of Amwell Road and Route 206."

In a cloud of dust, a speeding, old car screeched to a halt behind me. John rushed to my window, handed over an envelope, and said, "It's all there. Just go! We can take care of the details later." He knew I had to make a trip in twenty minutes that took thirty minutes in ideal conditions.

Out of breath and flush with anxiety, I placed the money on the sheriff's desk. "I'm sorry about this, Mr. Crane. I hope you understand I had no choice in the matter." The sheriff and his clerk continued to count the money, remarking, "We have never experienced a situation like this before."

I studied the receipt: *Received payment in full at 10:58, February 15, 1962, for sale number...*

"Sheriff, I'd like to know who instigated the strict enforcement of the payment for this particular sale."

"I'm sorry, Mr. Crane, an attorney placed the demand on behalf of his client. Therefore, the information is attorney-client privileged, and he would not disclose further details. But I can say, if you had arrived three minutes later, you would not own the property."

Relieved but perplexed, my mind raced to explain the extraordinary events of the previous twenty-four hours. Why had a payment notice been suddenly filed at 4:00 p.m. demanding fulfillment by 11:00 a.m. the next day? Who was the lawyer? Who was he representing for this deal? Why had I been told my loan preapproval was for $20,000, and then at 4:15 p.m. the day before the sale, I was told it had not been approved because of my very poor credit rating? Moreover, the bank had even refused to extend me a personal, short-term loan to save the deal. Common sense dictated that this was more than a coincidence. It plagued me for days while I anxiously awaited Mr. Benson's return from vacation.

"Hello? This is Mr. Crane calling for Mr. Benson. It's rather important."

"What seems to be the problem, Mr. Crane?"

"Mr. Benson, do you recall telling me my twenty-thousand-dollar loan request was approved?"

"Yes, of course. I was at the meeting. Is there a problem?"

"Yes, a big problem. I suspect some wrongdoing at your bank, but I prefer to speak with you in private and strictly confidentially."

"We certainly can have a private meeting, but I can't agree to confidentiality until I understand the seriousness of your insinuation. I would like to address your concerns immediately; can we meet at my office within the hour?"

"Yes. I'll be right there."

In quick succession, I set forth the pattern of facts that had created my suspicion. "Someone directly connected with your bank tried to sabotage my acquisition and steal my deal."

Alarmed by my blunt explanation that sounded more like an accusation than a suspicion, Mr. Benson quickly summoned individuals by name to immediately meet in the private conference room. "Please wait here, Mr. Crane. This won't take long."

An hour later it seemed, but he returned in less than fifteen minutes. Flush with controlled anger, Mr. Benson briefly stated, "Thank you, Mr. Crane, for bringing this matter to our attention. You have exposed a very serious situation here. Clearly, our reputation is at stake. I'm now asking you to keep this entire matter strictly confidential."

"Mr. Benson, I give you my word: nothing more will be said about it."

My mentor stepped forward to shake hands. "I don't know how to thank you enough, Mr. Crane, except to say we owe you one."

"I appreciate that, Mr. Benson, but please don't say it if you don't mean it, because someday, I'll be back once again to ask you for financial help."

In my office, just before noon, I received a call from Jack Bolby. "Hi, Jack. How's it going? Have you heard any word on my application?"

"As a matter of fact, I have. I talked it over with Dad, and he said you should contact his secretary, fill out the rest of the papers, and he's confident his bank can process a mortgage loan for you. There are no promises, of course, until he sees the entire application."

"Thanks, Jack, I appreciate your help."

Jack Bolby was my assistant in the internal audit group at Diehl Manufacturing. He is also an avid outdoorsman who thoroughly enjoyed pheasant hunting with me and my Labrador retrievers. His father was a director of the County Bank and Trust Company in Bound Brook, twelve miles from my office. During my scramble to connect with some money, apparently I had phoned Jack and explained my difficulty.

I rushed to the bank, filled out endless questionnaires and financial statements, and exchanged small talk with the bank director, Mr. Bolby. I barely knew the man, but he seemed quite sympathetic toward my plight and accommodated me in an unusual way. I suspect he was showing gratitude toward me for taking his son, Jack, pheasant hunting. He probably knew that unlike most people, I was not offended by Jack's crude, abrasive personality; it was just his way. Besides, his flaws were overshadowed by his talent as an expert marksman. Each time a startled pheasant launched into the sky with a noisy flutter, quickly gaining speed to forty miles an hour, Jack reacted instinctively to make a perfect shot through a tree line or a long-range, open field. In Jack's gun sight, no bird suffered; it was dead before hitting the ground. I recall our last outing. "Cock bird, cock bird." *Bang!*

"Nice shot, Jack, but I still can't believe you dropped that bird out of range, through the hedgerow, and with one shot. I couldn't do that, and I was an expert rifleman in the Marine Corps."

"It's easy, Ken. Just cut off an arm and use the other one to handle a long-barrel, twelve-gauge shotgun like I do." (Polio in childhood had left Jack with a fractional, useless arm, a strange piece of flesh with a hand attached, having no bone structure.)

Each time I entered my new office, formerly the kitchen of a small ranch house on two acres, I pondered the enigma of the prior six weeks. I wonder who had instigated the underhanded dealing at the sheriff's office. I wonder who had sabotaged me at the bank. But through it all, I marveled at John Pannitari, Jack Bolby, Mr. Bolby, and Mr. Benson, who were proof positive that a big problem is nothing more than a big challenge. But how can I show adequate appreciation and gratitude? It is comforting to know it will take more than my lifetime.

The Episode of Flight 851

"Good-bye, Grandma! We'll see you in ten days. The kids know we have to leave before they get up, so they'll be OK. If there's any problem, call the number I gave you. They will patch us through by ship-to-shore radio."

The cab driver remarked, "We made good time," as we arrived at the big house in Belle Mead around 12:30 p.m. "The trip takes about an hour, so I'll pick you up at six-thirty tomorrow morning."

"That will be fine."

As he left, Tammy ran from the house and jumped up to be caught in my arms. "You came back to get me!" Debbie and Ken were darting back and forth excitedly, yelling, "It's Mommy and Daddy!"

Grandma Snyder, surprised and confused, asked, "What happened? Did you miss your flight?"

"No, we'll be leaving tomorrow morning at six thirty. I'll tell you all about it while the kids take their nap."

Grandma Snyder was living in the converted chicken house next door, which had been our home before we traded properties with Mom and Pop. We had invited her to bring Gerald, fifteen, Carolyn, nine, and Charlotte, five years of age, to live with us after her alcoholic husband shot himself in the head with the .22 caliber rifle I had given their son, Gerald, on his twelfth birthday. This kind, gentle, unassuming mother-in-law often would babysit our children to break the chain of incessant crises that rendered our existence unimaginably impossible. Short vacations became our salvation. They became essential respites

from bill collectors, responsibilities to my clientele, and money short-
ages that challenged our basic daily life. Also, I was plagued by the news
that my brother Howard was the subject of a long-term investigation by
the Internal Revenue Service for payroll fraud. I was the informant.

The morning's events redirected my thoughts as I explained what
had happened. We had arrived on schedule at the Newark airport to
board Flight 851, nonstop to San Juan, Puerto Rico. Although we had
made this trip many times, Alice retained her fear of takeoffs and land-
ings. This trip was no exception.

The protocol was routine as we selected seats in the aft, on the port
side of the plane. Rumor has it that when a large plane crashes, the tail
section often breaks away, avoiding the conflagration and debris field.
It is irrelevant on which side of the plane one is seated, except for the
choice to avoid blinding sunlight when flying above the clouds.

The engines had sounded normal as we taxied for takeoff. Brakes
on, throttles forward, brakes off. The plane lurched forward, quickly
gaining speed, soon to be airborne a few hundred feet over major highways serving New York City. A steep, powerful climb brought the Twin
Towers into view a safe distance away.

Suddenly, at 850 feet and climbing, smoke filled the cabin. Flight
attendants rushed down the aisle, tossing pillows to grabbing hands.
An announcement from the cockpit temporarily distracted passengers:
"Ladies and gentlemen, please remain calm. Our engines are fine. We
are cleared for an emergency landing and will be safely on the ground
in a few minutes."

The reality of our situation had become apparent when the steward-
esses abandoned the pillow-tossing in front of Alice and me and fearfully
rushed to strap themselves into the forward seats. Thick smoke billowed
from the overhead air vents. The plane banked sharply to circle for a
landing. As the left wing dipped lower and lower, it exposed a clear view
of the activity on the ground, including ambulances, police, security
vehicles, fire engines, and flashing lights. People scurrying in all directions, especially from the hangar to our assigned runway, electrified a

chaotic scene that heightened the fear of our impending disaster. All other runways had been shut down and cleared of air traffic.

As the plane banked sharply, passengers saw the frenzied, frantic activity in preparation for our destiny. The sight caused passengers to react as depicted in those disaster movies such as *Airport* or *The Poseidon Adventure*. Some were silent, frozen with fear, speechless. Some were praying. Two college girls next to us laughingly remarked, "Oh look, tow trucks. We're going to get a tow job!" Suddenly, a middle-aged man in front of us grabbed the hair on each side of his head and ripped it from his scalp while screaming over and over again, "I don't want to die!"

The scene caused Alice to break into tears, but not hysterically. She sobbed, "What about the children? Mom has no money. Who will care for them?"

To break the thought pattern, I gave her a swift poke in the ribs with my elbow, scolding, "Get ahold of yourself. We have no control over this situation, so let's make the most of it. Besides, maybe we'll land safely, like the captain said."

Strangely, I had no fear. Perhaps the Marine Corps influences had created a naive belief that, regardless of the perils, somehow we'd get through it OK. Her head resting on my shoulder, my arm around her waist, Alice abandoned herself to me. In a soft, gentle voice, I reassured her, "We are safe, except for blinding smoke throughout the plane." I continued: "We are now lined up with the runway. We are about to touch down. Yes!"

The plane came in at high speed, engines roaring. Tires smoked as the plane skipped three times and then hugged the pavement. The plane shook violently, with engine power reversed and tires screeching under extreme braking pressure. We lurched back against our seat as the plane abruptly stopped, safely.

Instantly, emergency equipment surrounded the plane. The captain announced, "You must remain seated. Does anyone need medical attention? Regardless, you must be cleared by our medical staff before disembarking the plane." Calmly, he explained, "An electrical short developed in the air handling system as we climbed to 850 feet. This is a critical stage of the takeoff. Therefore, I had to increase power, causing things to appear worse than they were. The plane has great redundancy, and flight control was never impaired. I'm sure this has been a harrowing experience for all of you, but I assure you, we were never in serious danger. We must remain here until the FAA clears us to park the plane safely a short distance from the terminal. After the medical inquiry is completed, passengers are to disembark directly onto the tarmac and proceed to the Eastern Airlines ticket counter for further instructions. Passengers needing assistance for any reason, please remain seated. In the meantime, please accept snacks and drinks of your choice, compliments of Eastern Airlines."

The captain slowly proceeded down the aisle, shaking hands with the passengers while answering general questions about the mishap.

At the counter, several officials explained that a plane was being readied to complete our trip. I insisted we would not board another plane that day, because we would miss our connecting flight from San Juan, Puerto Rico to Saint Thomas, US Virgin Islands. Besides, I argued, when a racehorse hangs up in the starting chute, it's time to forget that race and bet on another one. After a heated discussion and under strong protest, a cab was dispatched to take us back home and return us the next morning, same time, same place, same Flight 851. Hopefully, it would be a different plane.

A Purse from a Sow's Ear:
The Hobart Farm, 1961-1980

"Son, you can't make a silk purse from a sow's ear."

"I don't understand, Dad. Who would want to even try?"

Many years later...

Here in bed, Alice snuggled closely as I pulled the covers around us. Sunlight through cracks in the siding caused fine, gritty snow to sparkle as it sparingly settled on and around us. Wind was howling outside. Inside, the rooms were frigid. Alice's sister, Betty, stoked a wood fire in the kitchen stove to perk an old-fashioned pot of coffee. Her husband, Dick, was out of work as a logger. No money, very little food, and their vehicle was about to be repossessed: we have a clear example of "poor, but not destitute." Forlorn and broken in spirit, existing in an old farmhouse in the Catskill Mountains of New York, twenty-five-year-old Dick looked up from his cup of coffee but did not respond to my question: "Dick, what the hell are you and Betty going to do with your lives?"

After much prompting, he replied, "What's the use talking about it? We have an eighth-grade education, no money, and no job."

"Well, Dick, it sounds like the only thing left for you to do is to dream. So, let's dream." I continued: "Setting aside all obstacles, what is your dream for the future?"

Slowly, pensively, he replied, "I guess I'll find a job on a dairy farm. That's all I've ever done. But right now, nobody is hiring."

"Why get a job on a farm? Why not buy one?"

Dick smiled, smirked, and remarked, "Now you're really dreaming."

"That's right, but most things start with a dream. Didn't you dream about Betty before marrying her? I dreamed about Alice for five years before we married. So here's what I want you to do. Monday, start looking for a farm to buy. We don't have any money, but you just never know what might happen by trying."

On the way back to New Jersey, Alice chastised me relentlessly, pointing out the obvious. "We have no money and no hope of borrowing it because of our poor credit rating. It's wrong to raise false hopes with baseless suggestions and wild dreams."

Two days later, eight miles away, Sy Maney offered Dick a nice home to live in while he worked full-time on Sy's dairy farm.

Shortly thereafter, Sy's neighbor, Horace Green, received the bittersweet news that his son, Bob, wanted to sell their family farm and become a traveling minister, guided by Jehovah's Witnesses. His struggle to pay for the 204 acres, house, barns, cows, and equipment, his father's retirement security, became meaningless because Armageddon would strike first.

Dick passed the news to me in New Jersey, including the tantalizing fact that the place was twelve miles from Howard's old farm in South Gilboa and barely five miles from Stamford High School, where I found my sweetheart. Incredibly, it was my old stomping ground. I am familiar with the entire area, having hunted wild game in the mountains and fished the trout streams for nine years.

After four hours of "getting to know you" conversation, the proposition for ownership was presented to me.

"My son is going to leave the farm with his wife and two young children. I'm too old to continue farming. If you pay Bob ten percent 'good faith' money—say, six thousand dollars, we will assign our contract for sale of the entire farm, including the cows and equipment, and convey clear title to you at a later date. But I need your answer within a week."

The five-and-a-half-hour return trip to New Jersey allowed uninterrupted contemplation of the possibilities. I accepted the challenges with great anticipation. I contacted Bill Fishburn, a former assistant in the audit group I had supervised at Diehl Manufacturing Company a year earlier. He had expressed his desire to invest money with me. The next day, I signed an unsecured promissory note for $6,000 and sent the money to Mr. Rose at the Hobart National Bank to be escrowed pending the execution of a "sale by contract" agreement.

In the spring of 1961, I acquired the entire business, lock, stock, and barrel, for the sum of $62,500. It included fifty-five head of livestock and the usual equipment to operate a small dairy farm.

Dick and Betty, with two sons and a baby daughter, moved into the small, two-bedroom farmhouse. Thus, a "Little House on the Prairie" was spawned. Except this was not a prairie; instead, it was a small valley high in the Catskill Mountains of New York, three miles from a little town called Hobart.

Trials and tribulations of farming sorely tested our resources. Our first corn crop, intended as silage for feeding to the cows during the long winter, was overtaken by weeds and deemed worthless. Expenses exceeded income. The personal aspects of farming continued to be my high and noble endeavor. During the following years, Betty worked harder and harder, but Dick worked less and less, relying on his two sons to pick up the slack. We struggled to overcome the obstacles by mechanizing the labor-intensive aspects of the business, such as installing a hydraulic, shuttle-action gutter cleaner and a pipeline milking system. We hired a dairy herd improvement specialist (DHIA) who maintained monthly individual milk production records setting forth the profitability of each cow.

I tried in vain to compensate for Dick's shortcomings by spending more and more time at the farm, resulting in detriment to my profession and family. The pervasive paradox of my being is that I never learned how to give up, quit, throw in the towel. As a young man, my tenacity had often been admired, but I did not realize until middle age that it was a major weakness in my personality. I loved the farm. I enjoyed the endless indoor-outdoor hard work, as did Alice and our three children, as did Betty and Dick and their three children (and another one on the way). But there was never enough money. This is a plague to most family-run farms and remained a scourge many years too long, perpetuated by a naive belief that "things will be better next year."

We renovated the small farmhouse to accommodate Dick's larger family. We increased production by remodeling the barn to accommodate more lactating cows. A new herd of fifty cows boosted income but also boosted the expenses. My primary goal was to encourage a way of life for Betty and Dick to raise their children within the range of their abilities and fulfill my plan, set at age seventeen—get an education and eventually own a farm. Economic forces beyond our control taunted our every decision, made worse by Dick's lack of ability to operate a dairy farm. But I believed he would learn to fill the gaps, especially as I delivered weekly information garnered from the accounting records of twelve highly successful dairy farmers I represented as a public accountant.

Severe criticism came my way for staying the course in an attempt to make a purse from a sow's ear, but to do otherwise would have been a defeat and would surely have put Dick's family back into a state of turmoil. Plus, I would have had to give up my dream to own a farm. Instead, I chose to continue, always believing that next year would be better. Fortunately, we maintained a healthy, open line of communication by concentrating on solutions through discussion instead of argument. In fact, we never had a shouting match, bitter argument, or derogatory confrontation. I shared ideas and offered suggestions on a regular basis, but I never issued work orders. My intention was to guide Dick, not lead him as an employee or indentured slave. Even so, humorously, I was labeled "the weekend warrior." I failed to heed the cautions offered by Confucius: "A low-energy person cannot be made a high-energy person." Regardless, I agreed to dissolve our relationship and accept the suggestion that generally, people will achieve much higher goals when the benefits and burdens of the effort are entirely theirs. "You reap the seeds you sow."

Debts at the Hobart Farm had to be renegotiated, but even Mr. Rose, president of the Hobart National Bank, could not extend me additional credit. Van Buren Feed Mill held a judgment lien and was seizing one-third of our monthly milk check plus a 10 percent sheriff's collection fee. We could not sustain the operation. Mr. Rose, a kind and gentle person, became my friend. He warmly advised me to give up the idea of farming on an absentee basis. Consequently, after detailed evaluation and friendly negotiations, I agreed to sell the farm to Dick and Betty. But sufficient funds were required to liquidate the farm debts in my name. Surprisingly, the Farmers Home Administration provided financing, but insisted that I remain personally liable for the farm debts; therefore, I conveyed the farm debt free. In conclusion, I absorbed all of the accumulated farm net operating losses and relinquished all right, title, and interest in the farm.

This amicable, happy resolve of the financial crises allowed Dick's family to maintain their lifestyle, guided by FmHA. My family could enjoy working on the farm and vacationing there indefinitely. Real estate values increased rapidly, and through inflation it became easier to liquidate old debts; clearly, time was in our favor, and we now had a win-win situation. The new arrangement allowed payment of the unsecured promissory note to Bill Fishburn, who had loaned me $6,000 for the down payment on the farm. Those were good times, but short-lived.

Within two and a half years under Dick's exclusive ownership and management, the farm plunged deeper and deeper into debt. Once again, we were caught in a financial crisis, and once again, the business could not be sustained. Understandably, Dick became demoralized, lethargic, and confused. An unbiased analysis of the day-to-day operations revealed the same old problems: poor hay quality, excessive feed costs, reduced milk production, and high machinery repair costs. Inefficiency and negligence was rampant. But why?

We reviewed the basic farming 101 I had learned at brother Howard's farm at age seventeen. The nutritional value of a cow's diet of hay, silage, and processed dairy feed is the primary factor determining the animal's productivity. Poor-quality hay lowers daily milk production. Poor-quality silage lowers the butterfat content, causing the milk to weigh less. Since bulk milk at the farm is sold by the pound, not by the quart, lower production coupled with lower butterfat inevitably results in a lower milk check each month. The US Department of Agriculture (USDA) fixes the monthly farm price for milk with 3.5 percent butterfat content and authorizes ten cents per hundredweight differential for milk deviating from that standard. For example, the price for 3.5 percent milk varies widely, but a well-fed Holstein cow may produce seventeen thousand pounds of 3.7 percent milk a year. Her gross income, therefore, would be $2,584 ($15 per hundred pounds, plus $0.20 bonus for butterfat above 3.5 percent). Thus, a seventy-five-cow dairy herd should gross $193,800 per year. The same Holstein cow, poorly fed, may produce twelve thousand pounds of milk with a butterfat content of 2.4 percent, lowering her gross income for the year to $1,168 ($15 per hundred pounds minus $1.10 per hundred). The same seventy-five-cow dairy herd, poorly fed, would therefore gross $125,100. Lower milk production coupled with lower butterfat content results in an annual loss in farm gross income of $68,700.

We analyzed our problems and concluded as follows: the nutritional value of hay deteriorates rapidly as it matures or if it absorbs rain during the drying process. Occasionally, foul weather is unavoidable, but in our case, hay was routinely mowed without adequate regard for the weather forecast. Hence, the saying "make hay while the sun shines" was not fully appreciated. The prime time to cut quality hay is May or early June. All too often, our hay was cut and stored during the summer and early fall, often after being soaked by rain. The nutritional value of corn silage is determined by its maturity at harvest time. Maturity is controlled by area climate conditions, generally expressed in "degree days." Sixty-five-day corn produces significantly less silage than 120-day corn.

Regardless, if the corn is planted too late, or if the corn, stalk and all, is harvested too early or too late, the fermented silage will be low in nutritional value. In our case, the corn crop often was planted too late and harvested too late. We concluded after much discussion that the harsh reality was that profitable farming is extremely difficult, even under ideal circumstances. This is evidenced by the slow, ominous disappearance of family farms throughout the United States. After more discussion, though, and against all odds, once again we decided to try to improve our circumstances. Mechanized efficiency appeared to be the only solution, and that would require a substantial investment of time and money.

In summary, this was our plan:
1. Modernize the operation
2. Remodel the back stables
3. Increase the dairy herd by fifty cows, each producing at least sixteen thousand pounds of milk annually
4. Purchase a full line of new farm equipment

Prompted by our obsession to salvage the Hobart dairy operation, as a last resort, Alice and I remortgaged our New Jersey home a third time and funded the planned expansion. Betty and Dick transferred the farm back to me, and in recognition of the inflationary value of the farm, he received a $40,000 promissory note payable if he turned a profit greater than their cost of living. I believed that the added money incentive, coupled with anticipated increases in real estate values, would secure the added investment, compensate me for absorbed losses in my name, and share the overall benefit of the venture. Naively, I also believed this plan would preserve Dick's chosen way of family life and at the same time allow my family to continue our happy involvement in farming.

We contemplated the following: each cow was milked twice a day with a milking machine that vacuum pumped her milk into a pail to be emptied into a portable dumping station behind two rows of cows. The strained milk was piped from the station into a six-hundred-gallon, refrigerated bulk tank. This labor-intensive procedure allowed one person to operate two milking machines, or three if another person carried milk pails to the dumping station and returned the empty pails to the operator. State health inspectors ensured that all milking equipment was washed and sterilized immediately after each use. So, we would replace that entire process with a push-button, self-cleaning pipeline system that transferred the milk directly from the cow to a refrigerated bulk milk tank. The upgraded system allowed one person to effectively operate four machines, thus cutting the milking time in half. Also, the new push-button cleaning system automatically washed and sterilized the equipment.

I located a young dairy herd in North Jersey and examined the DHIA records that certified each cow's monthly productivity, including butterfat content. The records reported an annual herd average of sixteen thousand pounds per cow with a butterfat content of 3.7 percent: excellent. The sales price was fair. Veterinary certificates and shipping costs were very reasonable and within our budget. We purchased new equipment, including a hay baler with a kicker that tossed the bales directly into a wagon, thereby avoiding hand-loading thousands of hay bales dropped on the ground as before. A New Holland two-row forage harvester with a grass head replaced our one-row, string-tie corn binder. I traded New York high-grade alfalfa hay to a New Jersey farmer client for a New Holland self-unloading forage wagon, using his truck twice a week to haul hay in one direction and equipment in the other. No longer did we have to gather the bundles of corn from the field and hand-feed them into a machine that coarse-chopped the corn and blew it into a fourteen-by-fifty-foot, upright, concrete silo. The new equipment chopped the corn in the field and blew it into the attached self-unloading wagon that would be unloaded directly into a blower by engaging the power takeoff handle on the tractor. No more belt-driven equipment; just stand by and watch the operation. We had modernized our farm. Milk production was up, butterfat content was above 3.5 percent, and our bills were paid. Happy days were here again. The future looked bright.

The next spring, we bought a new Ford 7000 tractor. Our two-row corn planter was replaced with a four-row planter that would cut the planting time in half, thus permitting the planting of hundred-day corn. If handled properly, it would produce significantly more silage than the lesser degree-day corn. The corn was planted on schedule, adequately fertilized, and with the proper use of herbicides, it was free of weeds. After the busy time as a public accountant ended on April 15, our family visited the farm every week or two. It was a happy, healthy change to work on the farm instead of continuously pushing pencils in the office. I noticed that milk production slacked a little, feed grain bills crept higher, and there was a sharp increase in the use of gasoline. A cursory review explained the cause and effect. Betty explained, "I have to drive the boys to school when they miss the bus."

"I understand that part, Betty, but why are the boys missing the bus?"

"They're not coming in from the barn in time. The trip drives me crazy," she replied.

The complete answer came much later, during an unscheduled trip to the farm.

"It's eight a.m. Are you OK, Dick?"

"Yeah, I overslept. The boys started the milking. The bus stopped at the end of the long driveway, waited a minute, then left." Dick followed me to the barn and remarked, "I'll relieve the boys operating the milking machines. You can grain the cows, if you don't mind."

"I don't mind, but I understand we always grain the cows before milking to settle them down in anticipation of being milked."

He explained, "The boys don't have enough time before school, so I finish the milking, then grain the cows before breakfast."

Puzzled, I scooped the processed feed to several cows and noticed the charts had not been updated. Our independent DHIA specialist provided monthly data for each cow, including the recommend pounds of expensive, mineralized feed to be fed to each one twice daily. Since the information cards over each stanchion had not been updated, the expensive feed grain was being randomly scooped out to the milking herd without accurate consideration of the amount recommended based on a cow's contribution to profit. Dick explained, "I know how much milk each cow gives and I know how much grain to feed her; I don't need those cards."

Under normal conditions in the Hobart area, the first and second cutting of hay generally should be completed by July first. It became obvious that we would once again be harvesting hay well into September. Our DHIA records indicated average milk herd production was predictably sliding downward. Six months earlier, our yearly herd average was fourteen thousand pounds of milk per month. Now it was twelve thousand pounds. The butterfat content was 3.4 percent, not 3.7 as before. Naively loyal to my brother-in-law, I considered it a nonthreatening, modest decline. I was wrong. My pleasure in farming and my concerns for Dick's family had clouded my judgment.

Our struggles at the Hobart Farm became so entangled with struggles in New Jersey that it became obvious I was expecting too much from my backup teams. I was spread too thin. Painfully excruciating but necessary decisions followed.

Richard Clampton negotiated a partial refund of a $1,000 deposit on the Noll Farm in Hillsborough, New Jersey. The contract included fifty-five acres of prime real estate fronting on a major highway and two secondary roads, a six-family colonial home with three magnificent white columns supporting a roof over balconies; off to the side was a modest, two-family ground-level cottage intended for my mother-in-law and her daughters. The price: $36,500. I held in hand an approved mortgage for $34,500 but could not raise another $1,000 to close the deal. Rich handed me a $900 deposit refund check and remarked, "If Bart and I were in better shape, we would have joined with you on this deal." Three months later, the house and five acres sold for $54,500. During the next six years, the remaining fifty acres was subdivided to allow single-family homes, office buildings, a day-care center, and an apartment complex with fourteen units per acre. After multiple subdivisions, the raw land alone sold for several million dollars. The $900 refund had saved my day.

Barbara Moffett, CPA, became my full-time employee.

Alice quit her job at Consumer Plumbing and Heating Company as assistant bookkeeper and agreed to babysit Moffett's two children.

My mother-in-law found full-time employment and vacated the "little house." The terrible choice to evict this wonderful person with two daughters, ages fifteen and four, weighed heavily on my conscience, but my home, too, was at stake. Ask any tax assessor.

Years later, in April 1973, under new management, a major expansion of the Hobart operation was planned.

For personal reasons, John and Carol Daniel moved from New Jersey to the Brown House on the Hobart Farm. The plan: John, our brother-in-law, a hard-driving, do-it-right person, immediately reformed the business consistent with good farming practices. Shortly thereafter, John flooded back negative management reports, embarrassingly true and all too often insulting my belief that somehow, a silk purse can be made from a sow's ear.

Angry and frustrated, he reported, "Dick won't get out of bed on time. Yesterday, I woke Dick and the boys, then rounded up the cows from the pasture and drove them into the stable. I expected someone to be there to close the stanchions. Instead, the cows drifted about, some in the wrong stanchions. Others sniffed around for the feed grain that wasn't there and came back toward me. Finally, Rick and Robbie (the boys) directed each cow and secured her in the proper stanchion. I grained the cows as indicated on the card above each cow. The boys began the milking. But it's six thirty a.m. Where the hell is Dick? Frustrated, I headed for the house, only to see him through the kitchen window toasting me with a raised cup of coffee. The problem is, it happens all the time. Dick said that no matter what, he's not getting up at five a.m. to milk cows. We had an argument, not a discussion."

John had insisted, "All right, then you take charge of the cows, and I'll do the fieldwork," and so it was. Fieldwork improved significantly, but our monthly milk check, the farm income, continued to decline. Our plan to acquire adjoining farms in the area and significantly expand the Hobart operation was abandoned. A new direction was required. It culminated with the acquisition of a farm forty miles east of Hobart, twenty miles south of Albany, in the diversified valley of Hudson, New York. The purchase included seven homes, six barns, eight silos, and five hundred acres to support three hundred head of livestock. Late summer, 1973, John and Carol moved from the Hobart Farm to our newly acquired farm in Hudson. As part owner and general manager, John would be responsible for all fieldwork, maintenance, machinery repairs, and supervision of his crew.

Regardless of the documentation of the Hobart Farm, I considered Dick my partner but never charged back his share of the huge Hobart Farm losses against the $40,000 promissory note executed years earlier. That fact notwithstanding, I asked Dick to be exclusively responsible for the dairy herd, including his selected barn crew. He would also receive a percentage ownership of B-Jack Farms equal to $40,000, the value of the note.

As a managing partner, he would not have to be on the job by 5:00 a.m. every morning. But it was not to be. Dick declined the offer, citing incompatibility as the reason. Clearly, he had made the right choice. Silently, I agreed, thinking, *How stupid can I be for even making the offer?* Dick, mild-mannered, lethargic, unexpressive, versus John, hard-driven, opinionated, strongly bellicose, each firmly set in his ways, left no room for compromises; such is the death knell for all partnerships, joint ventures, and marriages.

Betty and Dick remained in Hobart and continued the farm operation as before, while John and Carol energized the vacant, newly acquired B-Jack Farms in Hudson, New York. It was June 1973.

• • •

On November 17, deer-hunting season opened. Frost came in the middle of September as usual. Grass was dead brown, and so was our corn in the very late dent stage that should have been chopped weeks earlier. I deer-hunted one day, tormented by the events of this year. I drove the new Ford 7000 tractor to the upper cornfield in tandem with the new forage harvester and new self-unloading forage wagon, determined to bring in the remaining damaged corn crop. Dick was watching wrestling on TV that Sunday afternoon. Remember, I was the "weekend warrior."

As usual, I sang songs while driving the tractor. I knew my singing was not great, but safely, no one could hear it over the noise of the tractor, so it remained my fantasy pleasure. The air was clear and crisp, with frost on the brown corn that should have been chopped while green. But everyone was overworked and underpaid. I had no right to complain. The fifteen-minute drive up the switchback farm road leading to the elevated ten-acre field of corn was exhilarating, so I sang the song, "Oh, What a Beautiful Mornin'" as I gazed down on our precious valley farm below. I lined up the new two-row forage harvester with the rows of corn and engaged the PTO to spin the knives that chopped the corn and blew it into the wagon. Immediately, I heard a loud, ominous noise in the transmission of the tractor. I unhooked the field equipment and returned to the farmhouse.

"Dick, the new tractor is making a strange noise. Where is the owner's manual?"

"They were out of them when the tractor was delivered, and I still don't have one. They said everything was OK."

"But Dick, the tractor sounds like it needs oil in the transmission. Where do I check it?"

"I don't know. They said don't worry about it."

Not satisfied, I explored until I discovered a fill plug under the driver's seat and a gauge plug on the side of the tractor. The transmission critically lacked oil. After adding oil until it dripped from the gauge-plug hole, the noise immediately subsided.

The next morning at the breakfast table, much to everyone's surprise, I announced that I had decided to shut down the farm in the spring.

The cows and equipment were transferred to B-Jack Farms, and the Hobart Farm became inactive. During the transition, we paid Dick's wages while he searched for full-time employment.

• • •

As with all dairy operations, large or small, milk cows have to be replaced every three to six years. Federal income tax laws favored B-Jack's replacement of cows by raising them from birth instead of buying lactating cows or first-calf heifers at thirty months of age. Consequently, a separate heifer-raising program was established. Dick was overjoyed to run the new venture. He could live and work at the Hobart Farm, be his own boss, and sleep when he chose.

We initiated a crash program: repair fencing on the Hobart Farm, build new fencing on the adjoining Adams Farm, fill the barns with hay, fill the silos with corn, purchase and deliver a hundred yearling, high-grade heifers by June 15; all was accomplished.

The lush, green pastures predictably turned brown in October, then gradually white by December. Everything proceeded as planned, including operating well under budget estimates. John was running B-Jack Farms at full capacity with five employees. Dick was content with the heifer program. Alice and I purchased another fix-up rental home in New Jersey. Our freezer was full of venison. Another tax season successfully completed, followed by ten days vacationing in the US Virgin Islands on brother-in-law Chuck's charter yacht. Invigorated by unfettered optimism, I failed to see the perfect storm until it was upon us.

Winter temperatures often remain single digit in this high, mountain valley; therefore, dairy animals are allowed outdoors only for brief periods. During an unscheduled visit to Hobart, I discovered that the barnyard was covered with hay trampled into mud and frozen manure. Clearly, the animals had been fed outdoors instead of in the mangers inside the barns. Less than half the high-energy corn silage had been fed to the growing animals, causing them to be skinny and severely undernourished. They were severely stunted, worthless for the intended purpose.

I now know who is to blame for the nineteen years of travesties involving the Hobart Farm. It is a mistake to want more for someone than he wants for himself. Finally, I accept all blame for the financial losses and now know that "a low-energy person cannot be made a high-energy person." Also, I now know my Dad was right. "Son, you can't make a silk purse from a sow's ear."

Fortuitously, Tuttle, an area farmer, had recently sold his farm and rented ours for his son, Allen. The taxes, insurance, and mortgage payments would be funded with the monthly rent of $750. Dick would work on the farm for Tuttle and thereby support his family without my help. Betty would no longer be a slave to the property.

During the next six years, Tuttle never missed a rent payment, enabling me to pay all of our farm obligations on time. Dick became a model employee: in the barn at 5:00 a.m., breakfast at 8:00 a.m., clean stables, and then start the fieldwork. Their teenage boys went to school on the bus.

Surprisingly, even after losing over $100,000 in the heifer program alone, I harbor few regrets for having lived through this saga. For the enormous overall personal satisfactions derived at the Hobart Farm for my family, I gratefully credit Dick and Betty. Without them, it would not have been possible, even while they maintained their chosen way of life. We had many discussions, but no arguments, and we found lots of enjoyment, regardless of the many setbacks and hard labor. Dick and Betty continued to live on the farm with their family until years later. On Thanksgiving Day, Dick announced a newfound love: Tuttle's employee, a twenty-five-year-old barn girl.

We subdivided a choice, nine-acre wooded corner lot by a spring-fed stream, where Betty resides to this day, close to her children and grandchildren. In 1983, I sold the remaining portion of the farm to a developer for construction of mountain chalet homes on five-acre lots.

The net proceeds from the sale allowed Alice and me to recoup our multiple investments in the farm and repay most of the twenty-year accumulation of Hobart Farm net operating losses. B-Jack Farms absorbed the losses incurred by the heifer-raising program. Without the intended dairy herd replacements and first-calf heifers selling at an all-time high, B-Jack opted to sell its entire milking herd. Dick died in a house trailer eight miles from Hobart, broke and alone, at age seventy-four.

A Wasp Is More Than a Bug

What is a wasp? It is an insect, of course, but I have learned it is much more than a bug.

Mr. Webster defines a wasp as "a black-and-yellow flying insect that can sting." We know it can cause severe pain, even death by anaphylactic shock. It is a small, dangerous creature, justifiably feared. But it can also be the source of hilarious comedy—you know, that uncontrollable, piss-your-pants belly laugh. The following two incidents demonstrate that extreme difference between dead-serious stings and hilarious comedy.

Aurora, age thirty, a tenant at B-Jack Farms, a high school health teacher and part-time police officer, frantically beat on our kitchen door, vibrating a boom-boom-boom sound throughout the house. I rushed to the kitchen door as she turned toward her police car. "Oh, thank God you're OK! An emergency flash came over Andy's scanner requesting help for an elderly man who has just been stung by wasps and is in shock. He said the man's name is Crane. Andy is at the farm searching for you. I'll talk with you later."

Andy, a police sergeant and also a tenant at our B-Jack Farms, had notified Aurora of the incident. The heightened concern of both officers was justified, especially in view of the recent local newspaper front page showing the name, picture, and headline: "Tall, healthy lumberjack dies at age twenty-six, twenty minutes after being stung once." Weeks prior to his death, the young man had been warned to carry an antivenom hypodermic needle with him at all times. It can be carried safely in a sterile container, ready with serum for self-injection, even through clothing if necessary. The serum will reduce or prevent anaphylactic shock (which can cause inability to breathe). Tragically, the unfilled prescription was discovered in the decedent's pocket.

Suddenly, two police cars raced past our home, lights flashing, sirens blasting. They joined an ambulance ahead on the main highway. Their sound quickly faded and stopped at a distance that seemed to be the location of my brother Don's home. In fact, it was. At age seventy-seven, he had endured countless insect stings, spider bites, and such over time, as have I. But this time, it was different. Expert treatment at the scene and later at the hospital emergency room saved his life. He now carries a loaded antivenom hypodermic needle with him at all times.

Now add a *y* to *wasp*. Mr. Webster defines *waspy* as "waspish; an offensive term for a white person who has a Protestant, Anglo-Saxon background and is viewed as belonging to the dominant and most powerful level of society. (Informal insult.)"

According to my former client, former partner, and former friend, Bob Morgan, I am that person. "Beware of Crane the Wasp. You never know when he will attack and sting." It is unlikely that a consensus would confirm such an opinion of me, but I admit to satisfaction, having stung him in defense whenever he launched a provocative attack against me or others nearby. He felt my sting regularly for twenty-five years, beginning the week of our introduction and first conflict when he absorbed my wrath: "I had butter on my bread before I met you, and I'll have butter on my bread when you're gone. So, as of right now, Morgan, you go to hell!" Our personal and business relationship broadened as the law firm expanded to Morgan, Curtis, Spencer, Slagel, Hursh, et al., and we became guarded friends and partners in several very profitable business ventures. The relationship occasionally spawned a wasp's sting, which ironically produced hilarious pain and suffering.

• • •

Bob strolled into my office, eased back in the chair, and suggested, "Hey, Ken, let's go fishing again in Canada. We can use your car, because mine is too good for that purpose."

"Screw you, Morgan . I'll drive my car, because otherwise, I'd hear your bullshit for a month. Besides, you drive like an idiot over those mountain dirt roads."

"OK, Wasp, but make sure you fill the gas tank before we start sharing any trip costs."

"Don't worry, Morgan, I never pull that crap on others like you do." As usual, we were merely kibitzing, but "many a true word has been spoken in jest."

My four-door Chrysler Imperial was a preowned luxury car with 140,000 miles on it. Five hours into the trip, at 2:00 a.m., the headlights grew dim as we traveled the Northway, US Route 87, high in the Adirondack Mountains of New York, four hours south of Montreal, Canada. A glance at the amp meter gauge indicated a faulty generator was the culprit; the battery was not being recharged. I immediately stopped the car a safe distance off the highway to consider our options.

We were in a desolate area of the Adirondack Mountains, miles from civilization, no phone or CB. Traffic was sparse, less than one vehicle per hour passing in either direction. No problem; we'd wait for daylight to continue our trip.

Before I could say a word, Bob was bitching about our plight and my car, and "why wasn't it checked out," and it was entirely my fault that we would lose a day of fishing. His lawyer attack was relentless, scowling. "*No* way, I'm not sitting here until dawn hoping someone will come along to help us."

"Stop your bitching and complaining, Bob. We have no other choice."

Frustrated with anger, he yanked the key from the ignition and came to the driver's side. "Move over," he demanded, "I'm driving!"

"Forget it, Bob. It's too risky. I can see to drive as well as you, but what about the other guy?"

Bob latched on to the steering wheel, squeezed into position, and declared, "That's why the situation calls for a city driver, not a damn farmer!"

Notably, if the battery is discharging current to the spark plugs and nothing else, a vehicle can travel a great distance. By turning off the headlights this bright, moonlit morning and briefly flicking them on for an approaching vehicle, fortunately, with a very weak battery, we limped into Montreal at daybreak and parked at the bay door of an auto repair shop.

Exhausted by the four-hour, intense travel experience, we briefly drifted into deep sleep. At 8:00 a.m., the mechanic rapped on the car window and ordered Bob to move the car or drive it onto the lift for repairs.

A replacement generator could not be found in Montreal or any surrounding auto parts stores. However, Lady Luck was by our side. The exceptionally skilled owner could rebuild this one, but at a much higher cost and considerably more time. After breakfast and a stroll through the local natural history museum, we returned for the car at 11:30 a.m.

Bob always handled the pool money and insisted I handle the record keeping. Predictably, he started again: bitch, bitch, and bitch; there was no escape. "Ken, you have to put more money in the pool. I'm not paying for your damn generator."

Brashly, I warned, "Stop worrying, you cheap bastard! I don't have enough money with me, so I'll ante up when we get back to the office. Pay the man, and let's get the hell out of here."

Defiantly, Little Napoleon blurted out, "No way! That little frog is trying to pull a fast one on us."

I insisted, "Bob, pay the man. If you piss him off, he'll call the cops, and we'll be here the rest of the day."

"Screw you, Wasp!" he blurted. "The frog billed us in Canadian dollars but wants to be paid in US dollars." Now with increasing intensity, their shouting match exploded out of control as red-faced, bulging-eyed, out-of-control Morgan spoke English to a vicious owner speaking

French, each emphasizing their anger with sidesteps and talking hands. As the owner came closer, Bob was yelling, "You damn frogs are all the same—we saved your ass at Normandy Beach, and this is the thanks we get."

Bob popped the money in the owner's hand, and with the speed of a striking viper snatched the receipt from him and quick-stepped to the car, the owner charging close behind, shouting obscenities all the way. Morgan injected himself into the car seat, shouting, "Fuck you, frogs!" and slammed the car door shut with the lock button in place. Instantly, Bob let out a blood-curdling death scream. The shop owner, a few steps from the car, bent over in an uncontrollable, piss-your-pants laughing jag. Bob, wailing in pain, unlocked and opened the car door with his left hand and caressed the thumb on his right. While completely out of control, Bob had smashed his thumb in the door.

I loathe people who laugh when someone is accidentally embarrassed or injured, but often, unexpected, nonlethal circumstances cause such situations to be hilarious, especially while observing the likes of Bob Morgan . He was a short, late-middle-aged, balding Brooklyn lawyer who wailed in agony, begging for sympathy even when enduring only slight pain, but this was not slight pain.

We were underway, and Bob now had a captive audience. "You damn wasp, you have no idea the pain I'm suffering."

"I know exactly how it feels, Bob, and I know exactly how to relieve the excruciating pain."

"Listen up, Crane; you're not playing doctor with me."

"Bob, it's obvious the thumb is not broken. The extreme pain is caused by pressure under the nail. I have accidentally smashed my fingers and thumbs dozens of times while repairing farm equipment and tenant houses. All we have to do is drill a hole through the top of the thumbnail with this super-pointed fillet knife. A speck of blood will pop through the hole, relieving the pressure trapped beneath the nail. Instantly, the throbbing pain will be gone. Simply rest the knifepoint in the center of the nail and slowly spin it until you see blood. I'll do it for you, if you prefer."

"Stay the hell away from me, you sick wasp. You just want me to suffer more. Take me to the hospital."

"Forget it, Bob. I'm not going to sit around an emergency room while you pop pain pills and piss and moan about losing a damn thumbnail. You can drill the hole yourself, dip your hand in and out of a Ziploc bag of ice water, or go to the hospital. I'm leaving for Lac Rapide."

That night, we signed in for our reserved lakeside cabin on the Ojibwa Indian reservation. Bob continued to rant about his pain as he had done incessantly for seven hours. Relentlessly, he described my faulty driving, my junky car that had attacked him, and how only a heartless, wasp prick like me would let anyone suffer as I had done to him. Except for the two-hour power nap in Montreal, we had not slept in twenty hours. We quickly fell into deep sleep, but no human ever existed that could anticipate the next incident.

Bob's demeanor improved after a few days fishing from a boat aimlessly nudged along by warm, summer breezes. His thumb ceased throbbing but remained swollen and extremely sensitive. Several times a day, an exaggerated scream of pain echoed in all directions whenever Bob accidentally bumped his bulbous, rubbery thumb.

The lake was calm. The fish were biting. Loons echoed in the distance. Alone in the tranquil magnificence of this wilderness, peace transcended all worries, earthly problems, personal anger, and anxiety. Bob's Dr.-Jekyll-and-Mr.-Hyde personality momentarily morphed into that of an interesting, good, and decent person. He was my fishing buddy, my friend. Bob, being right-handed but not ambidextrous, was exceptionally tolerant to controlling the spool of the bait-casting reel with his left thumb. I felt a tinge of sympathy as he repeatedly untangled backlashes in the reel caused by improperly "thumbing" the spool. In the past, Bob's right-handed casts unerringly arced the bait toward the intended stump, rock, or floating pod, always splashing it near the target, often for a distance of forty or fifty feet. But, with him unable to deliver with his right hand, most of his left-handed casts fell far short of the mark.

I eased the bow of the boat up a small channel leading to a deep pool in the center of a floating bog, a perfect setting for a trophy northern pike. Surely, one was here. We floated toward the pool, our anticipation of landing that big one increasing with each word of instruction, exciting the moment for the happening. We eased ahead, silent as a shadow except for my instructions to Bob. "Get ready. I see nervous baitfish all around this bog. Stand up on the bow, I'll tell you when to make the cast. You'll have only one chance before the fish disappear under the bog after your lure splashes and sinks. I'll tell you when to make a long cast toward the loon's nest ahead about one o'clock. Do you see it? Do you see it?"

"OK, now I do."

"Don't cast until the bow turns slightly and you're about forty feet away, I'll tell when. Get ready—*now!*" Then came the unimaginable: a perfect cast, a huge swirl, the line taut, a giant pike. But Bob had not thumbed the reel, causing a predictable, tangled backlash. His familiar blood-curdling scream broke the silence as the pole and reel flew into the air, overboard. Bob fell back in his deck chair, holding his thumb, wailing in pain, screaming expletives too graphic for expression. I saw it coming, but it was too late. It was painfully hilarious. In perfect form, his arm had been slightly raised, elbow crooked, thumb straight up, ready to stop the spinning cylinder that prevents the hated backlash. A flick of the wrist, a splash, and a huge northern pike snatched the lure. At that precise moment, Bob convulsed with a pitiful scream of pure agony. His tender, bulbous thumb had been straight up, erect, ready to be zapped deep, three times, with venom from an angry wasp's ass.

Tears flowing, sitting, then jumping up and down, thumb in and out of the water, then he studied the thumb again and again while cradling it in his left hand. All the time, his screams echoed from every direction. This bizarre happening snuffed out my sympathy.

The suddenness, the surprise, the incredible odds against a swollen thumb innocently raised in the air, without provocation greeted by a venom-injecting wasp's ass: the thought and the sight of it all drove me into an uncontrollable, piss-your-pants belly laugh.

Bob moved to the center bench seat, leaned toward me, and shouted expletives over the loud hum of the outboard motor. As with the car, of course, his injury was my fault. His continued attack included, "You should have kept your damn mouth shut and not disturbed me. Without all your bullshit, 'do this, do that,' I would not have exposed my sore thumb." During the hour-long boat ride back to camp, Bob rehashed the events non-stop. Each time, he increased the number on the pain scale to unimaginable heights. Each time he did so, I tormented him more and more with my uncontrollable laughter. He chided, "Look, Ken, it's not a laughing matter. I lost my best fishing pole and reel. The biggest pike I've ever seen got away, and now my thumb is throbbing more than ever. It's not a laughing matter."

"I'm sorry, Bob. Do you want me to drill the hole in it?"

The calamity continued back at camp in the fish-cleaning shack as Bob told his story again and again—"How the big one got away." Each time, the pike grew bigger and bigger. Other fishermen gathered in a circle, Bob in the center, showing his thumb, emphasizing the size of the pike that got away. Of course, as always, I was to blame.

Annoyed, I could no longer tolerate his exaggerations. "Listen up, men. Mr. Morgan is correct. That fish was huge. Scientific studies prove that fish grow faster in the shortest period of time than any other creature on earth and that time is—from the time they are caught to the time they get away."

Bob reclaimed center stage and delivered his closing argument to the jury. "Our world is filled with great diversity. Most is very pleasing. Some is detestable, especially wasps. But the facts are clear: it was a record-setting, trophy northern pike that got away. I have a picture of it."

"It's true, guys. He has a picture of it. The big picture is in his small mind."

As the group eased down the path to the lodge, Bob rested his hand on my shoulder and quipped, "I agree, you're not an insect, my friend. But you sure as hell are waspy."

Don't Snap Your Fingers-It May Kill

Death by lethal injection is an inflammatory topic even among good friends. Regardless, considerate debate is valuable, especially when expressing honest differences of opinion.

Tony and I were traveling to a softball field with our wives when a news flash came over the car radio. "We interrupt this program to bring you an important message. So and So was executed by lethal injection at nine a.m. this morning."

Attorney Tony, in a rage, blurted out, "What the hell is this world coming to! Thousands of babies are killed each year by abortion doctors. Now the new way to murder is to pump poison into a helpless person strapped motionless in a chair." Tony, a devout Catholic, insisted the death penalty was not a deterrent to future crime.

Alice chimed in, "Besides, it's against most religions. Some countries have limited the death penalty, and others have abolished it altogether." Maria, Tony's wife, also a devout Catholic, strongly supported their viewpoint. *This is not good*, I thought. *Three against one*. To avoid being drawn into an open-ended discussion about religion or the death penalty, I briefly stated these points:

The general public considers the death penalty irrelevant as a deterrent, but it certainly does deter the executed criminal from further crime. Most religions impose various penalties depending on the severity of the crime. For example, Buddhists may flog individuals in public for relatively minor offenses. Muslims, in countries such as Saudi Arabia, behead women guilty of adultery. Even the current edition of the King James Bible is filled with controversy regarding death to certain transgressors.

I went on: "The Constitution of the United States demands a separation of church and state; therefore, matters of public concern, such as abortion or execution, should be determined on a basis other than the religious beliefs of lawmakers. Besides, you might feel different about it if you or your family became victims of a serious crime."

"Your point is well made, Ken, but that doesn't change my beliefs. It's wrong to kill unborn babies, and it's wrong to sanction murder because another person is guilty of murder."

"Nice try, Tony, but just be honest. Suppose you're accosted by three men in their late forties as you enter your home around ten o'clock at night? The long-haired, tattooed, toothless men handcuff you to a radiator in your living room. Two guys sodomize your eight-year-old son and then shoot him in the stomach with a .38-caliber pistol. Your son is twisting and turning in unbearable agony. The three filthy bridge bums rape and sodomize Maria and your twelve-year-old daughter on the floor ten feet away as Bernie dies, with his bulging eyes staring at you with a fixed gaze that pleads for help. Two hours later, drunk or high on drugs, the men stagger away, laughing and joking about the kid that took so long to die.

"Three months later, the perpetrators are apprehended while committing a similar crime in another home several miles away. The public defender assigned to the case has asked the Catholic prosecutor to plea-bargain to avoid a death penalty sentence. Shortly thereafter, you learn your wife and daughter are infected with syphilis and irreversible AIDS viruses. Both are pregnant. What do you want to happen next?"

Clearly frustrated, Tony carelessly stopped the car, jerked the keys from the ignition, and said, "Where the hell do you come up with this stuff? It's ridiculous!"

"It's my story Tony, so don't try to change the facts. What do you want to happen? You're not under oath, but I expect you to be honest!"

Without hesitation, Tony blurted out, "I want the dirtbags *dead*."

"What about the pregnancies?" I asked.

Now calm and pensive, Tony softly said, "I have to think about that."

"Time is up, Tony! Your wife and twelve-year-old daughter are in their second trimester."

Tony attempted to avoid the question by insisting the example was ridiculous. "That's not the issue. Opinions about controversial issues largely depend on 'whose ox is being gored.' Each situation should be considered case by case, depending on the seriousness of the crime and the public's need for justice. However, that does not mean we should revert to stoning people to death or dish out sentences as was done at the Salem Witch Trials during the sixteen hundreds."

"Well, it's easier for you to accept abortion and the death penalty because you're not Catholic and don't have strong religious beliefs."

Offended, I snapped back, "You may think you're a great attorney, Tony, but your summation sucks!"

High emotion and tension filled the air as we quietly waited for the traffic light to turn green. "You say I have no religion, Tony, but consider the death of a seagull."

"You're nuts, Crane!"

"No, no, it's a true story.

I was in the Marine Corps boot camp at Parris Island, South Carolina."

"When was that, Ken, just after the Civil War? Ha, ha."

"Don't be a wise guy, Tony; I'm trying to tell a true story."

"OK, I'm sorry. Go ahead."

"You were never in the service, so you probably don't know that marines are required to practice sewing."

"Oooh Kenny! That's—sooo—cute!"

"Tony, I told you, don't be a wise guy!'"

"All right, go on with your story."

"Basic sewing included replacing buttons, patching torn cloth-ing, and hemming trousers. Well, my buddy, Thomas, was a complete screwup. Every branch of the service has a few pathetic guys who simply can't do anything right. After weeks of training, Thomas just couldn't get with the program. One day, the drill sergeant suddenly shouted, '*Fall out, fall out, fall out!*' We realized a surprise inspection was seconds away. Thomas hurriedly slipped into his trousers, unaware of an error until he stumbled from our six-man tent to stand at attention in platoon formation. Everyone snapped to attention when the sergeant bellowed out, '*Tench—hut!*'

"Then he shouted, 'Private Thomas, *front and center!*' Thomas was shaking in his boots as the sergeant, in a rage, loudly shared his thoughts. 'This is what an asshole looks like. They round up a bunch of assholes like this and expect me to turn out fighting men in eight weeks. You people are lower than whale shit, and that's on the bottom of the ocean. All of you are spoiled punks, juvenile delinquents, and switchblade artists. Not one of you knows how to wipe your ass without asking your momma. Your soul may belong to God, but starting right now, your ass belongs to me! I will tell you what to do, where to do it, and when to do it. *Is that clear?*'

"Every marine responded, 'Sir, yes, sir!' He belched out, 'I caaaan't hearrr yooou. *Is—that—clear?* All together, we yelled, '*Sir, yes, sir!*'"

"Hey, Ken, that has nothing to do with religion. I suppose now you're going to tell us how you were wounded as you captured twenty-one of the enemy while saving Thomas's life."

"Cut it out, Tony! You know I haven't been in combat. Regardless, I guarantee, what I am about to tell you will shock all who doubt the power of prayer."

"OK, Kenny. I cannnnn't waaaait to hear this."

"The six-foot-three sergeant squared nose to nose with Thomas, still at attention and shaking uncontrollably. The sergeant blasted his smelly breath in Thomas's face through a menacing set of teeth, exaggerated by a huge overbite. He bellowed, 'You're a disgrace to the marines. *Get out of my platoon, private.*'

"He raised his arm and pointed toward the drill area. 'Get out there, on the double, and don't come back until you catch a seagull. If you stop for any reason, I'll come out there and personally kick the shit out of you. *Is that clear!*'

"Thomas loudly replied, 'Sir, yes, sir!'

"The parade field, the drill area, is like a twenty-acre parking lot, except there are no lines on the macadam. Parris Island is generally hot during the day and cool at night in late November. This day was exceptionally hot, which quickly warmed the macadam, causing flocks of seagulls to congregate in the sunny areas.

"I felt so sorry for Thomas, because he couldn't help himself. He was really a nice guy, but a complete klutz. My mind and heart was filled with sympathy for the little guy being intimidated by this big bully. Even so, I nearly broke out in uncontrollable laughter. Thomas looked absolutely ridiculous standing there at attention with one trouser leg cut twice, ending just below his knee, and the uncut leg doubled under his combat boot, trailing behind. He had hemmed the wrong trouser leg.

"Trembling nearly out of control, Thomas rolled the long leg up to his ankle, saluted, and dashed away. He ran, jogged, walked, and then ran again. I felt completely helpless while watching this sad charade. Sunday is our religious day, and I became overwhelmed with sympathy. I decided to pray to the Lord for Thomas to catch a seagull. I knelt down on one knee, bowed my head, and said a long prayer."

"Oooh, Kenny, that's *sooo* beautiful."

"Damn it, Tony, I'm serious, so knock it off!" I continued: "When I looked up, Thomas was running toward our tent area, yelling, 'I got it, I got it. I caught the son of a bitch!' The seagull was limp and still warm. Obviously, it had died moments earlier. Thomas had chased seagulls for hours and was about to give up when, as he put it, 'A miracle happened. I leaped at the sleeping bird, and it didn't move. It must have died on the spot. I still can't believe it.'

"'Believe it, Thomas. I said a prayer for you, and just like that'—I snapped my fingers—'the seagull died.'"I continued relating the events to everyone in the parked car, saying, "A nanosecond after the prayer "—I snapped my fingers—"the seagull was dead. So is there power in prayer? I say yes! But, I felt terrible for asking God to kill that innocent bird."

"That's a nice story, Ken. Now, I suppose you want us to believe you control life and death with the snap of your fingers. It's a tale filled with sound and fury, signifying crap. It was just a coincidence."

"Perhaps you're right, Tony, but a good Christian would never pass judgment so fast."

We quietly eased our way down a tree-lined sidewalk toward the ball field. A strange, inner urge forced me to have the last word. "Look, Tony, you said I have no religion. I'm telling you the complete truth of what happened, so help me, God. Believe what you want. I knelt, said a prayer, then the seagull died."

As before, when I said "the seagull died," I snapped my fingers. But this time, all four of us froze in our tracks. A squirrel came crashing through the tree limbs and fell spastic on the sidewalk, inches in front of us. Apparently, when I snapped my fingers, it had had a heart attack, and it slowly died on the spot.

Tony was spellbound as I chastised him, saying, "I have told you the absolute truth. Don't ever question my religion again, and never piss me off so I snap my fingers at you."

Seventy-three men had witnessed the death of the seagull. Four adults, including a skilled attorney, witnessed the death of the squirrel. The odds of such events happening are incalculable.

Was this all a coincidence, or is there power in prayer?

Trust

Trust can be a unique treasure or a curse. To own that treasure, one must also risk it becoming a curse. Trust is a matter of faith: faith in God, faith in something, faith in someone, and faith in yourself. It is a paradox: when to trust, whom to trust, what to trust, and to what degree. It is a lifelong conundrum partially explained to me as a young boy.

"Dad, you gave money to that blind man. How do you know he's really blind?"

"Son, you can't be sure every time, but I would rather give to a fake blind man than to miss giving to a real blind man."

Reconsider the saviors in my prior stories: Bill Fishburn, Mr. Rose, and Horace Green (the Hobart Farm); John Pannitari, Jack Bolby Jr., Mr.

Bolby Sr., and Mr. Benson (the office on Route 206); Richard Clampton and Bart Bennuto ("I Want to Be an Accountant"). All epitomize the wonderful treasure of trust that far outweighs the curses of betrayal. But where is the script that could identify Judas before he betrayed Jesus, or Salome, who requested that John the Baptist's head be delivered to her on a platter as a reward for her dancing? Where is the script that could identify Benedict Arnold before he betrayed George Washington and the American patriots fighting for independence? Where is the script or knowledge that can identify the betrayer before I am betrayed? Perhaps, like growing old, not knowing is the consequence of living.

Professor William Kunstler, my law professor at Pace College, fired hypothetical legalities at me in quick succession. Although I majored in accounting and business administration, his passion and flair inspired me to always search for answers beyond the obvious. This man inflamed my passion for legally challenging the law. Prof. Kunstler's ethos and downright brilliance gained him national renown in the 1960s and 1970s in the defense of the Chicago Seven, Black Panther Bobby Seale, and Stokely Carmichael, the prisoner accused in the aftermath of the deadly riots at the state prison in Attica, New York. He defended Mafia boss John Gotti and Sheikh Omar Rahman, who was convicted in 1995 of conspiring to blow up the World Trade Center. Prof. Kunstler encouraged me to major in the study of law instead of accounting.

Accounting and business management are extremely important, but the paramount question asked of small-firm public accountants is how to legally reduce federal and state tax burdens. Thus, we have the distinction between tax "evasion" and tax "avoidance." I became immersed in the law, believing everyone should pay their fair share of taxes, but always within the legal constraints set forth in the tax code and regulations. Be that as it may, in the 1960s and 1970s, specialized professionals saved their clients millions of dollars by suggesting they invest in legal tax shelters such as coal mines, oil wells, offshore corporations, cattle breeding, horse breeding, and leasing high-tech medical equipment, to name a few. My ultimate choice became cattle breeding and dairy farming. Hence came the Hobart Farm, Hillsboro Breeders, Inc., and later, B-Jack Farms. The simple purpose of most tax shelters is to legally convert ordinary income, taxed at 77 percent in 1969, to long-term capital gains taxed at 28 percent or lower. But the primary purpose must be business profits, not just to save taxes.

Technical application of this concept required expert knowledge of the US tax code and court rulings related to the subject matter. Tax laws throughout the world change day by day, week after week; therefore, continuing professional education is a must. Consequently, twenty-nine out of a field of 1,586 candidates successfully completed a two-day, four-part comprehensive exam sponsored by the Internal Revenue Service (IRS) and became IRS-enrolled agents (EAs). I was one of those twenty-nine.

An enrolled agent is a federally authorized tax practitioner who has technical expertise in the field of taxation and who is empowered by the US Department of the Treasury to represent taxpayers before administrative levels of the IRS for audits, collections, and certain appeals contesting technical rulings issued during an audit of tax returns. In addition to the stringent testing and application process, the IRS requires enrolled agents to complete seventy to ninety hours of continuing professional education every three years. Because of the knowledge necessary to become an EA and requirements to maintain the license, there are only about forty-six thousand practicing enrolled agents in the United States compared to 760,000 attorneys-at-law and 1.3 million accountants and auditors. Interestingly, of the 1.3 million accountants, approximately 8 percent are self-employed.

Thus, an amalgamation of my past—independent outdoorsman and tenacious hard worker, physically and mentally—I relentlessly converted problems into challenges. Impulsively, but with due diligence, I engaged in a variety of occupations. Star Breeders (remember—"Star" spelled backward is "rats") folded because of a lack of due diligence. I didn't know the meaning of one simple word (*pathogen*). But my understandings were different now, as I moved forward with a newly formed corporation registered in New Jersey under the name Hillsboro Breeders, Inc..

Hillsboro Breeders was formed in an attempt to prevent the sale of a small dairy farm in Neshanic, New Jersey, located thirty-five miles west of New York City, fifteen miles north of Princeton, and ten miles east of Flemington, the town where the world-famous Lindbergh kidnapping trial was held.

Bruce, the farm owner's son and also a beneficiary of a realty and insurance company that Bart Bennuto and I originated, had pleaded for my help to avoid a sale of the family farm. "If you can do that, we will take you in like a third son." I believed him. Bruce, then nearly thirty-three years of age, married, and a father of three children, had lived and worked on the farm most of his life as his father's employee.

After a lifetime of dairy farming, his father retired, and Bruce became unemployed. The entire family attended the Dutch Reform Church, where his mother and father worshiped for most of their life. As local farmers and lifelong members and treasurers of the church, the family maintained an impeccable reputation.

Plan your work and work your plan. The plan: using legal tax shelters, professionals in high tax brackets were guaranteed significant profits by purchasing high-grade, purebred, registered cattle for breeding purposes. The cost of maintaining the herd was deducted from their ordinary income, but when the herd was sold (including the progeny), the proceeds were taxed at capital gains rates. Thus, a skillfully crafted contract could legally reduce a taxpayer's annual tax liability to zero, depending on the sum of money he placed at risk.

Working the plan: Bruce and I, through Hillsboro Breeders, Inc., would purchase the family farm. Bruce, as general manager, would run the operation and receive a weekly wage. His father would receive consulting fees and a monthly payment toward the farm purchase contract. Investors would receive enormous tax benefits and use them to pay our company to care for their herd of cattle. Clearly, a proven, tested, win-win business investment.

Bruce cautiously questioned me, "How can I be sure you will accomplish this?"

I explained in layman's terms the responsibility we were accepting as partners in the farm and the pledge to his mother and father. I urged him to have his father's lawyer draw an agreement that protected all of us. Time was of the essence because I had deposited $40,000 in our account for the purchase of cattle at Col. Lee's upcoming cattle auction in Maryland. "I have two more contracts ready to go, but you have to complete the new cattle fencing. I'll have the first herd delivered in about two weeks, so let's get the farm ready and sign the agreements your mom and dad, you and Beth, and Alice and I have agreed upon."

"OK, Ken. But you have to realize, you're dealing with my home and family."

"Of course we are. That's why I thought you asked for my help as a 'brother.' Is there a problem? Has someone changed their mind?"

Together, attorney Clampton, Bruce, and I drove to Dayton, Maryland, to purchase thirty-five purebred Polled Hereford cows and one bull. Jim Linthicum, a newfound friend and rancher, assisted us with our choice of registered animal bloodlines. Jim, a twenty-nine-year old, charismatic young man, introduced us to a new bloodline called Modern Mesa. His prize cattle were of that bloodline and groomed daily, cooled with fans during hot weather, and hand-fed a diet prescribed by a veterinarian. Jim, a recognized authority in the beef-breeding industry, could not speak. Meningitis had destroyed his voice box, leaving him mute except for inaudible, high-pitched, squeaky sounds. I quickly learned the meaning of his gestures and expressions but never imagined someday we would be partners. Jim and his veterinarian assisted us at the auction and examined the veterinarian certificates authorizing interstate shipment of each animal as the herd was loaded, one by one, onto cattle trailers.

The eight-hour trip was uneventful. The animals raced for the hay and water in the secure barnyard while Mr. Church Man evaluated each animal for injury, all as planned. We were in high spirits and congratulated each other with a handshake. I remarked, "The cattle are here, but where is our agreement?"

Mr. Church Man replied, "Judge Algar will be here tomorrow at two o'clock with the agreement for us to sign."

The agreement set forth familiar, "boilerplate" legalistics until near the end of the document, where it stipulated, "Excepted from the afore-sited premises, 10 acres of land, all structures thereon, including, but not limited to, 3 residences, and farm buildings." The significance, of course, was to exclude from the deal 10 acres of land having significant road frontage and all the buildings thereon without reducing the ver-bally contracted price.

Stunned with disbelief, I realized I had been trapped. Bruce surrep-titiously had convinced his parents to change the agreement, but not to disclose the contents until the herd was unloaded at the farm. As presi-dent of Hillsboro Breeders, Inc., I reluctantly signed the agreement.

Bruce's wife handled the bookkeeping and diligently paid the com-pany obligations. The following year, we accepted two additional inves-tors that increased the herd to approximately 150 head, including calves from the original herd of thirty-five bred cows. We desperately needed a top-ranked bull and planned to acquire one in the near future, perhaps at the upcoming cattle show in Houston, Texas.

What a bull story...

A Bull and Horse Story

The Bull Story

Alice and I accepted a personal invitation to join a small group of dignitaries in a private, high-rise suite in Houston, Texas. The occasion was a national Polled Hereford Association convention followed by a show and sale of top bloodline cattle at the Houston Astrodome.

Alice and I, along with Bruce and Beth, sat in forward seats observing the prize cattle paraded onstage, glamorized and sold one by one. The loudspeaker blared, "And here is the grand national championship bull. Its bloodline is Modern Mesa. Notice the long, straight back, the square, heavy-muscled hindquarters, and especially observe the amount of daylight below the belly. This animal will sire high-quality beef, not fat as older breeds do. This is the desired look. This is the modern look. This is the bloodline of Modern Mesa." The auctioneer continued with instructions: "One-fourth ownerships will be sold at auction. Partial ownerships will be replaced by a full ownership if a bid price exceeds the composite sum of the one-fourth interests. Now, let's get started. What is your bid for one-fourth ownership in this magnificent sire?" He yodeled out his "Humminah, humminah, humminah...I have a bid of fifteen thousand dollars."

The bidding was fast and aggressive. James Linthicum, onstage, signaled me to come forward. An interpreter directed me to the rear of the stage, and when asked if I would be Jim's partner in the bull, I replied, "Yes."

The bidding continued, but clearly, the auctioneer was troubled by this backstage activity. The interpreter kept signaling Jim at each bid until finally he asked me how much of my money to bid. I quickly replied, "I will pay fifty-fifty with Jim."

The bidding slowed as Jim relentlessly and without hesitation said, "Yes. Yes. Yes."

The auctioneer paused and declared, "Going once…going twice… last call…all done?" The arena fell silent. "Sold, to James Linthicum of Dayton, Maryland, and Hillsboro Breeders of Neshanic, New Jersey, for thirty-two thousand five hundred dollars." No composite bid exceeded four times each one-fourth ownership bid ($130,000); therefore, the bull would be shared three months by each owner. All had to be trustworthy.

Back at the plush suite, little did Alice or I know that the purchase of the national grand championship bull would plunge us into the company of elite, high-roller, tax-shelter gurus. Approximately five couples, apparently well acquainted, greeted and reintroduced one another. A tall, well-dressed Texan offered a handshake and remarked, "Good luck with your championship sire. I'm Governor John Connelly. Welcome to Houston."

This time I did not humble myself, as had happened when I was in the Marine Corps, chest bulging to display my Good Conduct ribbon and Expert Rifleman medal and facing at attention a real marine with a full chest of awards. Instead, I humorously engaged Gov. Connelly by asking, "Is it true you grew up on your family's South Texas cotton farm as a 'barefoot boy walking mules that plow furrows'?"

Jovially, he replied, "That's an unusual introduction, but the answer is yes."

With extreme concentration, I suppressed the urge to ask questions regarding the Kennedy assassination or his injuries suffered at that time. Instead, I politely needled him about raising horned Herefords rather than Polled (hornless) Herefords as I did. It was a great honor to be a guest in his suite. Governor Connelly received a standing ovation following his appearance as guest speaker at the National Polled Hereford Association's convention.

The association's bylaws require members to maintain strict genealogical records of each animal registered as purebred. Certified birth certificates are issued to the owners of newborn calves, and the association maintains a lifetime record as ownership changes. An association official requested a meeting with us, the new owners of the Modern Mesa bull.

"Gentlemen, you are required to sign these documents and faithfully abide by the strict terms, conditions, and requirements contained herein. This agreement is intended to safeguard the health, safety, and well-being of this sire, for your benefit. Even a minor infraction will subject you to severe personal liability. I emphasize: do not overbreed this valuable bull. With our guidance and approval, you may establish a sperm bank for the pro rata benefit of the one-fourth ownerships. Health and accident insurance is required, but each of you will be personally liable for willful misconduct or negligence jeopardizing the value of this championship bull."

Hillsboro Breeders received possession of the Modern Mesa fourth in line because of our geographic location in Neshanic. Beef cows should be bred in August, causing birth nine months later in early spring, in open pasture during cool weather. The cow generally isolates herself, giving birth and causing the calf to suckle colostrum milk from her shortly thereafter. Colostrum milk provides a complete formula of vitamins, minerals, and essential immune-system supplements. All of this is extremely important to promote bonding and reduce the risk of diseases, especially scours, a deadly form of diarrhea. We agreed to rest the bull for six weeks prior to our breeding season, beginning late August. During his stress-free vacation, he would be pampered with a strict diet provided by a veterinarian, including grazing lush pasture grasses, special feed grains, and mineral supplements.

This bovine royalty arrived at our ten-acre home farm in Belle Mead, New Jersey, seven miles from his 150 potential lovers at

Hillsboro Breeders' 135-acre farm. At this location awaited a bacchanalian life for the Modern Mesa (eat, drink, and be merry, for soon you will be required to satisfy a meadow full of lovesick females). The pasture was well secured with four-foot-high welded mesh cattle fencing and a strand of electric wire on top. I was uniquely satisfied with the bull's safety, but carelessly negligent and ignorant of a potential life-threatening hazard. Our new kitchen window at the big house allowed a prominent view of the lush, green pasture in the area where my brooder coop home used to be. It was now a fenced-in swimming pool area. A twenty-four-foot above ground swimming pool would be acceptable for many families, but not for me. The previous year, my trusty backhoe had dug deeper and deeper, allowing the pool liner to stretch to a tapered depth of seven feet near the diving board. The above ground, steel-frame bed liner support became recessed to ground level. Thirty-six thousand gallons of water stretched the liner and frame into a secure position. I had backfilled the pool frame with the excavated material, then graded and seeded the surrounding area. My treasured brooder coop had thus become a lush, green lawn that Alice would cut with a gas-powered push mower. Or it could become a smorgasbord for Modern Mesa.

Alice busied herself in the kitchen as I savored a morning cup of coffee in the living room while observing the news and weather reports on TV. Suddenly, a blood-curdling scream vibrated throughout the home. "Honey, the bull is floating in the swimming pool!"

I bolted from the house, clearing four steps at a clip, shouting, "Get a rope from the barn and a short garden hose!" Modern Mesa was floating motionlessly near the edge of the pool. I lifted the bull's nose above the water and slipped a harness over his head. Alice held his nose above the surface as I hooked his front hoof over the edge of the pool frame. I grabbed the bull's tail and pleaded, "When I signal, pull as hard as you can." Miraculously, the hooked foot's reflexes powered the seemingly dead animal slightly past the fulcrum point. Slowly, ever so slowly, our adrenaline-fueled effort inched him out of the pool onto firm ground.

He was not breathing. Mouth-to-mouth resuscitation was not an option. I jumped up and down on his stomach, but this trampoline would not respond. The bull was bloated with water. A flashback to my experience as a farm boy compelled me to address the emergency. Instinctively, I grabbed the hose from Alice and forced it down the bull's trachea into the first of four chambers of his bovine stomach, called the rumen. It is the largest part of the stomach and contains millions of bacteria, yeast, and even mold to help break down the cellulose diet. For a bovine to get enough goodness from its diet, it has to chew its food several times. The second part of the stomach is the reticulum, which helps to regurgitate part of the stored food so it can be chewed again. This process is referred to as "chewing cud." The fermentation process continues through the third and fourth parts of the stomach, preventing the animal from barfing or burping. It can only release gas as flatus through its rectum.

The hose spewed water and stomach gases from the rumen under extreme pressure as I continued jumping up and down on the stomach, occasionally dropping onto my butt to add violent pressure. The bull rolled his eyes, gasped for air, and slowly began to breathe. An hour later, I led the drunken bull on unstable legs to safety. Alice locked the gate behind us and jovially remarked, "I'd rather cut the grass with my push mower."

Modern Mesa recovered completely and sired extremely high-quality calves. As the news spread, lucrative offers poured in, culminating with the sale of our ownership to Cornell University for an offer we could not refuse. Modern Mesa became an icon in the beef industry after a newly established sperm bank began selling his semen—at a very high price—for artificial breeding. Hillsboro Breeders' profits grew exponentially as clients desperately wanted to earn capital gains and legally reduce their income tax burdens.

Within three years, our breeding herd of forty cows expanded to over three hundred head, split between our Neshanic, New Jersey farm and a newly leased farm in Virginia. Suddenly, there was unexpected interest in our activity. We were invited to many prestigious cattle breeding facilities, including an estate in Dayton, Maryland (his son was a senior editor of *Reader's Digest*); Falkland Farms in Pennsylvania, whose owner had high-ranking authority in a major corporation.; D. farm in Duchess County, New York; and Black Watch Farms in Hillsdale, New York, which cared for an Angus bull named "The President" that sold for over $1M through a New York Stock Exchange company. Alice and I once declined an invitation from Gov. John Connelly's niece to visit the LBJ ranch in Texas; the list goes on. Strangely, we felt honored, but not impressed, to be in the company of such distinguished hosts.

Perhaps it was culture shock that caused me to reconsider the future of Hillsboro Breeders, Inc.

Neither Alice nor I knew the lofty social graces practiced with ease by the distinguished millionaires among whom we found ourselves. We admired their personal successes but fully realized we did not want to achieve their high, noble socioeconomic status. Also, circumstances at the Neshanic farm began to change. Unusually high expenses for gasoline, diesel fuel, and maintenance had to be explained, including personal items such as pool supplies and building material. Based on information and belief, the truth was revealed, and corrective action was taken.

While examining the herd records, I discovered unfamiliar bloodlines, and occasionally, the required registration identification tattooed in each calf's ear at birth failed to match the birth certificate authorized by the National Polled Hereford Association. Shortly thereafter, I was informed that my partner had purchased cattle on his own, blended them into the herd, and sold his cattle to potential buyers referred and directed to our main farm, Hillsboro Breeders, Inc.

A dilemma plagued me. How could I meet the responsibilities to our client investors by maintaining and expanding their herds, knowing my shareholder and equal partner was culpable of wrongdoing? I continued to work through the problem, not as a challenge, but as a matter of honesty, until I received a phone call from Bruce. "Hi, Ken, I have twelve first-calf dairy heifers on our stock trailer I received as a commission.

Do you want to buy them for your New York dairy farm? They're due to freshen any day, so they have to go to New York today."

Immediately, I contacted cattle dealer Ben Daniel, who had previously supplied quality dairy animals for our Hobart, New York farm, to obtain interstate health certificates required for him to transport the animals out of state. Ben interrupted me midpoint by saying, "Forget it, Ken, those heifers belong to Bruce's neighbor and will be considered stolen property. Rustling cattle is still a federal offense. Worse, the owner is totally blind but can identify each animal by touch."

My return phone call to Bruce was short and direct. "Get those heifers off of our farm and out of our cattle trailer immediately, or I'll call the police."

The next day, I informed him of my decision to shut down our beef-breeding business altogether. Regardless, together we would carry out our responsibilities as set forth in the option agreement to purchase the farm and use our profits in the company to carry out that obligation. Besides, an analysis of the ever-changing Internal Revenue Service code led me to consider a less glamorous but much more lucrative business than breeding racehorses, alpacas, chinchillas, or beef cows. All things considered, dairy farming became my choice, but not in New Jersey. High land prices had rendered dairy farming in the Garden State a dying business.

As the herd quickly sold, client investors reaped handsome profits, and Hillsboro Breeders Inc. retained earnings increased sufficiently to meet its obligations in the foreseeable future, even with the farm operation shut down. Bruce became a partner in the real estate agency and poured all his efforts into that business. Russ Duffy continued the insurance agency. Alice handled our expanded rental real estate properties with the purchase of two adjoining homes. My full-time CPA handled my burgeoning tax practice.

All was well, a win-win-win resolution for all concerned, until six months later. I received a phone call from a former auditor in my group at Diehl Manufacturing Company, my one-armed hunting buddy and friend, Jack Bolby.

The Horse Story

"Ken, I tried to go bird hunting today, but there are horses all over your farm. I heard you and Bruce are under intensive criminal investigation. What the hell is going on? Dad is worried about the two mortgages he arranged for you."

"Jack, I don't know what the hell you're talking about, but I'll find out right away." In fact, it took me several weeks to uncover the complete true story, an involvement so bad it became a matter of life or death.

Our Neshanic farm in New Jersey is located near a four-thousand-acre estate in Hillsborough Township owned by Doris Duke, the famous American tobacco heiress once called "the world's richest woman." The involvement started because of a rumored triangle love affair involving Dr. Kittleson, a beauty queen, and Dr. Tashen, a veterinarian, both employed by the Animal Medical Center of New York City; and the heiress, who has been the main contributor to AMC and chairman of the board of trustees since May 1973.

Miss Duke epitomizes the warning: "There is no wrath like that of a woman scorned." The press fanned the emotional flame by headlining irresponsible statements by experts, elected public officials, and attorneys- at-law. Consider the following headline in the March 27, 1974, Plainfield, New Jersey *Courier News*: "Hillsborough Horses Cause Concern." Paraphrased, it said that New Jersey's agricultural secretary, Phillip Alampi, intended to crack down on a New York research firm studying diseased horses in Hillsboro or oust it from the state. Outraged horse breeders feared an outbreak of swamp fever that could claim the lives of their herds if the research continued on the Bruce Ammerman Farm in Neshanic. The farm was adjacent to the Woodfern Road Elementary School. Miss E. Van Ness, a member of the New Jersey Agricultural Board, warned, "There are some very shady things going on there, and adjacent to a school playground, right in the middle of a horse-populated area."

Excerpts read: "Biting vectors transport the disease. Some kind of fogging devices are needed to kill flies and mosquitoes acting as carriers.

The small field used by the horses is a sea of manure, and the SPCA is after them. Township health officials reported there are no viable organisms present in the fecal material; therefore there is no transmission via ground water. Transmission distance appears to be 200 yards. The elementary school is less than 100 yards. There is a record of human infection in California. These horses are carriers of Equine Infectious Anemia (EIA), for which there is no cure or protection. The Animal Research Center has a budget of five million dollars to study the aging process of man by studying EIA's effect on blood vessels and circulatory systems of horses. Dr. Simpson, a virologist at Rutgers University, declared the EIA virus has been known to infect humans, causing a disease characterized by fever, diarrhea, bloody stool, anemia, and herpes-like skin eruptions in the lower abdomen area. The horses were kept and studied on the Doris Duke estate, but were suddenly forced off the property by armed security forces and mysteriously wound up on the Ammerman farm. Dr. Kittleson said there is no problem with spreading the infection and that a few rabble-rousers in the area are needlessly scaring the public."

Throughout the year, the storm intensified day by day. East Coast newspaper headlines read: "Diseased Horses Termed a Threat and a Danger to Humans"; "Former US Attorney 'Shocked and Outraged' at What Appears to Have Been a Star Chamber Proceeding"; "Horse Removal Is Up To the Judge"; "Mystery Intensifies around Sick Horses in Neshanic"; "Veterinarian Syringes Found Lying on the Floor at Woodfern Elementary School After Break-In, Sunday March 31"; "Dr. Kittleson's Absence Linked to Fear of Violence"; "Horsemen's Group files $10M Lawsuit"; "Duke Takes AMC to Court"; "AMC Fined $4,000"; "AMC Suit Against Doris Duke $1,775,000"; "Horse Issue Goes to New Jersey Supreme Court."

The year of lawsuits, claims, counterclaims, cross claims, and judgments culminated on January 16, 1975, with major newspaper headlines reading: "Research Horses Are Destroyed." Yes, the horses were gone, my partner's wrongdoing was exposed, and I was exonerated. The ten-million-dollar lawsuit continued, but I was dismissed as a named defendant, thanks to Jeffrey M. Morgan, senior partner of the law firm Morgan, Curtis, Spencer, and Slagel, who represented me throughout the ordeal. Bruce then attempted to disenfranchise me and Hillsboro Breeders by refusing to exercise our option to purchase the farm. The court ruled on the issue and ordered specific performance of the terms and conditions cited in the option purchase agreement executed by the parties, or Bruce would forfeit those rights to Hillsboro Breeders, Inc. and Crane.

A flash review of Bruce's dealings, not only with me, but also with others, confirmed my decision not to acquire the Neshanic farm but instead seek monetary damages. Having endured Church Man's betrayal and dishonesty for the last time, I ended all dealings and contact with that family after accepting the settlement offer of $125,000. Such amount delivered me no financial gain or loss but seared in my mind the enduring question, "Whom shall I trust?"

IV. Serious Business— and Serious Consequences?

The Pain in Spain

Episode One

While discussing business at a small restaurant called Alfie's in Madrid, Spain, Bob Morgan signaled his partner, Ben, to join us intermittently while greeting evening patrons. "We're not here on vacation, so let's get down to business."

Bob's demeanor and temperament typified the aggression that absentee owners in small businesses often display, firing questions at their partners before an answer is possible. Inevitably, hostility quickly ensued as Bob launched his prepared attack. "How many dinners and how many lunches did you serve today, last week, and last month? What's the total since we opened six weeks ago? And what the hell happened to all the money? Is the chef getting kickbacks from the suppliers? Are you giving free drinks to your friends and relatives? I'm telling you right now, Benny, I saved your ass from jail, so you better not be fuckin' around with the cash register. Ken is here to audit the books and find out what the hell you're doing."

"All right, Bob, that's enough. We can't settle anything with your shouting and table pounding, so here's how we will proceed. I want all of the restaurant business records here by seven o'clock tomorrow morning. If everyone cooperates, it should only take a day or so to verify the transactions. Then we can develop a business plan based on the verified financial data. Right now, we've had too much to drink, and I'm exhausted from jet lag. Benny, please call us a cab. Bob and I are staying at the Plaza Hotel across town."

Cab drivers unnerve me under ideal conditions, but fast, night driving in heavy city traffic makes it even worse, especially in Spain. I needed a distraction.

"Bob, what the hell was that all about back there between you and Benny?"

"What do you mean?"

"You know, your obvious suspicions that Benny might be trying to pull a fast one on you. Also, what does Benny owe you to satisfy your claim of saving his ass from jail? I'm here to straighten out the restaurant business, not free an indentured slave."

"Ken you have the wrong idea. Benny is free to run the business his way, but he can't be trusted."

"Why the hell did you go into business with a person you can't trust? Did it have anything to do with the fire in Flemington?"

"It's a confidential matter. I can't talk about it. You know, attorney-client privilege."

"Maybe so, but if there's something shady going on, I don't want to be involved."

"Stop worrying, there's nothing illegal going on. Besides, you're here to simply audit the books, nothing more."

"That's fine with me, but I smell trouble. You and Benny attacked each other in less than ten seconds, and I'm in the middle. I'll complete the audit and help with the business plan, but if you start any other crap, I'll board the next flight back to Kennedy Airport."

"Stop worrying; everything is under control."

In 1975, the flying time from New York City to Madrid was seven hours. Also, there is a time difference of six hours. My circadian clock would not correct the jet lag fatigue without ten hours of uninterrupted sleep. A quick shower and a place to sleep caused me to immediately drift into deep sleep. The next day, now well rested, with a clear head and in a quiet place to work, I began checking the list of records needed for the audit.

The restaurant had a medieval décor and a small bar at the far side of the dining area. Patrons relaxed on cushioned benches along the opposite wall while sipping wine and sampling hors d'oeuvres generously provided on each small table. Menus were offered and formally explained orally. A glance toward the *jefe* signaled "We are ready to order." Waiters, not waitresses, brought the food to the selected dining table. The headwaiter requested each party to be seated as a waiter delivered the remaining glasses of wine to the table and meticulously served each meal with dignity and grace. Food, décor, ambiance, and service were impeccable. After completing each task, the waiters immediately returned to line alongside other waiters, waiting to be signaled for a new task by the headwaiter: light a patron's cigarette, add wine to a glass, or serve fresh ice, cube by cube. Such tasks were carried out at prearranged signals from the headwaiter. Each patron was babied with speedy, efficient service to satisfy his or her every need without having to request it. While observing this routine, I became convinced that this establishment ought to be turning a profit as a good—but not gourmet—Spanish-American restaurant.

The restaurant was in a small part of a large, medieval building, a flashback to old Madrid, Spain. The dining area was three steps down from street level. There were no windows. As you entered, immediately to the right was a spiral stone staircase leading down to the lavatory and dressing room. Farther down was a wine cellar and an office furnished casually with a desk, file cabinets, a large sofa, and a four-by-eight-foot conference table with chairs. All of this would soon be etched in my memory.

Several hours into my work in the office, there came a knock on the door. Bob called out, "Hey, Ken, are you in there?"

"Of course, come on in."

"I can't. The door is locked."

Habit urges me from time to time to lock an office door, especially when it is two stories underground, damp, and poorly lighted. I opened the door.

"How's it going?"

"OK, but I have only half the records on my list. I need all of the information before starting the audit report. I can tell you right now, based on these records, this project cannot be completed in a day or two as planned."

As usual, Bob exploded. "I knew it, I knew it. That fat bastard is fuckin' around with us again. I swear, he is not going to get away with it."

"Bob, I told you once—and that should be enough—don't start any bullshit while I'm here. If you want me to continue, then stay the hell out of my way. You know me well enough to know I won't tolerate any of your courtroom antics."

"I'm sorry, Ken, but the very thought of him screwing around with the money infuriates me."

"That's my point, Bob. We don't know a damn thing about what he has been doing until we have all of the records. If you piss him off, he might lose the records, burn them, or hide them, if he hasn't already done so. Don't blow our chance to get all the information by acting stupid."

"OK, Ken, you're right. Sometimes I overreact."

"By the way, Bob, where the hell have you been all this time?"

"I went to breakfast with Emily, and then we walked around town for a while. I figured I could pump her for information about the business."

"Well, that's good, Bob. Go have another cup of coffee with her, but make sure that's all you pump her for. I'll talk with Benny."

Emily, a thirty-five-year-old native of Spain, had married Benny in Somerville, New Jersey, eight years earlier. Apparently, she had many relatives residing in Madrid.

Bob and Emily left the restaurant for an hour while I encouraged Ben to comply with my request for original source documents that would substantiate the financial records, especially those relating to income and purchases. I had met Ben several years before at my Somerville office and came to know him only as Bob's friend. Ben is a big man, over six feet tall and weighing 250 pounds, but he was as flabby as the lips on a camel and rubbery as a turkey's ass waiting to be stuffed. His fifty-year-old, pudgy cheeks and ruddy complexion belied his uncon-vincing attempt to be a tough, aggressive man with connections to organized crime. In fact, regardless of his charades, most people simply ignored his predictable, perfumed stage act. Occasionally, though, his size and demeanor could be intimidating, especially when conversing with a couple of strong-armed men probably posing as waiters.

Benny spoke fluent Spanish; I spoke none. Ben and I agreed on the protocol for my mission here. I had admitted that I didn't understand his remarks to the staff and really didn't care—but I also recognized that some of them understood English, and I didn't want them to know the details of our business. Consequently, I insisted he was not to discuss our business in their presence.

I continued: "Bob has asked me to develop a business plan for Alfie's that will eliminate your need for additional investment cash each week or so. To accomplish this, I need your cooperation. For the moment, Alfie's is my client, not Bob, and not you. My conclusions will be based strictly on the facts substantiated by the business records, documents, and your answers to my questions. I'm telling you the same thing I told Bob: knock off the nasty infighting, or I'll leave on the next available flight to the good old USA."

"Mr. Crane, you and I have always gotten along just fine. I have no problem with you and appreciate that you are here to help us, but Bob gets under my skin. His spies send false messages to him. Then he phones me every other day with the same questions: 'How many lunches? How many dinners did you serve each day since we last talked? How much is in the checkbook? What happened to the money I just sent you?' He doesn't know a damn thing about running this business but comes on like gangbusters, ordering me around. You have to get him off my ass."

"Ben, you and Bob settle your problems your own way. I'll settle Alfie's problems my way. Now, when can I have the rest of the informa-tion on the list?"

"Check back with me in two or three days—it will take that long for me to put it all together."

"OK, but do I have your promise to have it all together?"

"Mr. Crane, I promise you I'll have everything on the list, here at the office, in three days."

"Thanks, Ben. Incidentally, go easy on the 'mister' stuff; I prefer you call me Ken."

Exit Benny; enter Bob.

Bob is infuriated. "Every day for weeks, I told that shithead to have all the business records in order when we arrived in Madrid."

"Obviously, Ben didn't comply with your request. *So what?*"

"I reminded him time after time to be sure the records were up to date and available at all times. I'm telling you, Ken, that prick is up to no good."

"Maybe so, Bob, but he's trying to accommodate my demand to prove the cost of all purchases for food, drinks, and supplies. He has to contact his main vendors and obtain copies of the missing invoices, which certainly takes additional time."

"Stop making excuses for him, Ken. There should be individual vendor folders in the office file cabinet at all times. When he pays bills, the date and check number should be recorded on the paid invoice and then placed in each respective folder."

"Brilliant, Bob! That's all very obvious. I'm sure you learned that in law school, but I've moved beyond the obvious, and I remind you, I'm here to gather proof of the financial condition of this business, not to chastise Benny. What you do with the information is a subject for later discussions. Now, what are we going to do for three days?"

"You're right, Ken, we may as well enjoy our stay and do a little sightseeing. Let's rent a car and head south to Seville."

"Sounds great, Bob, but you'll have to drive. You have a lot more practice than I driving on the opposite side of the road. I drove an old Volkswagen on Saint Thomas in the Virgin Islands years ago, but that's all."

The hectic drive from the Plaza Hotel to the edge of town took only thirty-five minutes. Well-maintained roads through the rolling countryside revealed the casual, agrarian lifestyle of the people. Small villages moderately distanced ten to fifteen miles apart are scattered throughout the south. Homes are tightly clustered and randomly organized along paths or narrow streets. Many such streets will not accommodate vehicles.

Except for doors, windows, and roofs, the homes are constructed of stone, mud, or clay bricks and stucco. Such areas in central and southern Spain give proof of the severe energy crisis in much of Europe during the sixteenth century. The countryside is devoid of trees except for a large shade tree here or there in the center of a huge field. Usually, a bench encircles the tree trunk, providing a comfort zone for agricultural workers. Large areas of Europe were also denuded of trees to meet the heating and cooking needs of the general population. Occasionally, there is a castle on a hilltop surrounded by huge, tilled fields at its base. Similar flat fields can be seen in southern Texas. Clearly, these are fiefdoms from the past.

"Hey, Bob, let's check out one of these castles."

"Good idea. We'll make a toast to Thoreau. Do you remember his toast? 'A loaf of bread, a jug of wine, and thou.'"

"Of course I remember Henry Thoreau. He loved wine and nature and conjured up hundreds of famous one-liners from others, including 'A loaf of bread, a jug of wine, and thou.' But, you dumb ass, when he said that he was drunk from wine and was talking to a bird in a bush. We're out of bread, our jug of wine is empty, and there's no bird to talk to. Besides, we've had too much to drink, and I don't want to get stranded out here without food or water. And no speak-a-da Spanish."

A quarter of a mile off the main road, on the flat top of a long, sloping hill, sat an old castle. The slope ended abruptly with flat crop fields surrounding its base, a picturesque, medieval scene indeed. A few olive trees scattered around the castle and the courtyard added warmth and charm to this home fortress.

"Hey, Bob, don't you think we should get permission before we trespass?"

"How the hell can we do that? There's nobody here. Besides, remember, we 'no speak-a-da Spanish.'"

We descended to a lower level on stone steps beveled out from hundreds of years of use. The walls were worn smooth where a hand railing should have been.

"Hey, Ken, we hit the jackpot. Grab a tin cup! I told you we'd toast Henry Thoreau. The hell with the wine, there must be hundreds of barrels of liquor here. Man, this is the best brandy I've ever tasted! Here, try it."

"Wow, this is great stuff! Give me another cupful and let's get the hell out of here. I don't want to be arrested."

"Stop worrying, chickenshit; grab another cupful and let's look around the courtyard."

We staggered from the damp, dimly lighted liquor-aging basement into the bright light of the courtyard. We paused briefly at the entrance as our eyes adjusted to the direct sunlight beaming through spaces forming the half-moon of parapets surrounding the courtyard. I was awestruck to see a hundred or more archers ready to shoot arrows at the invading army below. They faded away as my eyes focused to see reality. Bob rounded the corner several paces ahead of me.

Instantly, a thunderous voice vibrated and echoed throughout the courtyard. "Cut! What the hell are you doing here?"

Unconcerned, Bob signaled me and said, "Ken, take a look at this." At the far end of the courtyard, approximately fifty yards away, stood dozens of people oddly positioned, oddly costumed, and oddly staring at us. They were silent except for one. He was blasting vulgar expletives in rapid succession at us through his screech horn.

"You stupid drunks! You just cost us a ton of money! Get the ___ off the set right now!"

Undaunted, Bob staggered forward. "Come on, Ken, we can be a stand-in or a prop."

I spun him around, saying, "The party's over, Bob. Let's get the hell out of here while we still can."

As I maneuvered Bob away, in an uncertain manner, he forced against my grip to look back over his shoulder. Still taunting, he shouted, "I'll have my friend Sir Lancelot on your ass by nightfall."

We rounded the corner and again savored the cool, sweet aroma of the brandy wafting from below. "Come on, Ken, let's have one more for the road."

"For the road? Screw you, Bob, let's have one for ourselves."

Having been born and raised in Brooklyn, New York City, Bob retained his driving skills while inebriated, far superior to mine when sober. We continued across the plateau down a long, gradual slope to the other side toward the main road, seemingly four or five miles away.

"Slow down. Are you OK?"

"Hell, yes, I'm fine, but I think we have a soft tire; I'll check it. Besides, I don't want to spill the rest of my drink. Damn, that's good stuff. I haven't had so much fun in a long time. We should go back, fill our jug, and toast Henry Thoreau's bird one more time."

"Forget it, Bob. We've had enough for one day. Besides, a town is not far off where we can buy dinner. Slow down. The hill is really steep at the bottom, where your lane narrows between those stone walls on each side of the road. Damn it, Bob, slow down!"

"Get off my ass, Crane. I don't need a peasant farmer telling me what to do."

Clouds of dust boiled up behind us between the walls of stone now six feet high. Suddenly, a T intersection loomed dead ahead. Bob jammed on the brakes while attempting a sliding turn to the right to avoid a head-on collision with the wall. Miraculously, he avoided sideswiping the left wall in the turn.

"You crazy ass, you're going to get us killed or landed in jail."

"Stop worrying, chickenshit; that wasn't even close. Ha, ha, did you piss your pants?"

"No, I didn't, but maybe my shorts have brown hash marks. How the hell do we get out from between these walls? There's barely room for cars to pass."

"Yeah, this is really weird."

While driving barely fifteen miles per hour and scanning the building tops outside the high walls, Bob exclaimed, "There's two gates just ahead."

"Good, let's get the hell out of here at that exit, but don't race around as if you're in New York City."

"Button up, Crane. You only know how to drive cows from a barnyard and nothing about New York City traffic, so don't tell me how to drive a car."

We passed through the gates, but there was no exit. We had found ourselves in some kind of arena. Like a pace car official, Bob slowly increased speed as he circled the enclosure, waving to the rapidly increasing crowd of people.

"Hit the gas, Bob. There are two clowns on padded horses charging after us carrying long poles with knives on the end! Quit screwing around, Bob, you stupid bastard, they're catching up to us!"

As the horsemen quickly closed in, Bob stopped waving to the cheering crowd, raised an isolated middle finger for the attackers, and shot across the arena at full speed toward the gates. The high, stone walls flashed scenes like the shutter of a camera.

"Slow down, Bob! They didn't follow through the gates. This is dangerous. There's no way you can stop in time on this dirt road." The side road we had come in on flashed by as Bob continued speeding recklessly onto a main thoroughfare. Bob made a sharp turn into a huge lot quickly being filled from several other directions. He eased into a parking spot among look-alike cars.

"Come on, Ken, just walk along with the crowd."

"You're crazy, Bob! Where the hell are we going now?"

"You'll see. Just don't act like a farmer or a stupid tourist." Laughingly, I replied, "Up your ass. I wonder who the hell they think you are, a stunted New York City bagel salesman?"

Bob handed me a playbill similar to those from Broadway plays. I followed behind as Bob arrogantly pressed on, looking for our center-aisle, fourth-row seats. People rose to let us pass, then quickly sat down. Bob continued: "Anybody here speak English? English, please."

"Yes, over here!" came a reply, poorly translated.

"Hi, I'm Bob Morgan ; this is my gardener, Ken Crane."

"Hello."

We exchanged small talk. "When will the fight start?" asked Bob.

"Shortly. It's been delayed by a jerk driving his car around in the bullring, waving to all the people in the stands."

"Why did he do that?"

"Who knows? Probably a wino or a stupid tourist."

"That's terrible. Did they catch the guy?"

"No, he left in a cloud of dust as the picadors ran him out through the gates. Actually, it was a bit funny."

Trumpets sounded. The crowd cheered as the bulls entered through that familiar gate. The bulls circled the ring wildly and then charged through an opening leading to the holding pens behind the announcer's stand. Spain's national anthem echoed through the arena and concluded with exhilarating applause from the crowd as they sat down. The sound of a long-stemmed trumpet ushered in the costumed matadors as uniformed riders pranced blanket-laden horses around the bullring. The pageantry continued as majestic matadors strutted their sculptured bodies to line up in front of the trumpeter. Each wore a short vest over leotards that outlined his genitalia like a huge sweet potato and his gluteus maximus like the marble ass of a Roman gladiator. But when spectators became impatient, each matador stepped forward individually, raised his strange hat, bowed in four directions, and slowly strutted back to the entrance below. The last entourage left the arena to loud applause followed by the audience's subdued anticipation.

Once again, the trumpet blared. The arena became ghostly quiet as the trumpeters quick-stepped to safety behind an eight-foot-high wooden barrier. The stadium came alive with a roar as the first bull charged into the arena wildly looking for a target. Regrettably, this magnificent animal filled with courage would soon be dead. The blood sport continued. But first, let me explain the tradition that causes this gory spectacle to endure.

The playbill explained as follows: Spanish bullfighting is a corrida festival. Traditionally, there are three matadors (killers). Each fights two bulls six years old and weighing no less than 1,014 pounds. Each matador has six assistants: two picadors (lancers) mounted on horseback, three banderilleros (flagmen), who, along with the matadors, are known as bullfighters, and a sword page. Collectively, they compose an entourage. The modern corrida is highly ritualized, with three distinct stages. The start of each is announced by a trumpet sound. The participants first enter the arena in a parade to salute the presiding dignitary. Accompanied by band music, the costumes are inspired by eighteenth-century clothing, and the matadors are easily distinguished by the gold of their "suit of light," as opposed to the lesser banderilleros, who are also called "bullfighters of silver." Next, the bull enters the ring to be tested for its ferocity by the matadors and the banderilleros, who wave gold capes, provoking the bull to a series of passes to impress the crowd. Next, a picador enters the arena on horseback, armed with a lance. To protect the horses from the bull's horns, the horse is surrounded by a protective, mattress-like covering. Without it, the bull could easily disembowel the horse during this stage, causing the number of horses killed during a fight to be higher than the number of bulls killed. At this stage, the picadors stab just behind a mound of muscles on the fighting bull's neck, weakening the neck muscles and leading to the animal's first loss of blood. If the picador is successful, the bull will hold his head and horns lower during the following stages of the fight. This makes the bull's charges less dangerous and more reliable, enabling the matador to perform.

In the next stage, "the third of flags," the three banderilleros each attempt to plant two banderillas, which look like sharpened bartender's sticks, into the bull's shoulders. These anger and invigorate the bull, which has been tired by his attacks on the horse and the damage he has taken from the lance.

In the final stage, "the third of death," the matador reenters the ring alone with a small, red cape and a sword. It is a common misconception that the color red is supposed to anger the bull, but in fact, the bull is colorblind. The matador uses the cape to attract the bull in a series of passes that serve the dual purpose of wearing the animal down for the kill and producing a display that causes the crowd to shout "Olé!" with each pass. The entire performance ends with a final series of passes in which the matador attempts to maneuver the bull into position for him to plunge the sword between the shoulder blades and through the aorta or heart. If the matador has performed particularly well, the crowd may encourage the presiding president or other dignitary to award the matador an ear of the bull by waving white handkerchiefs. If the performance was exceptional, he will be awarded two ears, and in certain rural areas, a tail may be awarded. If the bull has fought bravely, the bull's life may be spared, allowing him to leave the ring alive and return to the ranch from where he came. Then the bull becomes a stud bull for the rest of his life.

Back to the ring. The crowd shouted "Olé!" with each rhythmic pass as the bull weakened, slowing each attempt to gore his tormentor, but alas, he could no longer charge. Blood flowed profusely from the gashed neck muscles and jagged wounds from the six flagged banderillas. He stood motionless, his long tongue hanging out, gasping for air. The matador rose high on his tiptoes, with both hands on an elevated, thirty-inch curved sword, the point angled precisely toward the target. The two combatants were less than five feet apart, staring each other down. The matador challenged, "Toro, toro, toro!" The bull charged the red cape one last time, only to have the sword plunge deep into his body up to its hilt. The bull staggered forward, gasping, his long tongue flopping around his wide-open mouth, but he did not fall. The courageous beast managed several mournful bellows as the matador teased him to make short, quick movements right and left, like the pendulum on a clock. Predictably, the sword slashed flesh within. Seconds later, the bull dropped to his knees, blood gushing from his nostrils as his hind legs vainly attempted one last pitiful charge. The crowd roared with excitement; alas, the bull was dead. The brave matador strutted from the ring holding high one of the bull's ears in each hand. The carcass was tethered behind a team of horses and unceremoniously dragged away.

"Hey, Bob, I've seen enough animals slaughtered, so let's move on."

"No way, we have five more bulls to go."

"So what? This blood sport is disgusting. Let's head on down to Seville."

"Forget it. I'm staying until they knock off the last bull."

"This is barbaric. And you enjoy it? I suppose you would have been at the Coliseum in Rome to see the Christians fed to the lions."

"Yeah, I would—the more the better."

"You are one sick prick, Bob."

"Fuck you, Crane. There are sixteen thousand fans here having a good time, and one stupid farmer saying they're all wrong. So root for the bull instead. You're always rooting for the underdog or the loser."

"You're right, Bob. That's why I have hope for *you*; nobody else does."

Again the trumpet sounded, and a bull charged into the ring. "Hey, Ken, loosen up. Here, have a slug of brandy."

"Where the hell did you get that?"

"When you filled your cup, I filled my cup and also filled a bottle sitting between the barrels; I shoved it under my jacket."

"You filled a bottle? This bottle is half empty."

"You dumb bean picker, did you actually believe I was checking the car tires every half hour?"

The carnage continued. The crowd's primordial desire for blood and gore was never quite satisfied. I was perplexed by this enigma. While as a farmhand and lifetime hunter I have killed thousands of animals for much-needed food, I never fired a shot or used a club merely to see a panic-stricken animal suffer and die.

On the way to Seville, Bob was no longer full-out drunk, only partially inebriated. He passionately explained, "Seville certainly is one the most popular places to visit in Spain. The city was occupied by Moors for eight hundred years, and even today the Moorish architecture is quite evident. Winters are mild, and the region has about three thousand hours of sunshine per year. Phoenicians and Carthaginians settled here, and later came Romans. In fact, two of their emperors, Trajan and Hadrian, were born here. Don Juan started here to conquer the hearts of women across all Europe, while Columbus started from a port close by to discover the new world. Seville is the cultural center for flamenco music and bullfighters."

"Screw you, Bob. I'll see the flamenco dancers, but not another bullfight."

"Up your ass, Crane, I'm paying for this trip, so I'll decide where to go and what to see."

"Fine, you do that."

"Come on, Ken, get back in the car. Stop being a jerk."

"A jerk? You should know by now I'll never willingly allow any person, business, or situation to get their claws in my ass in an attempt to control me, especially you."

"OK, OK, forget it. Seville has a lot more to offer than bullfights. Besides, I'm only trying to put a little culture and sophistication in your life that's more interesting than plowing sod in the north forty."

"I accept your apology, but I fail to understand your obnoxious, complete lack of empathy. Besides, I'm trying to put a little decency into your life so that your culture and sophistication, as you see yourself, can be tolerated. It's probably your family background. Why else would you change your name from Feacleberg to Morgan ? Why wouldn't you contribute to your mother's support in her later years instead of having a judge issue a court order, forcing you to pay your sick mother twenty dollars a week? So, know this, when you dish it out to me, I'll give it back to you with as much respect as it deserves."

"Well, I'll have to admit, you've done more for me than anyone else I've ever known, and I want you to know I really do appreciate it. No matter what I say, always remember, I'm talking to you as a best friend."

"OK, Bob, enough of these heavy conversations. What's our next stop?"

On our way back to Madrid, Bob talked endlessly about the city of Toledo. "Well, we can spend a day in Toledo. I want to see the square called Plaza de Zocodover, a popular meeting point in the city where main streets of the old quarter intersect. It was once the location of a cattle market during the Muslim era but has now become a venue for bullfights."

"Bullfights, bullfights—that's all you talk about."

"Well, what you don't realize, Ken—every city and many small towns in Spain have bullfights and celebrate the life of a matador. But forget about those bullfights. I think we should see the cathedral. Toledo's cathedral is a colossal Gothic structure dating from the thirteenth century with a distinctive combination of Renaissance interior. The cathedral houses an exalted collection of paintings by master artists such as El Greco, Raphael, and Van Dyck. Also, I'd like to see Toledo's imposing hilltop fortress, which had been built and used by different peoples who conquered the city. If we have time, I want to go to Puerta del Sol, which was originally built at the end of the tenth century or the beginning of the eleventh. The Puerta del Sol's Moorish style, stone-and-brick archways were once the principal gateway into the ancient city of Toledo."

I paused momentarily at the cathedral, admiring the view of the village below, the scene as painted by the master artist El Greco years ago. Nearby, a sixteenth-century Renaissance hospice houses some of El Greco's famous works, including the *Assumption of the Virgin*, and other exhibits include paintings by Goya and ancient artifacts from different parts of the city. The day was culturally exhilarating. Bob was sober, genuinely inspired by our surroundings, and above all, admirably pleasant the entire day. Madrid is thirty minutes north of Toledo and it's another fifteen across town to the Plaza Hotel. We would arrive with sufficient time for a good night's sleep in preparation for a full day's work at Alfie's restaurant, starting at seven o'clock the next morning.

"Good morning, Bob. I'm about to leave for the restaurant, but you may as well sleep late. I prefer you don't come to the restaurant till I phone you."

"Really, and now I need your permission to visit my own business?"

"That's right. I have a lot of work to do in a short period of time, and I don't want to deal with a lot of bullshit between you and Benny."

"OK, but remember, I want some straight answers before we leave tomorrow morning. If I don't get the straight scoop from you, I'll choke it out of that prick Benny."

"You do that, Bob. I'll put your name up in lights onstage along with James Cagney. Remember: 'Yooouuu dirty rats!'"

"Get the hell out of here, Crane, and go do the work."

• • •

"Good morning, Ben. Do you have the information I requested?"

"Yes, most of it, but a few suppliers didn't want to bother with my problem since shipping invoices were left when deliveries were accepted."

A cursory review clearly indicated the financial records were in shambles. Entries in the cash receipts and disbursements ledger were helter-skelter. Subsidiary ledgers were nonexistent. There were no schedules listing purchase invoices or accounts payable. In fact, it appeared these records were hastily created during the past three days. I couldn't determine if Benny had "cooked the books," but clearly, the accounting records were worthless. I prepared opening entries in a new set of formal accounting records, realizing it would take at least a full week to complete the usual data necessary to produce reliable financial statements, particularly a profit-and-loss statement, a balance sheet, or a source-and-application-of-funds statement. Nevertheless, I worked feverishly throughout the day into the evening, barely completing the cash receipts and disbursements ledgers by 9:00 p.m.

Bang, bang, bang! "Open the damn door, Crane! What the hell is going on? Why didn't you call me? I phoned the restaurant several times and was told not to disturb you."

"That's right. It's the only way I could gather enough information to take with us and finish the financial statements back home."

"Fine, but where are the records you set up and sent over with Benny and Emily before we opened for business?"

"They're right here, but they haven't been maintained."

"That no-good son of a bitch, I'm going to break his fuckin' neck!"

"Look, Bob, I've been working nonstop for fourteen hours. I'm in no mood to deal with another round of bullshit, so calm down. We can leave Madrid tomorrow with enough information to completely evaluate the entire situation."

"I'm sorry, Ken; you're right."

"Thank Emily for keeping this pain in the ass away from here all day."

Bob laughed and continued: "Emily and I had a great time. We visited several art galleries, snacked at every tapas stand, and managed to see the bullfights at the Madrid bullfighting arena. It's the largest one in Spain and seats twenty-five thousand people."

"I'm glad you had a good time while I was here working my ass off."

"You chose your profession, but I'm glad you weren't with us today. Otherwise, I would have to deal with your wisecracks. Here, try a little Napoleon brandy with Emily and me."

"That's really nice of you, Bob—a little Napoleon carrying a little Napoleon!"

"Very funny, smartass. See, Emily, I told you he's a damn wasp and loves to sting me."

"Listen up!"

"Oh, hi, Benny, come on in. Thank you for getting everything together for me."

"I tried my best, but I don't know much about bookkeeping."

"That's OK, Ben. Sit down, have a drink with us. Bob has a vintage bottle of Napoleon brandy."

"I know. He took it off the shelf upstairs. I sell that rare cognac for ninety dollars a shot, and now I don't have enough money to replace it."

Bob snapped back, "If you had done what I told you to do, you would have plenty of money!"

"All right, you two, that's enough!" Benny and Bob sat at opposite ends of the four-by-eight conference table. Emily and I sat on opposite sides. Cautiously, I suggested, "Come on, people, this is our last night before leaving Madrid. Benny, put that Napoleon brandy back on the shelf, and let's have some bread and wine. Let's all toast Henry Thoreau."

"Screw Henry Thoreau. Emily and I have been eating bread and drinking wine all day." Viciously, Bob warned, "This cognac cost me a lot of money, so nobody touch the bottle."

Minutes later, a waiter delivered a platter of olives, *jamón*, and bread along with several bottles of wine and four long-stemmed wineglasses. Pleasant small talk favored the occasion with classic hors d'oeuvres and vintage wine. Bob eased a snifter glass toward me. "I want to improve your sophistication and help you acquire a taste for rare, expensive Napoleon brandy."

"No thanks, Bob. It smells like old socks or a wet dog. Alice says it smells like horseshit."

Humorously, he replied, "OK, peasant. If I gave you some, it would be like casting pearls before the swine or feeding strawberries to the pigs."

"What beautiful poetry. And that's the high cultural standard and sophistication you want for me?" All chuckled, knowing everything had been spoken in jest. "Well, folks, it's getting late, so drink up and I'll call for a cab."

"Wait a minute, Ken. I want to know where my money is."

"I can't answer that question right now."

"You can't, but Benny can, records or no records." As he pounded the table, Bob shouted, "I'm not leaving until I get some straight answers, so Benny, you better start talking right now!"

"Get off my ass, Bob. I have enough problems without listening to your bullshit."

"Bullshit? I have a small fortune invested here, and I have a right to know where my money is. Besides, I saved your ass from jail."

"Like I said, Bob, bullshit. The money was a legal fee that belonged to the law firm, not to you. The rest of the money belonged to my brother-in-law, Key-Key, so don't threaten me or I'll spill the beans."

"Hold it, you two! This has gone far enough. Everybody sit down, take a deep breath, and shut the hell up."

"No way, Crane, You take care of the books; I'll take care of prick-face. Now, asshole, where is my money?"

"Fuck you, Morgan !"

"I knew it; I knew it! You crooked bastard! You've been fucking me all along!"

"Why shouldn't I, you pathetic piece of lawyer shit? You've been fucking my wife all along."

Emily jumped from her chair and left the room without saying a word. Bob continued: "You don't know how to fuck your wife, and you don't know how to fuck me! I'll put your ass in jail!"

In his rage, Benny shattered his wineglass and instantly cradled the base in his palm, the long stem protruding between his fingers. Benny leaped across the table but landed on his knees in front of me, practically in a sitting position, shouting, "I'll kill you! You motherfucker, I'll kill you!"

Undeterred, Bob stood up and leaned forward, holding his suit jacket wide open with both hands and fiercely yelling, "Go ahead! Try it, you crooked, no good son of a bitch." As Benny lunged forward to stab Bob in the chest, I rose from my chair and fired a karate chop to Benny's larynx. He stiffened in place and then toppled off the table onto the floor, gasping for breath.

In the hall outside the office, Emily was crying hysterically. "That's it; I'm leaving! I don't give a damn what happens to either of you. You crazy bastards can sort out your differences by yourself."

A loud bang echoed throughout the restaurant when I slammed the door shut and quickly secured the medieval lock on the outside. "Ken, what are you doing?" screeched Emily. "Benny will kill him!"

"I've had it with those two screwballs. Whatever happens in there is up to them. Come on, let's get out of here and take a walk."

We walked and talked until exhausted. Tapas stands remain open late in Spain, a tradition dating back to the eighth century. In Spain, dinner is usually served between 1:00 p.m. and 3:00 p.m., followed by a siesta and then a return to work, usually until 8:00 or 9:00 p.m. Consequently, Spaniards often go barhopping and eat tapas in the time between finishing work and bedtime. Another common time for tapas is on weekends, as a means of socializing. It is very common for a bar or local restaurant to have eight to twelve different kinds of tapas in warming trays with glass partitions covering the food. They're often very strongly flavored with garlic, chilies or paprika, salt, pepper, saffron, and sometimes copious amounts of olive oil. Often, one or more of the choices is seafood, including anchovies, sardines, or mackerel in olive oil, squid, or something else in a tomato-based sauce. In several cities, there are entire zones dedicated to tapas bars, each one serving its own unique dish.

The serving of tapas is designed to encourage conversation—people are not so focused upon eating an entire meal set before them. Also, it is customary for diners to stand and move about while eating tapas. It is rare to see a tapas selection not include one or more types of olives, cheese, or bread. The tapas tradition continues to this day, and taverns are not allowed to serve wine to customers unless it is accompanied by a small snack or tapas. The wine, usually a variety of sherry, is stored in goatskin bags tied at each end. In their original form, tapas are served with slices of bread or meat and are used to cover your wineglass between sips. This is a practical measure meant to prevent fruit flies from hovering over the sweet sherry. The meat used to cover the sherry is normally ham, which is salty and activates thirst, helping the owner sell more wine.

The balmy night, spent strolling from tapas bar to tapas bar, sipping wine and sampling the variety of olives, bread, and cheese, calmed my flare of anger and soothed Emily's pent-up emotions as she poured out her troubles. "I don't know what to do with Benny. He's drinking all the time. He was in the hospital for ten days after being gored by a bull."

"What are you talking about? Benny is no bullfighter."

"I know. In Spain we have a tradition—spectators are given the chance to jump into the bullring, sit motionless with a blanket covering their heads, and experience a very young, small bull's charge. Afterward, a matador distracts the bull, and the man under the blanket escapes behind a wooden barrier. Most of the time, nobody gets seriously hurt, but Benny was drunk and wouldn't leave. He sat back down several times, and then he was taken out of the arena on a stretcher. It's supposed to prove manhood and bravery, but I think it proves stupidity."

The restaurant was eerily quiet as I descended the cold, stone staircase to the second level, past the restrooms, then to the third level, past the wine cellar next to the office. The voices from within fell silent as the medieval lock noisily released the door.

"Hi, Ken. Where the hell have you been? It's nearly three a.m."

"That's not important. Let's go. I have a cab waiting. Besides, Ben and Emily have things to talk about."

"Don't worry about it, Ken. Bob and I have an understanding."

"I don't want to hear about it. Enough has already been said. Let's go, Bob. *Now!*"

Our return trip to Kennedy Airport was unremarkable. Alice was waiting for Bob and me at Peggy's high-rise apartment overlooking Johnson Park in North Brunswick, New Jersey. Her passionate kiss was followed by, "How was your trip? You look terrible!"

"I'm just tired. I'll tell you all about it later."

"OK, honey, but I worry when you travel with that man. He humiliates me in public. I don't trust him, and I don't like him."

"I understand how you feel, but this is my profession. This is what I do. Bob is involved in a difficult situation with Benny Fernando, and I fear this is just the beginning."

Episode Two

The law firm Clampton, Bennuto and Morgan became Clampton Morgan after Bart Bennuto accepted a New Jersey Superior Court judgeship and divested his interests in the law firm and new office building. A year later, Morgan 's intolerable personality inspired Clampton to dissolve his own interest in the law firm and new office building and accept the appointment of Somerset County prosecutor. I sold my interest in Hillsboro Breeders, Inc. and the Route 206 office building, purchasing Clampton's 50 percent interest in the new law office building at 32 High Street in Somerville. Thus, I became a fifty-fifty partner in real estate with Bob Morgan . As owner of the building and manager of the law firm, I occupied a plush corner office, and shortly thereafter, the firm expanded to become known as Morgan, Curtis, Spencer, and Slagel, et al.

My personal intercom sounded. "Mr. Crane, Mr. Morgan wants you to meet a client in his office."

Bob stepped forward. "Mr. Crane, have you met Mr. Keke, Benny Fernando 's brother-in-law?"

"No, I don't think so, but I do remember Benny mentioning your name."

"Well, we won't be related much longer."

"Oh, why not?"

"Mr. Crane, do you remember the fire in Flemington last year that totally destroyed Mona Records?"

"Yes, I'm aware of the fire but never followed the details."

"Well, Benny owned that business and was charged with arson. After the fire, he begged me to cosign a promissory note at the Raritan Valley Savings Bank for the sum of seventy-five thousand dollars. It was to be repaid with the proceeds from the fire insurance settlement. Shortly thereafter, Benny took off for Spain. Recently, he said he's not coming back, and the money has been lost in his restaurant business. Now the bank is demanding payment from me as the only cosigner. You know the bank president and chairman of the board of directors. Can you help me?"

"I'll think about it and get back to you in a day or so."

Keke left. I continued: "Bob, were you aware of Keke's problems? His situation threatens to expose a number of serious negative implications, most obvious of which is your conflict of interest. Ethically, we cannot represent Keke in this matter. We should immediately apprise him of that fact by phone and confirm it in writing. I'm also concerned about my potential conflict of interest by representing you personally at the same time I represent the firm."

Aggressively, Bob replied, "So what? One thing has nothing to do with the other. They are separate entities, completely unrelated, and Benny is lying about the legal fee. Consequently, no conflict of interest exists."

"Perhaps you're right, Bob, but I recall Benny's threats regarding a legal fee he paid to you. I would like to explain my position at a full partnership meeting and address the concerns your partners may have as we clear up this mess with the restaurant and Benny."

"That's OK with me so long as you speak in generalities, but I don't want you to divulge my personal business. It has no effect on the firm."

Privately, the eight law firm partners thanked me for keeping us above reproach, but they expressed an ongoing concern for Bob's involvement with Benny Fernando, especially as it related to the fire that destroyed Mona Records. Strangely, a short time thereafter, it was rumored that Bob had had new carpet installed in his home following a different suspicious fire that destroyed a small carpet supply company in Somerville, New Jersey.

Bob's personal and professional demeanor became very perplexing. For example, while sitting directly opposite from me at a table in a booth eating lunch, Bob suddenly contorted his facial expressions to look fiercely aggressive.

"What the hell is your problem, Bob?"

Ignoring me, he snarled, "I'm going to eat your ice cream!" Instantly, a four-year-old boy in the booth directly behind me began crying in fear.

His mother, paying her lunch bill a few feet away, scolded the child for crying and angrily said, "I told you, no more ice cream!" She clenched his arm roughly and led the boy from the store, warning, "I said stop crying, or I'll give you something to cry about!"

Still smirking, Bob smugly commented, "Did you see that stupid kid? And the mother didn't even ask why he's crying. I have no respect for people like that."

"Bob, you need help; you're one sick bastard." Similar incidences occurred regularly during my twenty-year association with "Little Napoleon."

The following year, Keke received a judgment in absentia against Benny for $75,000, plus attorney fees and court costs. Bob entered my office. "Hey, Ken, guess what? My war buddy and former law partner, Bart Bennuto, has cautioned me to secure Keke's losses with Ben's interests in my restaurant. He knows it's listed for sale, but Benny refuses to sell without first knowing how the money will be split. We'll have to go to Madrid and convince Benny that the business must be sold, regardless of the money split."

"Why should we go?" I asked. "The records clearly show large sums of money have been misappropriated. Your complaint, therefore, is against Benny, Emily, or both."

"You're right, but there may be trouble, so I'd like you to be there. Also, perhaps you can convince Big John to come along."

"Why bring John? What kind of trouble do you expect?"

"There won't be any trouble, as such. Bigmouth Benny is threatening to 'hire some muscle to settle everything.' There won't be any trouble, because Benny is full of bullshit, but I prefer you and John be there as a precaution."

John Daniel was my brother-in-law and one-third partner in our six-hundred-acre, joint-venture dairy business at B-Jack Farms. Originally, Bob, John, Alice, Carol, and Ken, all together, were involved in the venture. Like most people, John didn't like the "little bastard" and complained relentlessly whenever in his presence. "Ken, explain to me why I should accept a paid vacation with Morgan when he knows Carol and I hate his guts."

"It's simple, John: you're six feet two and weigh two thirty. Bob is five feet two and weighs one thirty. In fact, his head would fit nicely in the pit of your outstretched arm."

"That's where it belongs, so I can pinch it off. So what's the catch?"

"Bob is concerned that we could encounter difficulty while attempting to sell the restaurant in Spain. He wants us along as a precaution. Besides, I'm sure it will be a memorable experience."

• • •

John nervously paced back and forth in my Somerville office, remarking, "Where the hell have you been, Bob? You're late. Reports warn of heavy traffic around Kennedy Airport."

Not responding, Bob ranted, "Some lousy son of a bitch stole the hood ornament off of my new Cadillac!"

John fired back, "So what? You can't see over it anyway!"

"Ha, ha, very funny. Get your ass in the car, and let's go."

Bob drove like a maniac at high speed with utter disregard for courtesy, carelessly racing around a traffic circle near the airport. John, in the front seat, yelled, "Don't cut in front of him, Bob!"

With reckless abandon, Bob floored the gas pedal and fired back, "Bullshit! We'll miss our flight!" The Cadillac lurched forward to exit the circle, and while passing, sideswiped the car in the right lane. Undeterred, Bob held his course and came to an abrupt screeching stop. He then bolted from the car to confront the driver, shouting, "What the hell are you doing? You ignored my blinking turn signal! I'm an attorney, and right now I have to catch a flight to Europe, but when I get back, I'll have your ass in front of the judge. Here's my card; I'll deal with you later." Clearly intimidated, the driver remained speechless and absorbed

Bob's wrath. In less than thirty seconds, Bob returned. "Write down his plate number and description of the vehicle. I'll deal with that prick when we get back. Just remember, you two are my witnesses."

"That's right, Bob," replied John, "But the accident was your fault, and I'm not going to lie for you."

"OK, you two, we have a long trip ahead and a lot of scores to settle, so let's not take on a new issue at this time. Besides, we only have a few minutes to catch the flight."

At the check-in counter, Bob cut to the front of the line, demanding immediate service as the loudspeaker blared, "Last call for boarding, flight number...to Madrid, Spain." A female attendant hurried through the procedure but lost precious seconds by repeatedly pushing her eyeglasses back above the bridge of her nose.

"Come on, lady! Give me our baggage claim tickets. You can put the tags on later and get a nose job to hold your glasses in place." Bob grabbed our documents casually placed on the counter by the expressionless check-in clerk. The flight attendant greeted us and sealed the cabin door as we eased into our assigned seats.

"Bob, that was a rotten thing you said to that check-in girl. You seem to enjoy being nasty and tormenting people—it's not normal."

"Yeah, did you see the nose on that broad? With a face like hers, she should not have a job in public. Every time she looked down to tag a piece of luggage, her glasses slid down that huge banana nose. People should be criticized and ridiculed; otherwise, their faults will never be corrected."

John couldn't resist. "That's bullshit, Bob. You're fifty-five years old, and none of your faults have been corrected."

"That's because I have no faults, and people love me the way I am. Isn't that right, Ken?"

Facetiously, I remarked, "Absolutely! Including Benny, who claims you were in bed together. Now let's have a couple of drinks and get some shut-eye." Surprisingly, we had no problems with the stewardess, but a confrontation was about to erupt at the baggage claim office in Madrid.

"Where the hell is Mr. Crane's baggage? We have important business meetings all week! Mr. Crane has only the clothes on his back. Where's the manager of this airline? I'm a lawyer, and I'll sue for Mr. Crane's excessive losses due to your negligence, along with other damages including legal fees." Now on the attack, Bob paced back and forth, ominously face-to-face with the claims manager as he fiercely presented his case.

"Calm down, Bob, calm down!"

"Stay out of this, Ken. I'll handle it. The board of directors of this airline know—or should have known—about the rampant incompetence of their employees serving the public. That ticket agent at Kennedy Airport couldn't see through those big-rimmed, Coke-bottle glasses flopping on her huge nose good enough to handle the baggage-claim labels. I doubt she could see the luggage, let alone the claim tags."

The manager sidestepped and calmly said, "I assure you, Mr. Morgan, our employees are highly trained and skilled. But we don't live in a perfect world, and mistakes do happen—"

Bob rudely interrupted, "Yeah, yeah, yeah. Will I have to sue you, or do you want to settle this right now?"

The manager calmly replied, "As I was about to say, we have a standard company policy to compensate our passengers who have been inconvenienced by lost luggage—"

Once again, Bob rudely interrupted. "Yeah, yeah, yeah. How much money will you pay?"

The manager, still calm, continued: "We will pay Mr. Crane five hundred dollars to purchase essentials until we locate his belongings, which usually only takes a day or so."

"There is a huge difference between locating it and returning it to my client. We're scheduled to appear in public throughout Spain over the next seven days."

I nudged Bob to the side and whispered, "I didn't bring anything of great value. Let's take the five hundred and get the hell out of here."

Bob was on a roll. "I told you I'd handle it, so don't say anything." He continued: "Mister, you can't be serious! My client's damages exceed four thousand dollars, and you have the audacity to offer five hundred? Don't insult me again. To settle the matter right now, he will accept a payment of two thousand dollars."

Now somewhat annoyed, the manager stated, "That amount exceeds my authority. Besides, Mr. Crane declined our offer to insure his valuables against loss or damage."

Bob reacted immediately. "Brilliant. A passenger should spend extra money to protect against *your* negligence? How much is your authorized compensation limit?"

Clearly annoyed, the manager replied, "That's confidential information, which I cannot disclose." The manager turned away while saying, "Please excuse me while I make a phone call." He returned shortly and declared, "I have been authorized to pay you fifteen hundred dollars. Take it or leave it."

Little Napoleon, having won the battle, held his ground. "This is your lucky day, Mister. We'll take it, on the condition that Mr. Crane's undamaged possessions entrusted to United Airlines are delivered to him at the Plaza Hotel in seven days." As we left, Bob smugly and condescendingly remarked, "Do you get the point, Ken? By being nice, you would have settled for five hundred. I'm nasty and got fifteen hundred."

"That's right, Bob, but it's 'ill-gotten gains.' The stuff isn't even worth five hundred. Besides, if you hadn't abused the check-in girl, the baggage probably wouldn't have been mistagged. I'll buy a few necessities, and you keep the rest of the money toward the trip expenses."

"You heard him, John…I get the extra one thousand!"

The next day at the restaurant, the stage was set for the coming events. I explained the detailed audit report to Bob, Emily, and John, and contrary to my advice, Bob argued with Benny by phone throughout the day, point by point, dollar after dollar, until it degenerated into a screaming match, threat after threat. Impatient and disgusted, I lashed out, "That's enough bullshit, Bob. You're wasting our time while making matters worse by the minute."

Red-faced, with bulging eyes, he blurted out, "I can't help it! The fat prick pisses me off with each lie, trying to explain away your audit facts. I'll have the fucker jailed! But first, I want to get my hands on him, and you and John can kick the shit out of him."

"That's ridiculous. You're talking crazy, and we're not here to mug anyone or help you get revenge. Emily, call Benny and explain to him we have to have a meeting."

"I'll try, but it's unlikely he will meet with us. I've been with relatives for a week to test the idea of divorcing him."

We returned to the hotel to await Emily's reply. When we arrived, I received Ben's handwritten message: *Urgent. Call me ASAP. I will speak only with Mr. Crane.* Although I was curious, it was too late to call. I'd call him in the morning.

Bob insisted, "Call the prick right now and find out what he's up to."

"OK, OK, all right…Hello, Benny? I received your message. What's up?"

"I'll meet with you only, Mr. Crane, and nobody else. Come to my apartment tonight, alone, and I'll discuss the whole matter privately."

"Ben it's twelve midnight; let's meet tomorrow."

"No way, it's tonight or not at all."

"OK, Ben. I'll leave as soon as you send a cab. Remember, I don't speak their language."

The driver nodded yes, acknowledging he understood the address I had handed to him. Thirty minutes later, the door popped open the short length of a security chain and Ben whispered, "Are you alone?"

"Of course." Ben released the chain, looked right and left down the hallway as I entered his well-furnished apartment. Immediately, two men came toward us. "What the hell is going on, Ben? You and I were to meet privately."

"They're OK, Ken. I wasn't sure you would come alone."

A tall, cowboy-type man dressed in Western clothing offered a handshake and said, "Howdy! I'm James Philbrook. This is my stuntman. Whenever we're shooting movie scenes in the area, we eat at Benny's restaurant. After dinner, Benny wanted us to see his apartment. We have to work tomorrow, and we're about to leave, so I'll say nice to meet you and good night." Benny locked the door behind them and reconnected the security chain.

"Ben, I've had enough of this cloak-and-dagger stuff. Who are those guys?"

"Jim is a famous movie actor, and his stuntman teaches karate. I told Bob I'd hire some muscle to deal with him if he starts any trouble."

"Ben, you're in enough trouble already without getting in deeper with this gangster crap. There is a mountain of evidence to prove you are guilty of embezzlement, misappropriation of funds, and fiduciary criminal malfeasance. Perhaps I can convince Bob not to file criminal charges against you if you cooperate. Regardless, the business must be sold, and you will have to make restitution."

"You won't get away with this, Mr. Crane. That's extortion! I'll spill the beans. Bob and his law firm will be in big trouble. How much money do I have to pay back?"

"It will be a negotiated settlement based on the merits and proofs relating to each charge. But it will be determined later, after the restaurant is sold. It's the only way to resolve the issues with Bob and settle the money dispute, once and for all."

"It can't be as bad as you're saying, Ken, so I have to see the records before I agree to sell off everything. This is all I have left in the world."

"Fine, meet me at the restaurant tomorrow at nine a.m."

"OK, but just you and me, not Bob and the other big guy."

The trip back to the Plaza Hotel was uneventful. Bob and John were fast asleep. Greatly relieved to be back safely, I pondered: *I've been out in a foreign city, can't speak their language, across town alone, at four o'clock in the morning, dealing with a hostile situation. I must be out of my mind!* Sleep came quickly.

I awoke from a deep sleep to find Bob already out of control. "Let's go!" he insisted, "It's eight a.m. I can't wait to get my hands on that crooked bastard!"

"Forget it, Bob. There's not going to be any more of that while I'm around. Benny understands his grave situation and has agreed to cooperate with the sale of the business and make equitable restitution. I agreed to meet him alone at the restaurant around nine. He specifically stated you and John are not to be there, or he won't show up."

"Bullshit! The prick steals my money and then has the balls to tell me he won't sell the business. I'll put his fat ass in jail before the day is over."

"That's your prerogative. Just remember Benny's threats to spill the beans and cause serious trouble for you and the firm."

"His threats are bullshit. He has nothing on me or the firm. Let's go get the crooked son of a bitch!"

"Bob, didn't you hear me? Benny won't show up. We'll just be wasting another day sitting around."

Emily joined us for breakfast at the restaurant around 8:45 a.m. We talked and drank coffee and tea for more than two hours.

"This is ridiculous, Bob. I'm not sitting here any longer waiting for a no-show. I'll hire an interpreter and tour parts of Old Madrid during the afternoon. What do you say, John?"

"Sure! I'm tired of hanging around here, so why not go?"

As I headed for the men's room, Bob teasingly remarked, "Go ahead, farm boy…run out on me! But remember, I have the return flight tickets."

I descended the now-familiar winding stone stairwell to the lavatory. It was eerily cool and quiet, strangely peaceful. Suddenly, I heard the repeated rumble of distant thunder. The sound came from directly overhead. I rushed upstairs, only to see John standing in the lounge area laughing, while red-faced, bulging-eyed Bob scooted around unpredictably, waving his fists and arms in an uncontrolled frenzy. "Some help you are, Ken! Just when I need you, you walk out on me."

I opened the door to the street and peered up and down the sidewalk. Benny, twenty feet away, spotted me and began running, ignoring my shout, "Benny, come back! I just want to talk to you!" While speed-walking a short distance, I repeated my request several times.

Without warning, Benny grabbed a fierce-looking Spanish girl who threatened me with a knife and screamed in broken English, "Leave us alone! Don't come any closer!"

I immediately returned to the restaurant, realizing the entire sequence of events had happened in little more than a minute. Shortly thereafter, the police entered with Benny and the Spanish girl. Tempers flared, followed by a rapid Spanish-and-English verbal exchange. The police quickly took charge. Bob, clearly unnerved, stood quietly to the side with John and me. Emily became our advocate. Approximately thirty minutes later, the police left with Benny in handcuffs and escorted the girl to the street. Emily ordered an ample supply of wine and a tray of tapas and rejoined us in the lounge.

"What the hell happened here, Emily?"

Bob interrupted, "It's all right, Emily, go ahead and tell him."

She explained, "Bob phoned me and insisted I be here before nine o'clock. I told the maître d' to tell Benny that Ken was waiting for him to review the audit reports. If he asked about Bob or John, he was to say they weren't here, just Ken."

"That's a lousy trick, Bob. Why didn't you clue me in?"

"Simply because you would have tipped off Benny and met him alone elsewhere."

Emily continued: "I told the police Benny was stealing from our business and that our accountant and lawyer were here from the United States to press charges. Bob owns fifty shares of the company; Benny and I each own twenty-five. I told the police that Bob and I had controlling interest in the corporation, and we had decided to sell the business. That Benny was told to leave and never come back, and then a scuffle broke out. In Spanish, the officer had asked, 'What kind of scuffle? Tell me what happened.'" Emily continued: "When Benny and his girlfriend entered the restaurant, Bob immediately told them to get the hell out of here and don't come back. In quick succession, Benny rushed toward us, only to hear Bob say, 'OK, John, do your job.'"

"That's what you told the police. Now Bob, tell me what *really* happened. Remember, while I was downstairs, I heard the thunder."

John, amused and enjoying the excitement, urged, "Go ahead. Tell him what happened."

"OK, but first let's have more wine and toast Henry Thoreau. Crane can be the bird without a bush."

"Very good, Bob. Now what the hell happened?"

Bob explained: "When Benny stepped from the bright sunlight into the restaurant, at first he couldn't focus on us. I told him to 'Get the fuck out of here and never come back!' Right away, the fat, chicken bastard started his tough-guy routine by shooting off his big mouth: 'If you think you can throw me out, come on and try it.' I leaped toward Benny and yelled, 'OK, John, let's kick the shit out of him.' Now focused, Benny stumbled and fell as he carelessly turned away. I rushed forward and kicked him in the ass while he was on his hands and knees. When he tried to stand, I jumped on his back and pounded the piss out of him while riding him across the floor, up the steps to the doorway. He grabbed the door handle and stood up, dumping me to the floor. Then you came upstairs."

"That's quite a story. At least he gave you a piggyback ride. And you got in a few licks. But where was John all this time?"

"I couldn't believe it," Bob replied. "John never moved. He just stood there, laughing his ass off."

John continued smirking as Bob repeated bits and pieces of his exaggerated moment of euphoria. I winked toward John to signal my appreciation for sticking to our agreement not to be drawn into a fight except to defend against extreme violence. We polished off another jug of wine and toasted Henry Thoreau as we listened to Bob retell his story over and over, each time lengthening the tale and embellishing the drama that had actually lasted less than twenty seconds. While basking in his moment of triumph, Bob reverted to his obnoxious kibitzing, commenting, "And let this be a lesson for you two country boys. This is the way business is handled in the city."

"We get the point. So let's get back to the problems at hand. You need a written agreement from Emily, a real estate broker, and a local attorney to handle the current issues. Also, we have to find my luggage."

Bob quickly replied, "Banana-nose sent your luggage to Puerto Rico, but a day later it was forwarded to Madrid. I told the claims manager you would retrieve it on our return trip to Kennedy Airport."

John sarcastically quipped, "Thanks for keeping us informed, Bob."

During the next two days, we secured Emily's commitment to lead the effort to sell the restaurant as quickly as possible. Bob retained an international law firm with offices throughout the world, including New York City and Madrid. They would also handle Emily's divorce and all matters related to the sale of the restaurant. Benny was in jail. The intended purpose of the trip was over. It was time to go home.

John nervously paced the floor, waiting for Bob to free up the bathroom. "Let's go, Bob—it's getting late. You can put on your perfume and play with yourself later. There's exceptionally heavy traffic on the way to the airport, and we also need time to get Ken's baggage."

"You have nothing to fear but fear itself," replied Bob. "They'll have Ken's baggage retagged for Kennedy, and his claim ticket will be at the counter when we check in."

A long line of travelers at the check-in counter slowed the process to a snail's pace. Bob, clearly frustrated to the limit, moved ahead in the switchback lines of people with luggage, carry-on baggage, canes, and four-pronged walkers, only to be quickly escorted back to our position. Finally, we reached the check-in counter one at a time. Bob received our flight tickets, boarding passes, and baggage-claim tickets, but not my claim tickets. The powder keg between Bob's ears exploded. "I was told Mr. Crane's lost baggage would be on this flight, and the claim ticket would be here when we checked in."

The clerk completely ignored Bob's nasty remarks and replied, "I'm sorry, sir, you will have to retrieve your property from the lost baggage room. *Next!*"

Bob attempted to maintain a position in the security line while John and I searched for my luggage. Time slipped by as we checked identification tags on dozens of look-alike suitcases scattered over the floor throughout the huge lost-property room. "There it is!" I exclaimed. "At last. Hurry, the flight is already boarding."

Back at the terminal, we could see Bob ahead of us in a crowd moving through the security checkpoints. A warning sounded: "Last call for boarding Flight 456 to the United States, New York's Kennedy Airport."

John and I both yelled, "Bob! Wait up!" He didn't stop but ran faster until out of sight after stepping onto the moving sidewalk.

In a heartbeat, four armed, uniformed government officials surrounded us. "May I see your flight documents, including your passports?"

"I'm sorry, sir, for yelling like that, but our attorney has boarded the plane with all of our paperwork. We have to get on that plane."

"Forget it," he replied, "the plane is about to be pressurized, ready for departure." We were escorted to the side, ordered to keep our backs toward the wall; three officials strategically positioned in front of us slowly paced back and forth, sternly warning, "Don't move."

Half an hour later, the fourth official came strolling toward us, with Bob speed-walking behind. I couldn't resist laughing at the scene; thinking of it now reminds me of Danny DeVito and Arnold Schwarzenegger in the movie *Twins*. I mused at a *Mutt and Jeff* comic strip I remembered about a pygmy and a goliath. The officials diligently checked our picture IDs, verified each passport, and returned our travel documents. I dared not repeat the verbal exchange between us after the officials bade us farewell.

Seven hours later, we secured the remaining standby seats on a midsize jet with three seats separated by an aisle. It was operated by Iran Air. Bob was mortified. Every seat was occupied except three in the rear of the plane. John sat next to me, leaving Bob to sit between two Arabs directly in front of us. In fact, all the seats behind the wings except ours were occupied by Muslims. Little Napoleon was terrified. His ploy:

"John, I have to talk confidential business with Ken, so you take the other seat."

"Screw you, Bob, I've had enough of your crazy bullshit. I'm not moving."

"Ken, you know how important this is. Ask John to move."

"We've completed the business for this trip, so take your seat and relax. This is not your Waterloo since you changed your name to Morgan, unless you go stupid on us."

John quipped, "How do *you* like it being on the receiving end, Bob? It's no fun, is it?"

"Not now, John, he's really terrified. Why don't you trade seats?"

"No way, forget it. He's getting just what he deserves."

Bob squeezed in between the two Arabs and remained motionless the entire trip. In fact, one hour into the trip: "John, watch this." I flipped a fat, one-inch-long cigar ash into the bald spot on his head; he didn't even flinch. Bob was a perfect example of the cliché "scared stiff."

When the parking brakes locked into position at the terminal, the plane lurched forward slightly. Instantly, the Arab next to Bob stepped into the aisle to open the overhead storage bin. In a flash, Bob was hiding behind us in the rear of the plane until all passengers disembarked. The ash from my cigar was still in place on the yarmulke-sized bald spot on his head. It sat there undisturbed, like an unburied cat turd. Bob's six-hour, life-threatening experience on Iran Air momentarily transformed him into a gentleman: no teasing or snide remarks. For no clear reason, he praised the American stewardess as we proceeded to the baggage-claim carousel. He generously tipped the porter and politely asked John and me to wait curbside while he secured the car from the long-term parking lot.

The remainder of the trip was uneventful except for Bob graciously expressing his appreciation for our help and understanding. He emphasized, "I couldn't have gotten through all of this without your help. I'm grateful to have friends and business partners like you and John."

John responded politely, "That's nice, Bob. But I don't understand why you constantly insult people. You know what I mean, the put-downs."

"Most people don't understand," Bob replied, "but it started a long time ago when I was growing up in Brooklyn. Wherever I turned, I had to fight back. Someday, maybe Ken will explain it all to you."

Episode Three

Bob rushed into my office, excitedly declaring, "The restaurant is sold! All I have to do is sign a release and pick up my money."

"That's great news. I'm surprised it took a year to complete the deal, especially since the sale was for all the company's shares of stock held in escrow by your lawyer. It was a simple sale of shares of stock, the same as in all corporate ownership, large or small. Can you finalize the deal in the United States, or do you intend to go to Spain?"

"I have to settle a few money snags, so I want you to come along with me."

"I would rather not go, but if you honestly feel it is absolutely necessary, of course I'll go."

That evening as I broke the news to Alice, she unequivocally expressed her displeasure with a stern review of our past, present, and future relationship with Bob Morgan, alias Bob Feacleberg.

"I have no defense against your enormous disdain for the man, except to encourage you to understand him. He thinks the world of you but doesn't know how to show it."

"Oh, really? Is that why he spread the rumor, 'Whenever I'm invited to dinner at the Cranes', Alice serves me bread and beans'? And what about the time we attended a formal dinner at Richard Clampton's new home, with all the lawyers from the prosecutor's office, along with their wives? Bob changed seats three times to sit next to me so he could embarrass me at close range. Do you remember what he said?"

"Yes, I do. But do you remember what *you* said?"

"Of course. The next day I ruined a bedsheet and two of your shirts while ironing his face."

"Honey, you don't understand. He was only joking."

"Well, I wasn't joking after he said to everyone at the table, 'I taught Alice's kids how to eat sweet corn. They should bite the corn from the cob in circles, rather than from left to right or right to left. Next, break off the tip and suck out the juice.' That infuriated me, and my Irish temper caused me to answer, 'That's right, Bob, but I told our children to never do that. We leave that part for the pigs.'"

"But you don't understand, dear. He's just being facetious. It's a practiced Jewish trait called 'kibitzing.'"

"I don't care what it's called; he can't be trusted. I don't like it, and I don't like him. Why don't you make him stop abusing me instead of expecting me to grin and bear it and try to understand the little *rat*?"

"OK, dear, you're right. I'll discuss it during our trip to Spain."

The trip to Madrid was unremarkable. Bob was jovial and in good spirits. He promised to be more considerate of Alice's lack of formal higher education. There was no kibitzing. Emily received her agreed share of money at the law office and thanked everyone for helping her through this difficult period. After signing a release, Bob looked at a pile of money in the kind of large bag used to carry exhibit documents into court. His lawyer asked me to leave the room. Upon my return thirty minutes later, he sternly warned, "We have concluded our legal representation pursuant to Mr. Morgan 's instructions and according to Spanish law. When you leave here, no one from this firm will have further contact with either of you for any reason whatsoever. Mr. Crane, do you understand what I have just said?"

"Yes, of course, but why?"

He stepped forward; we shook hands as he politely commented, "It's been a pleasure doing business with you. Good luck."

Based on my knowledge of and belief about Bob's dealings with that firm, he had acted professionally, courteously, and without discord. "What the hell was that all about, Bob? You alienate people every day and piss off somebody by the hour. Did you try to chisel on his legal fee?"

"No, no," Bob replied. "It's technical, lawyer stuff. I'll tell you all about it later." Bob was relaxed but pensive as we strolled toward his car rented at the airport. He mused, "Things are over with here, so let's do a little sightseeing. I've sketched out a travel plan that includes cathedrals, castles, and villages in northern Spain. We definitely should see the viaduct in Segovia, which is about an hour from Madrid."

"What about the money?" I asked. "Shouldn't you deposit it in the bank immediately?"

"No, it's locked safely in this satchel. I want to visit Segovia today, spend the night farther north, and cross into southern France early the next morning. I plan to tour the wine country and then book a room at the King George Hotel in Paris."

"That's all very nice, but I told Alice this would be a quick trip. 'Bob will sign the papers, get his money, and we'll be home the next day.'"

"I'm sorry about that, Ken. There could have been snags in the deal, so I booked our return flight for next week. Besides, you advised me to vacation a little while on a business trip so as to deduct the cost for tax purposes. I'm only following your advice."

"You are one sneaky bastard. You should have told me so I could be honest with my wife."

"You *were* honest with her. That's why I didn't tell you; otherwise, you might not have come along."

"Benny is right. You are one sneaky bastard. How can you brag to others about our friendship and then pull this kind of crap on me?"

Humorously, he replied, "What do you think friends are for?"

As we traveled, I received a history lesson. Bob continued: "Segovia is a major part of Spain's history. It was first settled under Roman rule in 80 BC and was on the front lines of Muslim and Christian conflict until Christian forces captured the city in 1085 AD. The Cathedral of Segovia was completed in 1577 and now is open to the public seven days a week. Every tour-guide book ranks it as a must-see when visiting Spain."

Bob and I consumed the marvelous architecture and stonework of Alcázar Castle of Segovia, built during the Renaissance period. Later, the Romans had fortifications on the site. In 1862, a three-day fire destroyed the roofs and framing. The building was restored in 1896. We left each site reluctantly, but with excited anticipation went on to the next. The magnificent splendor of it all flooded my mind with spirits of the past. I had boarded a time-travel machine. Next stop was the Segovia Aqueduct, built in the first century. It is a marvel of Roman engineering, and the one in Segovia is the best preserved in all of Europe. It has sixty-six arches and 120 columns. Until recently, it was still in use.

In a flash, I traveled forward to the present. Too tired and hungry for more travel, we enjoyed a dinner of lamb chops cooked on an open-pit fire, followed by a liberal supply of wine. Henry Thoreau became our mentor. Sleep came quickly as Shakespeare joined us on the world stage: "To sleep, perchance to dream."

The next day, we eased our way through the mountains of northern Spain to within ten miles of the border. During the daylong trip, we shared our knowledge of European history. Also, Bob desperately wanted me to better understand him personally by explaining the history of prejudice against the Jews in Spain. He continued: "My heritage is filled with hate for those who have attacked, killed, and maligned Jews throughout the world, from the beginning to the present. Spanish Jews, especially Sephardic, once controlled one of the largest and most prosperous Jewish communities under Muslim and Christian rule in Spain."

Bob ad-libbed between reading excerpts from dozens of pamphlets offered at each historical sight. "You know the Germans murdered six million Jews in a period of less than six years around the time of World War II. But did you know that Jews settled and prospered in Spain as citizens of the Roman Empire around 95 AD? They engaged in a variety of occupations, including agriculture. Until the Roman Empire's adoption of Christianity, Jews had close relations with the non-Jewish population and played an active role in the social and economic life of the province. Spain was the medieval 'golden land of opportunity' for the Jews. Then the barbarian invasion came by the Visigoths in the fifth century, devastating the lives of Jews for the next two thousand years.

"In 653, Jews were required to convert to Christianity or be put to death along with their brethren who relapsed back into Judaism. There were brief periods of prosperity, however, until 1212 to 1300 AD when the Crusaders began indiscriminately robbing and killing Jews in Toledo. On account of their industry, knowledge, and wealth that aroused jealousy and provoked hatred, the Jews had to suffer greatly as anti-Semitism forced many Jews to emigrate elsewhere. The massacre of 1366 came, killing no less than eight thousand people. Some laws were strictly targeted against the Jews. The final blows came as all the Jews were expelled from province after province, before and after 1492, dislocating an estimated population of three to eight hundred thousand people."

"Thanks, Bob, for the history lessons, but even as a 'country boy,' as you put it, I know about the Visigoths, the Spanish Inquisition, the Holocaust, and about Jew-hating discrimination throughout the world. But I fail to understand why you are so arrogant and condescending. Jewish history, steeped with prejudice, cannot justify your obnoxious conduct. In fact, your put-downs, insults, and rudeness are what give Jews a bad reputation. Jew-haters, as well as many others, then often stereotype Jews because of people like you. You personify the Hebrew attitude and belief that promoted the Jews as 'God's chosen people' and everyone else on the planet as 'Gentiles.' In other words, Jews like you from early on began to think of themselves as better than everyone else. You have no right to attack the people around you merely to exploit their weaknesses in search of their jugular veins, especially when in the company of my wife and our friends."

Bob exploded, "Crane, if you weren't my best friend, I'd stop the car and kick the shit out of you right now."

Sternly, I quipped, "Oh, sure, you and what army? The fact is, the truth hurts, but you won't change your ways. Do you really think in all cases that the best defense is a strong offense? By the way, what about the money? We've been traveling for two days through Spain with the money locked in the car. Why the hell don't you deposit it in the bank? To do otherwise is crazy."

"Don't worry about it, Ken. It's my money. Tomorrow we'll be in Paris, and I'll deposit it at that time. Let's look for a motel, have dinner, and leave early in the morning."

That night, Bob dumped the satchel of money on the bed, nervously commenting, "The Basques in Northern Spain are a bunch of thieves. We have to cross the border without them knowing about this money."

"Oh, that's great, Bob. Suddenly you've come to your senses. Let's find a bank and deposit the cash, then cross the border."

"Why are you so damn stupid, Ken? I need your help, not your criticism. We have to cross the border with the money. There is no other way."

"Is this the 'money snag' that demanded my presence to wind up your business affairs in Spain?"

Bob didn't answer but paced back and forth, exposing his confusion, worry, and fear. Pleadingly, he asked, "Ken, what should we do?"

"It's your money. You make the decision."

He speculated, "Let's carry it on our person. Most likely, they'll check the car but not frisk us." We stuffed the money inside our shirts, in our pockets, in our jackets, and on our backs under our belts.

"OK, let's practice your idea. A border guard may order you to step out and put your hands on the car." Instantly, I lost control, laughing while exclaiming, "Bob, this won't work. You're too damn short! You look like a baby hippo standing on its hind feet. Besides, with your hands on the wall, the money flashes below your suit jacket."

"Stop your laughing. There's nothing funny about this situation." Once again, Bob paced back and forth like a caged animal full of fear, looking for a way out, begging for an answer. "Ken, what should we do?"

"You already have my advice. But you insist on crossing the border with the cash rather than banking it. In that case, I think the best way is to be very obvious rather than surreptitious. Put the money back in the satchel, but leave it open, with a shirtsleeve draping out of one corner. Let's carelessly toss our shoes and jackets on the back seat alongside the clearly exposed money bag."

"That's too risky! Maybe you shouldn't be here. Where did you get such a stupid idea, planting corn?"

"As a matter of fact, I did. I was listening to a portable radio while planting corn. The commentator reported that a middle-aged man was arrested after a six-week investigation while crossing the border from Canada into New York State. He crossed over three or four times a week, and customs agents searched him every time with body scans and X-rays of his bicycle, including the tubes and tires. It was known that he used illegal drugs, but it took them six weeks to figure out what the man was smuggling in. The guards overlooked the obvious: he was smuggling bicycles! Regardless, why the hell are you so worried? The closing statement proves it's not drug money or a stash of counterfeit bills. How much 'funny money' are we dealing with?"

"There's eight million, one hundred twenty-five thousand *pesetas*."

"Cut the crap, Bob. How much American?"

"It's a hundred and twenty-five thousand dollars."

"Bob, you're crazier than I imagined! Here we are, touring foreign countries, our whereabouts unknown by anyone else, with a hundred and twenty-five thousand in cash in our possession. People have been killed for a hell of a lot less money. If I had known your plans, I would not have come on this trip. Do you remember? Do you even care? I have a wife and three teenagers counting on me. Alice was right: you can't be trusted."

I just stood there, listening to this pathetic little man, periodically repeating time and time again, "I'm sorry Ken, please forgive me. I'm sorry, I'm sorry. You shouldn't be here. You cross the border in a cab, and I'll meet you on the other side with the money."

Then I saw a flash of my past. This was not a problem, just a challenge! "Forget about the cab. Let's get going. But first, call Peggy and tell her where we are and the route we'll take to the King George Hotel in Paris. Tell her my Social Security card is in the sock on my right foot. But she's not to mention that to Alice."

We rounded an eighty-degree curve in the road where, instantly, a billboard warned: "Border Crossing, All Vehicles Stop." Around the sharp bend came a view I have experienced only in movies. We could not avoid the narrow, elevated bridge crossing a very deep canyon. Ahead, at the far end, was a guard shack with retractable barriers blocking entry and exit to the bridge. There were five uniformed border guards with pistols and automatic rifles, two on each side of the road and one atop the flat-roofed guard shack manning a heavy machine gun.

Bob's hands turned grayish-white as he clenched the steering wheel. Sweat beads glistened above his lip and down his brow. He was nearly out of control with fear. Shaking like a leaf, he babbled, "Ken, what should I do?"

"Calm down, or they'll arrest you on suspicion. Maintain your speed until just before stopping, but ease to a stop. Wipe the damn sweat off your face and relax. You look guilty as hell. Here, put your share of cigars in your breast pocket. When we stop, put one in your mouth to light, quickly grab another one, and offer it to the guard. For Christ's sake, stop shaking! You're making me nervous."

Fifty yards ahead, we saw two guards holding automatic weapons horizontally, waist-high, signaling us to stop. The heavy machine gun swung toward us. I remained calm and unconcerned; after all, we had done nothing wrong. Besides, in case of attempted robbery, I was prepared to state, "We are expected at the Andorra Consulate's office within the hour."

Bob glanced at the machine gun pointed at us and started freaking out. I had observed him remaining calm and decisive under extreme pressure in a courtroom, but his behavior now was strangely uncharacteristic. I wondered why. "Don't lose it now, Bob. Slow down to stop. Remember the cigars."

In a matter of seconds, the machine gun swung past us to a vehicle approaching the bridge on our left. The two guards, now thirty feet in front of us, leaped across the divider and surrounded the other vehicle. "What should I do, Ken?"

Before I could answer, the barrier swung open, but with all of the guards concentrating on the other vehicle, no one waved us through. An opening was in sight. This caged animal raised his foot from the brake pedal and was about to speed away, quipping, "Let's get the hell out of here!"

He groaned in pain when the toe of my shoe sank deep into his leg muscle. "This is no time to go stupid on me!" I warned. "Stop, then slowly increase your speed and maintain it at the posted limit." Fifty yards later, we rounded another sharp, eighty-degree turn with a large billboard flashing, "Welcome to Andorra."

Bob, now anxious to put a great distance between us and the border guards, began speeding recklessly around horseshoe turns high in the mountains. "Slow down, Bob! We're out of danger unless you wreck the car or get stopped for speeding." After several stern warnings, he slowed to speed limits while traveling nearly twenty miles to a small, mountain village. A restaurant, several tapas bars, and gift shops formed the center of town. Park benches circled a huge, ancient oak tree shading several small water fountains. "Pull over. It's time for a break."

"Good idea. I'll buy bread, cheese, wine, and olives." He returned with enough food for ten people. All tension disappeared in this tranquil village uniquely nestled high in the Pyrenees Mountains of Andorra that separated northern Spain and southern France. Andorra is one of the smallest countries in the world, having a total population of barely 830,000 people. There is no military. The literacy rate is 100 percent, male and female, confirming the benefits of the quiet, peaceful existence of this kind, gentle people. Their life expectancy is eighty-two and a half years, second in the world. Tourism is 80 percent of the economy, providing high employment, mostly in service industries. Passers-by acknowledged our presence with a nod, smile, or a gesture signifying "welcome"—I guess.

As we snacked, we exchanged interesting conversation as good friends often do. "Bob, we have a lot of money with us. I'm asking you to forget the France Grand Prix Race and drive sensibly from now on.

We don't need any more cliffhangers or high drama as at the border crossing."

"OK. We've been lucky so far. I'll drive at the speed limit. Besides, the worst is over. We should have no trouble on into Paris."

"Trouble? Why have you been so worried about having trouble?"

"Let's enjoy the trip, Ken. I'll explain it all later." And enjoy the trip we did. Conversation centered on the elegance of the vineyards, the diversity of wines created by blending grapes grown in the Pyrenees mountain foothills compared to grapes grown in different types of soils throughout the wine country of France. Occasionally, business matters involving our office building, farm operations, and particularly the law firm were interspersed with other subjects throughout the day. Bob had morphed into an astute businessman, caring partner, and above all, a gentleman. Perhaps the disparaging but measured criticism of his partners (except for me) was fogged by events of the day, but not nullified. He injected, "John is doing a good job at the farm, but we have to assert more control over him. Spencer must be warned to take fewer vacations. Tony is destructive. He's not a team player. Arturo is not meeting his full responsibility to the firm by working on files at home instead of at the office. Hursh and Slagel are technicians doing monkey work, but their timesheets should be checked each week to keep on top of their billings." I didn't respond to his gentle but unkind remarks. Little did I know, these casual words were precursors of the tumultuous events to come. Regardless, Gentleman Bob drove casually for seven hours through wine country to the suburbs of Paris without incident. During this time, the beast in him was subdued, replaced by a knowledgeable, kind, and gentle person.

As we neared Paris, clouds formed as traffic increased. Bob's demeanor changed in direct proportion to the number of cars and people near him. The beast became defensive, poised for an attack. He weaved in and out of traffic, dangerously close to cars at all times, shouting, "Get out of the way, old man! Old lady! Stupid kid!"

"Come on, Bob, slow down! We have plenty of time."

"Don't tell me how to drive in the city. You farm boys just don't get it, so keep your damn mouth shut."

I snapped back, "Don't talk to me that way. Remember, I had butter on my bread before I met you, and I'll have butter on my bread when I don't know you."

He smiled and commented, "Yeah, I remember. You're the only person I know that thumbs his nose at easy money."

The car lurched forward, then slowed as Bob pumped the gas and then the brake pedal in quick succession, tailgating at all times. I felt the urge to pray, but under the circumstances opted for humor. "Hey, Bob, do you know the difference between you and a female pygmy marathon runner?" He didn't respond. He drove down the Champs-Élysées threatening most vehicles with close encounters of the crash kind.

At the hotel, Bob ordered me to get out. "Ken, grab the bags, and let's go." He slid across the seat to exit on my side, nudging me out as he did so. I stood there momentarily while Bob snatched the moneybag from my grip.

"Wait a minute. What about the car you just sideswiped in front of the hotel?"

"The hell with him. He shouldn't have double-parked, leaving the possibility of an empty curbside parking space after the other car left."

"You're crazy, Bob. I can't believe this!"

"Believe it. Let's go."

A generous tip wrapping the car keys persuaded the concierge to graciously follow Bob's instructions: "Call the car rental company and have them retrieve their vehicle here at your hotel. We will be leaving in the morning, so give us a wake-up call at seven thirty a.m. Also, have a cab waiting for us by eight."

"I've had enough excitement for one day, Bob. When you phone Peggy, ask her to notify Alice of our schedule. I'll ask room service to deliver hors d'oeuvres and two bottles of vintage wine."

Minutes later came a rap on the door. "Room service!" In broken English, the bellhop said, "Shall I open and pour the wine, sir?"

Predictably, Bob eloquently replied, "Yes, indeed," and with a gentle wrist motion slowly eased a minor swirl of wine to circle the glass. His buzzard beak drew in the aroma just prior to sampling the beverage, as professional wine tasters do. His meaty lips locked in a proper portion of wine that splashed back and forth between rubbery cheeks. A professional couldn't have done it better. The little guy was in his glory. He continued: "I like its bouquet. It's quite interesting. The flavor is a bit fruity, but quite satisfactory. I recognize the vineyard. Their aged blends are recognized internationally as one of the finest that vintage year. We have been touring the wine country of Spain and southern France, you know." Once again, a very generous tip served its intended purpose.

"That was quite a show, Bob. Do I dare drink your wine? Or would it be like casting pearls before the swine, or feeding strawberries to the pigs?"

Jovially, he clicked my glass and said, "For most people, it would be. But for you, my friend, nothing is too good. Drink up!"

Learning about Jekyll and Mr. Hyde requires caution, as does learning about Mr. Morgan . "Thanks. Is everything OK at home? Did you remind Peggy to call Alice?"

"Of course I did! Have you forgotten I'm a lawyer?"

"Hell, no. You make that impossible. By the way, what about the car in front of the hotel that you sideswiped?"

"What about it? You saw what happened. I was parked at the curb. The guy cut in front of me and raked the side of his car with my front bumper. I wrote down his license number before we checked into the hotel."

"That's rotten. Don't count on me for that dishonest, cunning stuff. I guess you really don't know the difference between a small, tricky lawyer and a female pygmy marathon runner."

"You asked me that once before. So what's the answer?"

"Well, a female pygmy marathon runner is a running cunt. A small, tricky lawyer is a cunning runt."

"Very funny, wiseguy."

Sleep came quickly, as did the wakeup call. I proceeded gingerly, longing to see Alice and our children. Events of the day were unremarkable: a continental breakfast, taxi waiting, money in the bank, and we are in the air waiting to start the movie *Old Yeller*. Seat backs reclined, we casually sipped measured libations. Bob settled in and sighed, "This was an exciting trip, but I'm glad it had a happy ending. Do you agree?"

"Yes, but the trip isn't over. Besides, I can do without that kind of excitement, especially the risk of carrying all that cash with us. Our bodies could have been dumped in a ravine without ID, money stolen, and no one knowing our whereabouts. It was all *so stupid*! Why the hell didn't you deposit that money in the bank in Madrid?"

"Well, Ken, that's the 'money snag' I referred to when I asked you to come along. While you were out of the room at the lawyer's office, I counted the money and signed a release. Also, I was again reminded of a strict federal law prohibiting the transfer of money out of Spain. The money had to remain in cash—pesetas—otherwise, it could be seized by the government on its way out. I was warned of potential criminal charges for such offenses that could impose fines, prison time, and forfeiture of the money as contraband. Since the money is lawfully mine and you have no knowledge of the events, you could not be held responsible as an accomplice. It's over now, but in retrospect, I should have insisted you cross the border in a taxi, and I alone risk crossing with the money. I'll be forever grateful to you for not deserting me while under such extraordinary pressure."

"Save your gratitude. It's obvious I would not have been here if I had known your illegal, unscrupulous intentions. I have lots of choice words that could be said, and lots of choice words that should be said, but this is your lucky day. For now, I'll just say you pulled a dirty trick and used me, so don't patronize me by saying you're sorry."

Old Yeller started baying as the sharecropper in the Deep South raced through the woods to catch up. The movie ended. Sleep ended. The flight ended. But new trouble was just beginning.

Our luggage was in order. We cleared customs without incident. Bob notified Peggy of our arrival and asked if Alice would meet me at their high-rise apartment overlooking Johnson Park in North Brunswick, New Jersey.

While resting on our suitcases at curbside, waiting for Bob to return from the long-term parking lot, the large hippocampus in my brain highlighted salient episodes collected under the title "Pain in Spain": two automobile accidents, lost luggage, a terrified Jew on Iran Air, Seville, history reviews of Toledo, Segovia, El Greco, Picasso, Goya, and of course, Thoreau. Altercations with Benny, tapas bars, flamenco dancers, bullfights, crashing a movie set at the castle, attacked in a bull-ring, and the ultimate act of stupidity, smuggling money out of Spain. The review surfaced feelings of pleasure, excitement, satisfaction—but always tainted by the fact that I had been used. I am a schmuck.

Forty-five minutes later, Bob stopped in front of the curbside. One look, and I sensed trouble. "What the hell is it now? They seized your money?"

"No, no. I wired the money to my bank in Somerville before we left Paris. Get in, let's go!"

"So what's the problem?"

"The girls had an argument. Security guards have detained Alice in the lobby for questioning by the police. We'll discuss it after the weekend when things cool down."

Alice rushed to me with open arms and tear-filled eyes. After the hugs and kisses subsided, a guard closed in, warmly suggesting, "I think it's best if you take your wife home."

• • •

Monday, at my office: "Hold all my calls, and tell Mr. Morgan I want him in my office the second his feet touch this property. We are not to be disturbed."

• • •

"OK, Bob, what's the story?"

"There's no story. Peggy said Alice threatened to kill me, so she called the police. Talk with Alice and let them work it out. Let's not get involved."

"That's impossible. We are involved. Peggy phoned Alice as you instructed, but pulled one of your stupid tricks by telling Alice, 'The boys will be delayed a week. I guess they're having a good old time. I heard girls in the background.' Alice lashed back, 'You don't have any children. We have three teenagers. Bob had no right to plan on keeping Ken away from his family for an extra week without telling him in advance.' Alice's hot, Irish temper demanded retribution and caused her to say, 'If I get my hands on a gun, I'll kill that little son of a bitch.' Such behavior cannot be condoned; neither can Peggy's, yours, or mine. Someday I'll explain the complete story to her, but for now, only you and I know the truth. One thing is certain: there were no girls involved, except for you screwing Benny's wife. Because of you and Peggy, I have to repair the damage at my home. But it's like blaming the bank for bouncing a check."

"I'm really sorry, Ken."

"That won't cut it, Bob. I have to decide if I'm a token goy, a schmuck, or just plain stupid. Until then, just shut up and get the hell out of my office."

Left to right: Ken's client, John Pannitari; Bob
Morgan ; insurance company CEO, Jack Boyd

Bob Morgan Is Little Napoleon

Little Napoleon's battle tactics were predictable and based on his belief that the best defense is a strong offense. You know—as Bob would say, "Damn the torpedoes, full steam ahead!" In spite of being a skilled trial lawyer, Bob's attacks against the unsuspecting were often harmful, humiliating, shameful, and lacking empathy. In short, they were pitiful.

During and after each attack, I intervened physically or with severe admonishments, viz: Bob's threats to take the little boy's ice cream, his ruthless insults to waitress Coke-Bottle Helen Keller, his heartless verbal abuse of Banana-Nosed Airline Ticket Clerk, and let's not forget his incessant, misguided teasing of Alice. At this point, you may be asking why I befriended him. Hundreds have asked the same, including me. Why? Because I understood his childhood pain, the warped, bifurcated personality that suppressed his kind and gentle traits and exposed his vicious, cruel, obnoxious, hateful, repugnant, detestable, insufferable, abhorrent attacks against all vulnerable people. "Weaken the witness, then cross-examine" became his philosophy; "the best defense is a strong offense" was his theme.

Bob often talked nonstop in an open boat deep in the Canadian wilderness, waiting patiently for his pole to bend, his reel to sing, fueling his dream of adoration, to catch the big one, a respite from his tormented past.

But these temporary interludes of tensionless activity would inevitably succumb to the overload of cruel, detestable traits so deeply embedded in his personality. He could not escape his heritage as a five-foot-four Jew, born and raised in Brooklyn, New York City, relentlessly bullied until adulthood. His pudgy face accentuated a sloping forehead. His first-to-sunburn proboscis, which teenagers called a "beak," often wound up bloodied after skirmishes with neighborhood boys. His full, meaty lips complemented the stereotype and prejudice of the time that contaminated his mind and soul—"Bob Feacleberg looks Jewish."

He was not unattractive physically, and at age fifty-eight, he married his very young secretary. But he did not mellow with age. Instead, each new negative event in his life further poisoned his already paranoid belief that "the best defense is a strong offense." In fact, he would attack without provocation, thus becoming universally disliked and much despised. The attacks generally set a warlike emotional boundary few people dared to cross. I crossed that boundary with empathy toward this middle-aged man who did not heal from old wounds.

He became my lawyer. I became his accountant. We became partners in numerous real estate ventures, including ownership of a law-office building in Somerville, New Jersey, several parcels of land south of our office, and each one-third partners in a six-hundred-acre dairy farm with seven homes located in Hudson, New York (B-Jack Farms). And for a span of twenty-plus years, we were "fishing buddies."

I felt sorry for Bob, believing I could make a difference by entering his realm and diverting his feeble attacks, causing him to learn and accept the responsibility of genuine warmth and compassion. I expected nothing in return, remembering Sunday school teacher Mrs. Pearson's warning: "No good deed goes uncriticized."

Bob longed for meaningful friendships but pathetically lacked the skills to deserve, acquire, or safeguard such treasure. He sensed my weakness for pursuing business ventures, personal involvements, and "causes célèbres" for the challenge, the satisfaction, the pleasure of success, but not primarily for money. I warned, "Bob, if you continue this alienation madness, you will wind up with no friends, only money."

In a flash, he responded, "I'll take it!"

Content to share the money while hoping he would change, I acquiesced as he intruded into all aspects of my life. His perpetual, heartfelt efforts to become part of my family failed because he could not escape the impenetrable shield put around him years ago by his own family, his environment, his culture, and society. But I too have an impenetrable shield: "I am what I am because that's what I am. So says Popeye the Sailor Man." So said Dad; so says me. But I am happy with my shield and do not want to change. On the contrary, Bob was surrounded by countless wonderful people, but he was alone. I felt sorry for him. Naively, I was in his realm, always with my protective shield: independence. He could not "get his claws in my ass" to control me. My dad became smarter and smarter as I grew older and older. Often, his thoughts became my thoughts: "You can't change the spots on a leopard. You can't make a silk purse out of a sow's ear. An unhappy person cannot be made a happy person." These thoughts buffered my careless trust of friends and family. And Bob and I became trusted partners and loyal friends, much to the chagrin and vexation of others chafed by "Ken's foolish association with Morgan ."

Over time, the offended became aware of their common plight and often formed a fragmented coalition to expand my responsibilities, including an unexpressed, pivotal role for one purpose: "handle Morgan ."

The risks were high. All too often, Morgan 's misguided conduct threatened the financial and emotional stability of my clients, partners, associates, friends, and family, especially my wife. There were few exceptions. The abused included Richard Clampton, Bartholomeo A. Bennuto, Cliff Curtis, Sheldon Spencer, Jack Slagel, Kenneth Hursh, Arturo Armanno, Tony Chismento, and dozens more. All were lawyers. All were my clients. Each was my friend. There were many more victims, too numerous to list. But extraordinary tolerance "beyond the call of duty" compels honorable mention: my associate CPA, Barbara Moffet; my brother-in-law, John Daniel, a partner in B-Jack Farms; and especially my high school sweetheart, my wife.

Intriguing stories involving Morgan, each member of the cast, and me could extend for many years the episodes on the weekly TV program *LA Law*. Instead, consider the nuances shadowed in the following skirmishes leading to Little Napoleon's Waterloo:

"Hey, Ken, let's get the hell out of this office and go fishing in Canada for a week. I'll bring my toaster oven and cook up a pile of lamb chops. Remember, like the ones in Spain?"

"I sure do. They were great. I'll check with Alice; she won't agree, but I'm sure it will be OK."

"She won't agree? I think the world of Alice, but I'd like to know why she resents me so."

"Bob, the fishing trip is for only a week."

"OK, Wasp, I get the point."

In the boat at the north fork of the French River in Ontario, Canada: "Hey, Mack—"

"Don't call me that. My name is Bob!"

"I know your name is Bob, and I'm aware lots of Jews change their names. But why did you change yours to Morgan when it's actually Feacleberg? Did your family take umbrage?"

"Hell, yes, especially my father. He disowned me."

Hours flew by as Bob poured out his heart, explaining the ever-increasing burdens he could not unload. Burdens of a small-man complex, coupled with his perception of relentless discrimination against Jews, made more evident by Hitler and manifested in Bob's character when he enlisted in the army to fight the Germans.

Bob continued: "No matter where I am or what I do, I can't drop my guard except when you and I are fishing or discussing things in private."

"I understand all of that, Bob, but you walk around half pissed off, poised for attack if the chip on your shoulder falls off or is deliberately made airborne."

"Maybe so, but I can't help it. For example, I wanted out of Brooklyn, so I joined the army. Would you believe it, my squad leader, an anti-Semite, was also a German-American sergeant! His racial slurs kept me wired and pissed off until the day he called me a 'damn New York City kike.' I lost it! I chased the bastard out of camp, waving a hatchet and screaming, 'I'll kill you, you lousy kraut!' I never saw him again, but to this day, I seethe about it."

"You need anger management. Otherwise, sooner or later, you will self-destruct."

I continued: "So why did you change your name?"

"Ken, you're a naive country goy, but that's what I like about you. You won't understand that I could no longer deal with all of that Jewish-stereotype crap, so I became Bob Morgan and later studied Italian. Besides, as a lawyer often traveling to different countries, especially the Middle East such as Saudi Arabia and Iran, it's a lot safer not to have a Jewish name."

"Yeah, I know all about that stuff. But I really don't give a damn what your name is. The trouble with you is that you're trying to fake your life by denying your heritage. That's a huge insult to your father."

"The hell with him, the hell with the whole damn family—and the hell with you, too! The last time I tried to explain it to that son of a bitch, he barely opened his eyes while speaking his final words: 'So you came to make sure I'm dead? You're not my son, you get nothing.' I touched his hand, he pulled away and died."

"What about your mother?"

"The hell with her, too. She never trusted me, especially after I screwed the neighbor girl under her daddy's back porch. We were only kids, you know, just fooling around. Then she showed me where to stick my pecker, so I did. But then the little bitch lied and said I forced her. Everybody blamed me, including my mother, so the hell with her, too! Years later, my sister and an uncle filed a lawsuit in Somerville demanding I pay twenty-five bucks a month to help support the old lady." Bob turned away to hide his broken heart, a hurt more painful and lasting than his World War II battle wounds. Thankfully, the fish started biting.

We eased toward a small island to enjoy a shore lunch. Bob cleaned the fish as I gathered white birch bark for starter paper, small pine sticks for kindling, and larger chunks of wood to provide red-hot coals after blazing. Bob popped several thick slabs of bacon into our heavy cast-iron frying pan along with a full stick of butter. Once that melted, he removed the bacon and deep-fried the heavily peppered, fresh fish fillets, walleye and northern pike. I added diced onions to our second cast-iron frying pan and dumped in a quart of Campbell's pork and beans. Bob equally divided the crispy, brown, square fillets and served it up. Bob always served the food to control his worry that someone might take more than their share, regardless of the number of people present.

The open fire, bacon and onions sizzling, and coffee brewing blended a familiar, intoxicating aroma that wafted about this warm, windless day on a remote, miniature island deep in the Canadian wilderness. The isolation, tranquility, and stark beauty, complicated only by the forces of nature, once again disarmed the demons in Bob's mind.

Relaxed and melancholy, his back against the tree, Bob mused: "Hey, Ken, let's buy a small island out here and build a cabin on it. Whenever I have the urge to tell somebody to go to hell, we can come here."

"That's a good idea. The only trouble, is you would go broke making that many trips."

"Don't be a wiseguy, Crane!" We drifted into deep sleep, a power nap.

"Hey Ken, get the hell up! It's five o'clock. Dusk is at ten fifteen, so let's fish our way back to camp, and while you clean the fish, I'll broil a pile of lamb chops in my toaster oven."

Calmly, I suggested, "Bob, I don't think you should use that toaster oven. It draws fifteen hundred amps. The big generator in the woods runs every night until eleven, but I don't know its full capacity."

Bob snapped back, "You clean the fish, and I'll cook dinner. That's the way we've always worked it, so mind your own damn business. Besides, I've already checked with Pierre." That was the camp manager.

After many fishing trips with Bob, I understood his short fuse. I smiled and quipped, "Yes, sir! Right away! But remember, I drove the boat and still caught all the fish, except those two minnows of yours."

Ghostly shadows danced about as I gilled and gutted the day's catch as required by law when transporting fish from Canada. Suddenly, dead silence: the entire camp was dark. But it wasn't eleven o' clock. At the fish house, in French-Canadian English, barely understandable, Pierre shouted, "Where is that little guy in Cabin Twelve?"

"I don't know, Pierre, but he should be right there. What happened?"

Pierre paced back and forth in a rage, flailing his arms and shouting, "Where is he? Where is he? I told him not to plug in that electric oven! That's a twenty-five-thousand-dollar generator! It's ruined, and he has to pay for it!"

"Calm down, Pierre. Let's find out what happened."

We rushed to the cabin, only to find Bob fake-sleeping in his locked car. Pierre fiercely pounded on the window with one hand and yanked the door handle with the other, shouting untranslatable French. I moved dangerously close to stop an altercation. Angrily, Bob fake-waked and launched his attack:

"How dare you accuse me?"

Pierre tried to go around me, first to the right, then to the left, as I pleaded, "Please, Pierre! Please calm down. Let me handle this. Why don't you check the breakers and cartridge fuses?"

"I already did. They were blown, so I replaced them. The generator is burned out."

"Pierre, most generators are also protected with a reset button in a heat-resistant relay switch. Did you check that?"

"No. I was so damn mad I forgot all about it."

Spring-loaded screen doors clapped in rhythm as each cabin emptied and dozens of handheld flashlights cast dizzying, undulating beams of light that pierced the darkness. Pierre found Bob's toaster oven hidden under our cabin steps and unceremoniously flung it in the air.

"Nice going, Bob. Now what are we having for dinner? Or should I 'mind my own damn business?'"

"Don't be a wiseguy, Crane. I don't need your waspy bullshit."

"Of course you do, Bob, and you also need every 'I told you so'—the more the better."

We returned to our chores at the sound of a diesel engine struggling to start. It groaned several times and then gained rhythm, controlled by the engine's governor. Soon, the generator kicked in at high speed. "Let there be light—and there was light." We left camp at dawn, never to return.

The private environment together for days in an open boat and fourteen-hour car trips prompted the one-on-one, unstructured interaction Bob so desperately longed for. He would begin with modest observations that gained emotional momentum, often to a fury, as he moved from past to current issues. He criticized his family life; war days with Bart Bennuto; the law firm Clampton, Bennuto and Morgan ; John Daniel, our partner at B-Jack Farms; and each lawyer in *his* law firm, Morgan, Curtis, Spencer, et al; always accentuating the negative while slowly isolating his prey.

Then his orders came, followed by all of his solutions: do this, don't do that, you have to do this, I have to do that, and we can't let so-and-so handle the problem. Most of his fragmented complaints lacked a composite evaluation of the good and bad aspects of a particular matter. Some would say he was always whining; others called it bitching: bitch, bitch, bitch. But generally, he simply made mountains out of molehills. You know, like Humphrey Bogart as Captain Queeg in the 1954 movie *The Caine Mutiny*: he relentlessly nitpicked his crew over minor infractions, culminating in a paranoiac investigation to determine which crew member took more than his fair share of canned strawberries locked in the ship's store. The mutineers were court-martialed; the complainant, Captain Queeg, also a star witness at the trial, painted himself into a corner by explaining the logic of his discipline. But Humphrey Bogart as Captain Queeg exposed the error of his tortured logic while ranting on and on, exaggerating the importance of extremely petty issues with his crew as he clicked three shiny steel balls in his hand.

The movie portrays an epitome of self-destruction caused by a Napoleonic complex—the paranoia of Captain Queeg was much like Bob Morgan 's.

As we motored through the Adirondack Mountains from Montreal, Bob continued to dwell on his past.

"Bart Bennuto and I were war buddies and close friends all through law school. He had lots of friends while in the service and lots more after shrapnel severely wounded his legs. Everyone likes Bart, especially women. Then he tried to dump me by starting a law practice with an Italian named Richard Clampton. Bart is a nice guy, we all know that, but he didn't have the balls to even let me know about his partnership until I saw the sign: 'Clampton, Bennuto : Attorneys-at-Law.' I was crushed. I had it out with him. Soon after, I moved to Somerville and the sign read, 'Clampton, Bennuto, and Morgan, Law Offices.'

"Once I was there, the practice increased by leaps and bounds, so we built a two-story office building at 32 West High Street. The partnership lasted two years, and then Bart ran out on me again by accepting a judgeship paying less money than his salary at the firm."

"In all fairness, Bob, Bart didn't run out on you. He's a calm, kind person and detested the outrageous bickering over money. Don't forget, I negotiated the settlement of his equity in the law partnership and office building. Also, I remember the bitter arguments over that damn ashtray in his office."

"Well, you were wrong on that one, Ken. The firm paid for all the furnishings, including the ashtray. It was not his. But maybe it's a good thing Bart left. He and Rich always stuck together, making me a third rung.

"During the next three years, we hired the right people to work the expanding petitioner's cases and insurance defense practice. Things were great; we were making big money and our bills were all paid. But what happened? Rich bailed out of the firm, leaving me holding the bag so he could accept a lower-paying job as Somerset County prosecutor."

"Come on, Bob, be fair. Rich was the driving force, the seed that flourished and expanded the firm. His efforts alone brought into being the new office building at 32 West High Street, permitting you to have a plush corner office instead of that third-floor coat room area over the post office. Rich didn't bail out on you. He left for the same reason Bart left. Don't forget, I also negotiated Rich 's equity settlement in the law firm and office building. I clearly remember the nasty disputes, especially that time I walked into the large conference room as you drove Rich to such rage he nearly threw a chair at you. Besides, everybody moved up a notch, and you became 'numero uno.' You took full control, the big boss."

Bob had refused to buy Rich 's share of anything, including the new office building. Consequently, Cliff Curtis and Sheldon Spencer acquired Rich 's equity in the law firm. I purchased Rich 's interests in the building for the amount declined by Bob and moved into a corner office shortly thereafter.

The firm continued to grow with Bob at the helm and me as financial manager. Still, Bob was a live wire, a loose cannon, and mostly unpredictable, except by me. I'd come to know his every move well in advance. I was his confidant, his best friend, perhaps his only friend.

During the formidable years of our relationship, 1962 through 1971, from age twenty-eight to thirty-eight, during lunch, on fishing trips, or at the office, I shared my belief in the deceased country comedian Will Rogers's advice: "Own land, son, they ain't making no more of it." Also, with some exceptions, I concluded, wealth is a state of mind. But many professionals are so heavily taxed (up to 70 percent of adjusted gross income). They make good livings but cannot build sufficient wealth, the amount I call "go-to-hell money." Simply put, it allows you to say, "Your proposal carries very little risk, and clearly it will make a ton of money.

Unfortunately, your proposal strongly offends me. Fortunately, I don't want the money, so to hell with your deal."

My attitude was a constant reminder to Bob of what I had said: "Remember our first conflict? I had butter on my bread before I met you, and I'll have butter on my bread when you're gone, so as of right now, Morgan, you go to hell!" At that time and for many years thereafter, I was broke. No money, but after all, wealth is a state of mind.

During the same period, Bob watched with envy as Alice and I continued to acquire real estate in our spare time. In ten years, we had acquired five homes, half interest in a 125-acre farm through Hillsboro Breeders, a ranch house through foreclosure (later converted to a small office), and a 204-acre dairy farm we called the Hobart Farm. Will Rogers had forced me to purchase half interest in a law office building and accept Bob Morgan as my partner. "There's no such a thing as a bad person; it's just that some are better than others."

Bob looked on with envy as this country boy and his wife accumulated wealth far beyond his own. Our friendship grew, our trust firmly bonded, illuminating the benefit of pooling our talents for mutual enjoyment and financial gain.

Bob became enamored with the possibility of reducing his annual income tax liability. During the 1960s and 1970s, tax avoidance continued to be a prime objective for taxpayers in high-income brackets. Converting ordinary income to capital gain often became the chosen way to safely reduce one's high income tax liability and build equity. Although less sophisticated than racehorses or beef ranching, technical analysis of the concept clearly indicated that dairy farming would return significantly higher profits with considerably less risk. The horse-and-bull story ended, only to be replaced with a story of dairy cows.

Still inspired by Will Rogers, I traveled throughout New York State in search of a farm to serve our unique purpose. I received a phone call from our Somerset County agricultural agent informing me that a middle-aged, hard-driving man had fallen into a silage blower (similar to a wood chipper) and had died in seconds as half his body was chopped with the corn silage through the machine into one-inch pieces. His large farm would soon be listed for sale as part of his estate. I immediately contacted the executor, hired a real estate broker for a modest fee, and directed the broker to negotiate a purchase contract on our behalf.

In 1971, we purchased that farm consisting of eighteen structures (including seven homes) and approximately six hundred acres in the Hudson Valley, twenty miles south of Albany, New York.

Our timing was perfect. Real estate prices were flat, causing the executor to accept a quick sale price of $450,000. We named the entity using the first letters of the first names of each partner and his wife: Bob and Peggy, John and Carol, Ken and Alice. Rearranged, the letters formed the name of B-Jack Farms.

All was well, except that Bob's friendship and greed became more and more troublesome. "Ken, you're the firm's accountant. I don't want you to include any outsiders in our deals, especially my partners."

"I don't understand why not. It's time we bring them along and share the wealth. Besides, they're not just my clients; they're also my good friends. Also, there's unrest in the partnership caused by my exclusive dealings with you. They've expressed resentment that we own the office building, yet they're working their asses off to pay for it. We should offer equal ownership of the building and have the rent set by unanimous vote."

"No way, Crane, that's the trouble with you. You're always giving away the store."

"I'm not 'giving' them the building. They'll pay for it, the same way you and I do."

"Don't be stupid, Crane, you know what I mean."

"I'm not stupid, and I know exactly what you mean. And so do your partners, especially Cliff Curtis. He's a brilliant attorney who has done a fantastic job with the firm for fifteen years. His credentials are impeccable: Yale Law School graduate, Hillsborough Township attorney, and now a Montgomery Township Municipal Court judge. We have to share the benefits and burdens of our involvements. Otherwise, your house of cards will crumble as your partners defect for greater opportunities."

"Bullshit, Crane, I'm keeping my fifty percent. Curtis and Spencer split Rich 's interest in the firm, so now they already have more than enough. They're not getting a part of this office building."

"Be realistic, Bob. I'm not talking only about the firm and office building; I'm talking about sharing some of the real estate deals. You've made nearly a million dollars on deals I've shared with you."

"How do you figure that? I haven't seen a dime."

"No, you don't have the cash; you have the equity, the net worth. Anyone can see that, including the lawyers around you. The other day at lunch, after completing the legal work for B-Jack Farms, Royal Mac Corporation, and five other entities in the works, Cliff commented, 'You and Bob now own acreage equal to that of Highway 22 from our office to New York City'"—thirty-five miles—"'but I'm doing all the legal work.'"

Bob ranted, "So what? You always made sure the firm was paid generously for its service. Cliff is jealous and wants to horn in on our deals. That's never going to happen."

"Bob, this is 1972, not two thousand years ago when disciples understood parables: 'Therefore, I speak to them in parables: because they seeing, see not; and hearing, they hear not, neither do they understand.'"

"Look, Crane, don't try to dazzle me with your brilliance or baffle me with your bullshit. Nobody else is going to get a piece of our action, now or ever."

Cliff became my lawyer, I his accountant. We were close friends. Alice and I often dined with him and his wife, Sue. We vacationed together, notably in the Virgin Islands, or at bar association conventions in Puerto Rico, Acapulco, and Paradise Island in the Bahamas. We shared confidences and joint family cookouts with him, his wife, and three young children.

Bob bitterly resented any and all new or strengthening friendships Alice and I fostered or accepted in our professional or personal lives. His intrusion grew menacing: "You went to the farm without telling me. Oh, you had a cookout with the Curtis' Why is Alice hanging around with my partners' wives, but not Peggy?"

One day, Bob caught me by surprise. "Hey, Ken, how about riding into New York City with me? I have to pick up a suit at Barney's clothing store."

"Sure, when do you want to go?"

"Right now."

"OK, my calendar is clear for the afternoon, so I'll call Alice and be with you in a minute."

Kibitzing, Bob quipped, "You are frigging henpecked!"

Examining his new suit, Bob remarked, "Look at these suits on sale. Why don't you trash your old college suits and buy some decent clothes? Look at these terrific sales."

With surprising ease, suit after suit was marked and fitted. Short- and long-sleeve shirts were laid out, together with neckties carefully tucked inside each suit jacket for a perfect match. I admit, I really got carried away like a kid in a toy shop, but reality struck when I saw the bill.

"Hold on, Bob. I don't need all of these clothes, so put the formal overcoat back on the rack."

"Come on, Ken, you can wear clothes like this. I can't."

"Bob, I don't care for it."

Teasingly, he educated me. "It's an exquisite, formal, full-length overcoat called a Chesterfield."

"Oh, really? I thought Chesterfields were cigarettes. Besides, just look at the damn price tag."

Sternly, he insisted, "Shut the hell up, peasant. At least try it on."

I eased into the silk-lined coat as Bob reached high and slipped the blended, white-and-gray material over my shoulders. A rich, black-velvet collar rested smartly as Bob admiringly patted it into place, saying, "This is a garment fit for royalty. Ken, you have to have it."

A glance in the mirror confirmed my thoughts: *This coat is perfect for a Mafia boss, but not for me.* I tossed it aside, only to have it reappear two weeks later. Unbeknown to me, and in complete violation of my known personality, Bob had paid the full cost of the entire wardrobe. That violation penetrated deep into my soul, linking up with his advance forces of intrusion into every aspect of my life. I feared he was outmaneuvering me, fracturing my protective shield, my pride, my self-respect, my independence.

"Bob, I can't accept this. I don't want you or anyone else buying my clothes. I appreciate the thought, but this is just not right. Here, take this check."

Smiling, he sidestepped and whispered, "Stick it up your ass! Sorry, it's too late. This is one way, but obviously not nearly enough, for me to thank you for all you've done for me. So, my friend, I'm asking you to accept my gift to you."

Early that evening, Alice served me a mixed drink. "You look troubled, honey. What's the problem?"

Our agreement, mutual promises at our ages of twenty-two and twenty-one: "Never let the sun rise on yesterday's dispute. Accept the resolution. Do not dwell on or ponder those perpetual thoughts 'I should have done' or 'I should have said.' In short, cleanse your mind. End the dispute."

Alice sternly, emphatically, stated her position: "You're entitled to a hell of a lot more than those clothes, so take whatever he has to offer and make the most of it."

"But, honey, you don't understand. I feel I'm making a pact with the devil. You know, claws in my ass."

"Forget it, sweetheart. You made that pact a long time ago, so get over it."

I have come to know the antidote for my intelligence, higher education, and association with smart people. It is my high school sweetheart's *native* intelligence. We snuggled tightly in each other's arms and kissed warmly. It was 3:00 a.m.

Later that morning in Bob's office: "I want to thank you for those gifts. I was totally surprised and shocked by you spending so much money on me, especially when you're always bitching about my fees." We shook hands and patted each other on the back. "Thanks, Bob, that was really nice of you."

Smiling, he said, "I'm preparing for a trial, so haul your silly ass out of here."

Embarrassing compliments came from the lawyers, their staff, my clients, my friends—not for me, but for the appropriate suits, shirts, and ties. It was rumored that Bob had "the hots" for me. The Chesterfield, protected with a plastic cover, remained hanging in our closet, unused except briefly to and from the firm's annual formal Christmas party at Fiddler's Elbow Country Club. A gala event indeed, attended by exclusive guests, mostly clients, high-ranking CEOs, their wives, and, of course, Alice and me. Bob, impressive as master of ceremonies, sparred with comedian Henny Youngman, famous for his one-liners: "Take my wife, for example—somebody take her, *anybody* take her." His appearances always included a few strokes on a violin, followed by more jokes.

Bob was in his glory. "Thank you, Mr. Youngman, for gracing us with your presence—late, as usual. But we forgive you. Our check is in the mail!" The guests, now wined, dined, and entertained, vigorously applauded, following with a standing ovation. Relishing the moment, Bob locked his handshake far too long while saying, "Thank you, Mr. Youngman! I'll have a tree in Israel uprooted and forever tilted in your honor."

With gentle music in the background, unchoreographed, Bob eloquently praised his guests, signaled the firm to join him on stage, and proudly introduced two new partners: Jack Slagel and Barry Hursh.

What a great time.

But storm clouds were rumbling. I saw dark clouds in the distance. Another fishing trip was required to track the storm, but in a different province—and Bob without an electric toaster oven. A predictable pattern emerged through private conversation year after year. Seldom interrupted except by a fish, Bob would methodically present his case to the jury (me), name by name, charge after charge: count one, count two, count three, and so on. Two days for opening statements (far too long). "Bob, I've heard all of this too damn many times. For God's sake, give it up!"

Third morning at the cabin, Bob's instructions: "We're starting late, so let's eat sandwiches for lunch instead of wasting time building a fire for shore lunch. I skipped breakfast and will be famished by lunchtime, so load up my sandwich with lots of lunchmeat and cheese. I have to take a walk."

"Did you say make the sandwiches? Bullshit! I've packed the shore lunch every day we've been here. It's your turn."

"Too bad, Ken. I have to walk. Tell your brother-in-law, John, to help."

"He's at the dock, getting the boat ready."

"Don't you understand English? I have to take a walk." With that, the screen door banged closed as Bob left the cabin. So, as ordered, I prepared the shore lunch: coffee, thick sandwiches, and cookies for dessert. But I intended to get even with that little twerp.

The bone-chilling, wind-driven rain continued all morning into late afternoon. Our hooded rain gear kept us dry, except for our hands that grew colder and colder, as did our bodies. This was John's first and last fishing trip with Bob, primarily because John is not a fisherman and Bob is an unsympathetic agitator. Bob continued his pleading. "Hey, guys, the fish aren't biting. Let's have an early lunch. I'm starving!"

The leeward side of this island allowed access to protected pockets beneath an outcropping ledge of rocks. We squeezed together just inside the drip edge of the rocks, Bob to my right, John to my left. Rain was gushing over the ledge, occasionally splattering inside.

Bob started: "John, quit jerking around, give me my sandwich! I'm starving."

"Screw you, Bob, Ken and I are eating first. You were supposed to help with the shore lunch."

"Quit screwing around, John, give me the damn sandwich."

"Sorry, Bob, you'll have to wait, just like you made me wait two miles from the farm while you played figure-eights with the tractor and empty forage wagon."

John continued: "Let's see, now, each sandwich is marked. What is your password?"

"John, give me the fucking sandwich." John waved the sandwich back and forth tauntingly. "Oh, this one says 'Bob'—Bob, Bob, Bob— Bob up and kiss my ass! You're not getting your sandwich until Ken and I finish eating."

Like a serpent, Bob snatched the tightly wrapped sandwich, hands dripping wet, and ripped open a corner of the wrapping. In a feeding frenzy, Bob chewed a huge bite and swallowed. John and I looked on, stunned in disbelief. It was incomprehensible, impossible. His little rat teeth had bitten clean through two slices of Jewish rye bread, two thick slabs of salami with its casing, and three squares of Kraft cheese still in their plastic wrappers! Bob, still in a feeding frenzy, a full coffee container in one hand, the sandwich in the other, sank his teeth deep and pulled hard. But this time it was hilarious.

The sandwich pulled apart. Cheese, salami, and plastic wrappers hung from his teeth, bread and mustard squeezed between his lips, fingers, and hands, all gooey-wet with the water from his hood, dumped when he had leaned forward. John and I quickly finished lunch to the tune of Bob's unspeakable vulgarity, dulled by our laughter.

All was quiet. Bob reached forward, rinsed his hands, and watched his coffee cup and bread float away. The cheese and salami sank. The afternoon sky cleared. The warm sun and breeze dried us. The fish box was full. Our self-inflicted wounds healed quickly.

• • •

Back at my office: "Ken, during our last fishing trip, I explained in detail the problems with Cliff Curtis, but I'm puzzled you did not defend him as you do with everyone else. Ever since we came back, Cliff has been acting weird. What the hell is going on?"

"Bob, go easy. We have a very serious matter to settle. Saturday, Cliff received my ultimatum: voluntarily resolve this issue with your partners by next Thursday, or I will submit the report to them on Friday."

Tension within the firm escalated nearly out of control. Bob demanded an emergency partnership meeting on Saturday, January 12, 1980, at 5:00 p.m. Absence was not an option.

Cliff arrived thirty minutes late, pale and resolute. He offered no apology. No one offered a "Hello, please sit down." Without preamble, Bob presented the case, summed it up, and moved directly to the penalty phase in less than ten minutes. Immediately thereafter, a unanimous vote expelled Curtis from the firm. He was to leave that week, taking with him his personal client files, his office furniture, and a cash settlement to be negotiated in seven days. The meeting ended abruptly. All left in silence, Cliff first.

I had never felt quite so low. It must have been obvious to Bob. "Here, Ken; let's have a Napoleon on the rocks." He raised his snifter glass for a toast. I turned away, gulped down the rare brandy, and dried my teary eyes. He quickly poured another drink. "Come on, Ken. I didn't think he meant that much to you."

Sarcastically, I replied, "Your action word is *think*. Cliff's fifteen years of service to the firm ended in ten minutes. You prejudiced the situation, predetermined the penalty, and intimidated the others into silence except for a yes vote.

"Only Sheldon Spencer expressed a broken heart, deeply saddened, when he said, 'I'm sorry, Cliff,' then looked toward you and said yes. The quick result: fifteen years wiped out in ten minutes. And you can live with that?"

"You're damn right I can. Anyone I can't trust will not remain my partner, and all the other partners feel the same way. Don't try to play attorney, Ken, you're not very good at it. You know how Curtis and Spencer always stick together against me. I didn't want them to team up and risk the firm being split in half. Anyway, it's all settled now, so let's have another drink and move on."

Exhausted, emotionally weakened, I received more than a buzz from the vintage brandy, which apparently stimulated a New Jersey state trooper. My heavy, new Chrysler station wagon swayed more than usual as I exited I-287 twelve miles from home. Spinning cherries appeared from nowhere. As usual, the trooper asked for "License and registration, please. Wait here, please." Quite by accident, my firearms permit and contact card for the New Jersey Bureau of Criminal Investigation had stuck to the driver's license. He returned and asked, "Mr. Crane, what is this all about?"

"Well, sir, Mr. Sapienza requested my help in an investigation he is handling. I believe Trooper Bill Doyle is also involved, but I haven't talked with him lately."

"No wonder. He's my sergeant and is extremely busy with several sensitive cases. Are you OK to drive?"

"I believe so, but if you'd rather, I'll call my wife to come get me."

"That won't be necessary, Mr. Crane. Drive carefully, and pressurize those air shocks to avoid future stops, because the vehicle is swaying unnaturally."

A week after our meeting, Cliff moved and remained as a sole practitioner for twenty years. Not long after I was invited to a meeting. A psychiatrist, Sue, and I all listened intently as Cliff told his story, in regards to what happened at the firm, glancing towards me from time to time for confirmation as he unfairly laid full blame on Bob Morgan .

"Excuse me, Cliff; I know you'd like to put a bullet in his head, although—"

Cliff interrupted, "I don't want to put a bullet in his head. He wouldn't suffer enough!"

"I'm sorry about all of this, Cliff, but surely this is not entirely Bob Morgan 's fault."

The psychiatrist stood up, saying, "I've heard enough. You can stay as long as you want." The psychiatrist left the room; all fell silent for thirty seconds. Gently, I pressed one hand on Sue's shoulder and the other on Cliff's. Compassionately, I said, "I'm so sorry." I left, never to have further contact with the Curtis'. Although to this day, I miss their friendship, it was not strong enough for me to orchestrate a cover-up involving full restitution, thereby so much agony for so many people.

Cliff's net worth in the firm was purchased by Jack Slagel and Kenneth Hursh, making them junior partners. The law firm sign changed from "Morgan, Curtis, Spencer " to "Morgan, Spencer, Slagel, and Hursh, et al." Business increased yearly, requiring more attorneys, more secretaries, and more support staff needing more office space.

The road ahead was clear. The firm was secure and prosperous, but not sufficiently for Bob to delegate mundane administrative tasks. Bob's complaints included, but were not limited to, use of firm credit cards, missing office supplies (notably pencils), personal abuse of the telephone and postage meter, and mandatory employee breaks. His concerns were generally valid, but his aggressive solutions verged on abhorrent.

Bob became obsessed with reducing overhead costs far below the carefully prepared budget. Gloria, age twenty-six, Bob's newly hired assistant, policed according to his directives and reported her findings exclusively to him. She became known as his "little spy," which was also the label for her replacements.

● ● ●

I finished a round of golf at Fiddler's Elbow Country Club with Bob and Joe Duncan. Joe owned a TV cable company nearby. After two golf games, Joe answered all of my probing questions. I now knew I was ready for the next challenge. Hillsborough Township was ripe for improvement: abandon those ugly antennas in exchange for one tower enabling clearer signals to every viewer in the franchise area. The process was not difficult, just extremely time-consuming—time not available to me unless it encroached into allotted family time, something I would not allow except in an emergency.

Veto Margolo, my client, a graduate of Princeton University and former mayor of Hillsborough Township, accepted my invitation to join with Bob and me to serve this fast-growing suburban area. I explained, "The process should go smoothly with you as CEO, Bob Morgan as legal counsel, and me as accountant." As with all of my joint ventures: "I suggest each owner receive interest on his investment, fair pay for services rendered, and last, split the profits equally." Veto was elated. I was excited to enlist his talent and reputation.

Thirty days later, the local newspaper headline read, "Former mayor files application for cable TV franchise to serve our fast-growing community." It further read: " Daniel Kingsworth, architect, Jeffrey Morgan, legal counsel, and Kenneth Crane, public accountant have been elected to the board of directors."

Bob stormed into my office, livid. "Crane, what the hell is this all about?"

"What can I say, Bob? I trusted the guy."

"You asshole, I told you not to allow anyone else in our deals!" Still raging, Bob ranted on, "Now the cable company belongs to Margolo, and he has the balls to elect you, your client, Kingsworth, and me to serve on *his* board of directors. Unbelievable!"

"Simmer down. I've already ended my business and personal relationship with Veto . Also, he is to retract the headline and has disavowed our association with the cable company. There's nothing more we can do."

"That's probably true, Ken, but I'm so pissed off you didn't at least have him sign a letter of intent and have me set up the corporation. You're smart, Ken, but it burns my ass when you play lawyer."

"I'm sorry. I don't blame you for being outraged. I feel the same way. But I only asked him to consider our offer; there were no promises and no handshakes on the deal. Apparently, he surreptitiously ran to another lawyer, formed a corporation, and quickly applied for the franchise license—all behind my back. And one more thing: Contrary to your opinion, I don't try to play lawyer. You're a fine example of why I'm not very good at it. Regardless, you must agree: I allowed Veto to expose his true character before we put our money at risk."

Building Equity

In time, my professional expertise with the US tax code and IRS regulations coalesced with my expertise in dairy farming and the State Farmland Assessment Acts. The combination created the opportunity to own land at much lower carrying costs than usual. I explained the concepts to Bob. My plan:

Invest cash (capital) in a partnership. The partnership agreement would establish ownership on the ratio of each capital account to the total funds invested. Interest per annum would accrue on each capital account at 2 percent above the prime rate.

The partnership would loan cash to new corporations formed solely for acquiring specific parcels of land. The loans would be secured by first mortgages bearing interest at the rate of 15 percent per annum (a fair charge at that time), and would be recorded simultaneously with the conveyance of land to the corporations. If a corporation defaulted on the mortgage, the partnership would foreclose in court and secure a clear title with a sheriff's deed.

With great excitement and enthusiasm, Bob declared, "Let's go for it! I'll handle the real estate laws, and you handle the tax laws. We'll work together to handle the finances."

Remember, 1980 was a recession year. At age forty-seven, with great anticipation, I worked my plan—and—here we go!

On June 11, 1980, Grundy Corporation acquired a twenty-acre prime parcel of land directly across from the Hillsborough, New Jersey high school.

On June 27, 1980, Ken Vern Corporation acquired 7.2 acres of vacant land, also near Hillsborough High School. Our ownership in the two corporations cost $100,000, financed and mortgaged through B-Jack

Farms. Three years later, in a nonrecession year, we conveyed the titles for a combined total of $936,000. Bob was elated but nervous. I was elated but not nervous. I continued working our plan even with storm clouds closing in on us.

Morgan as Captain Queeg

Captain Queeg ruled the firm, but mutinous expressions abounded. Barry Hursh, a young attorney with a fractional interest in the firm, told me, "I think I'm about to be fired. Bob summoned me to his office. I became more than irritated when he blurted out an entire diatribe that ended with 'Anything you can do here, I can do better.' Sarcastically, I said, 'Oh really? Try this.' I turned away to leave and put my hand on the top of the doorframe." Bob's insecurity and greed plagued our daily existence.

Each year for many years, Bob and I fished in Canada as the firm expanded and we increased our net worth by acquiring choice real estate. I enjoyed the challenge. Bob enjoyed the numbers, but it was not enough; Bob wanted more, faster. Slowly but surely, his past distilled a potent paranoia that surfaced a supreme choice to acquire money by expensing friends. "I remind you, Bob, that unless you change, all you will have left is money and no friends."

Instantly, he replied, "And let me remind you, Ken: I'll take it."

Fully aware of Bob's insatiable quest, I adroitly summarized the plan outlined years ago: "Bob, I have contracted to acquire two additional parcels of choice vacant land adjacent to Hillsborough High School. The deal is complicated, so as before, I'll use a partnership to accept capital contributions. The money will be loaned to newly formed corporations secured by the real estate each acquires. Through direct negotiation with the current mortgagor and mortgagee, I plan to stop the impending sheriff's sales. I'll need five hundred thousand dollars in seven days."

"Ken, are you nuts? We're already out of cash."

"Bob, the attorneys here want to invest in the companies, and Spencer 's friend from Germany has pledged the balance. I'm going in with a hundred thousand in borrowed money."

Bob exploded, "I'm appalled by your action. You've gone behind my back to include outsiders in our deals. I told you not to do that, especially with my partners."

"Bob, nothing is complete, I'm not going behind your back, and they're not outsiders. They're my clients. Also I told you I want to share the benefit of these great opportunities, knowing we alone can't take advantage of every situation. Always remember, Bob, you will never get your claws in my ass, and you should know it's fruitless for you to give me orders. Just answer without a lot of bullshit: do you want in or not?"

Without hesitation, Bob replied, "Shove it up your ass, Crane."

Bob steadfastly refused to share the benefits and burdens of my joint ventures. Undeterred, I forged ahead, and on October 15, 1980, the economy still in recession, Mogul Investments, a newly formed partnership, started business with assets totaling $576,568. Bloomingdale Estates, Inc., a newly formed corporation, borrowed $100,000 from Mogul Investments and purchased 14.6 acres of choice real estate, including a six-acre lake. Pleasant View Estates, Inc. borrowed $400,000 from Mogul Investments and purchased 118 vacant acres. Both parcels were close to Hillsborough High School and very near the parcels Bob and I controlled. Several years later, these two corporations conveyed title for a combined total exceeding $2.5 million. The intervening years were extremely troublesome for Bob.

Morgan Hooks the Big One

The Ecstasy of Winning

Bob's search for the Holy Grail—happiness—continued one perfect spring week. Our catch of walleye and northern pike was the stuff of dreams. In four days, we filled a three-by-five Igloo travel cooler with our legal possession limit, all big fish. Exhilarated, we fished two more days. Bob repeatedly stopped the birds chirping and the squirrels barking as his voice echoed in the wilderness, "Fish on, fish on!" Suddenly, his dream came true. "Get the net, Ken, it's that big one! The one I have pictures of from years ago."

"Hot damn, Bob, that's the biggest pike I've ever seen. Let's take a real picture back to camp instead of the last picture framed in your mind that everyone laughed at and called bullshit."

Bob proudly admired the big one that didn't get away, exaggerating its weight and size by grimacing as he strained to hold the heavy fish toward the camera at arm's length. "That's one hell of a big pike," I exclaimed, and added, "Render unto Napoleon that which is due Napoleon."

"You dumb farmer. It's 'render unto Caesar,' not Napoleon."

"I know that. But Caesar was taller than Napoleon. By holding the fish way out in front of you, it appears you are almost as tall as the fish."

Bob was in his glory. "Piss on you, Crane. Just admit it. At the end, I always come out on top, the winner." I quietly stowed the Polaroid camera and then gently pumped the trophy fish back and forth, flushing its gills with water. Seconds later, a swish of its tail, a swirl, and we let the big one go free.

Still shaking with uncontrolled excitement, Bob became a gentleman, a true sportsman. "Ken, I'm really happy that our last two days fishing have been catch and release. It would be a damn shame to kill a fish like that. Besides, this way you'll have the opportunity to catch the same fish, assuming the unlikely prospect that you improve your skills to my level."

"That's not a problem, Bob, just a challenge."

While traveling three hours in the car, the theme was happiness, glorified with euphoria. "Ken, this was a hell of a nice trip. Perfect weather, lots of fish, and I caught the biggest ones."

"Yeah, it's been a good trip, Bob."

"Good? It's been great! We've made lots of trips together, but without a doubt, this has been the very best of all. We should buy an island and build—hey, Ken, look at all those cop cars ahead!"

"Yeah, two more just pulled in there as we passed by. Oh hell, Bob, it's a diner. They're just having lunch."

"So what? It's against regulation for the cops to gather like that while on duty." Bob grabbed the CB microphone. "Hey, Smokey, why the hell are all of you eating at the same time? You frogs never learn. I'm telling you to get off your lazy ass and get to work!"

"Are you out of your damn mind? Hang up the mic!"

Bob continued laughing and slapping the armrest while blurting out disparaging one-liners characterizing the mentality of the Canadian police.

"OK, Bob, knock it off. You'll just get our ass in trouble. Get off the air!"

"Lighten up, Ken, I'm just having a little fun with the stupid bastards. Besides, they're having lunch and can't hear me."

"You are one piss-poor eyewitness. Two cars parked as we drove by, but only one officer left toward the diner."

Bob, still in high spirits, began needling me. "Stop worrying, chickenshit. There's no way they can track us. Remember, I'm a lawyer, and you're a farmer. Come on, Ken, step on the gas. You're driving like an old lady, always looking in the rearview mirror."

Toyingly, I slowed down to five miles under the speed limit. We were a hundred miles from the border. "The faster you become a pain in the ass, the slower I'll drive."

We laughed and kibitzed until we reached the border checkpoint. The guard questioned us. "What is your name? Where were you born?"

I answered honestly, politely. Bob, still euphoric, answered as a wiseguy. "Billy Bob. Alabama…maybe Georgia."

"What is your citizenship?"

"I'm not sure, but I'm a New Jersey attorney.""Why are you leaving Canada?""We've had a fantastic fishing trip, and we're going home.""Do you have any fireworks or contraband?""No; we like Canada, but we love the United States.""That's nice to hear. Park your car in bay number three.""What for? I'm an attorney!"

The border guard pointed and sternly ordered, "*Bay* three; drive there *now*."

Authorities immediately surrounded Bob's Cadillac.

"Step out of the vehicle.""Why, what for? You have no probable cause. I am a licensed New Jersey attorney.""Get out of the car *now*!"

Standing with the driver's door open, I admonished Bob, "Shut your damn mouth and get the hell out of the car."

Authorities ushered us into a huge detention room to fill out a long questionnaire. Two hours later, my patience exhausted and Bob at the boiling point, we reloaded our property randomly scattered around the car. "Hey, Ken, look at this. Those pricks checked every fish. The ice is nearly gone." Seething with anger, Bob backed out and peeled away onto I-87, aka the Northway, speed limit sixty-five miles per hour. Bob was doing ninety.

We rounded a sharp curve where two vehicles blocked the road; one remained in the fast lane, the other in the slow lane. Both were traveling at sixty-five miles per hour. Adrenaline-driven road rage controlled the moment with tires screeching, horns blasting, and Bob yelling, "You fucking idiots, get over!" Tailgating, Bob laid on the horn, zigzagging in and out of the right and left lanes, relentlessly screaming obscenities. "Ken, write down the prick's plate numbers."

An adrenaline surge compelled me to yell at Bob, "You stupid bastard! Give it up. Pull over. I'll find a safer way to get home."

Cherries flashed—announcing the New York State Police. The usual procedure followed. "Driver's license and insurance card, please. Wait here."

As the officer returned, I warned Bob, "Don't start trouble. This time, keep your damn mouth shut."

"Do you know why I stopped you?"

In a flash, Bob became a courteous, nice guy. "I didn't realize you stopped me. We were about to change drivers when you pulled up behind us."

"Mr. Morgan, I have to cite you for traveling thirty miles an hour over the speed limit."

Bob was convincing. "I'm glad you stopped, officer. I wasn't speeding; it was a maroon car that zoomed past me. I'm an attorney in New Jersey and own the state police barracks on Route 22 near Somerville. You can apprehend the vehicle if you radio ahead. He's a real danger to the public. Here's his plate number." The officer ran to his car and sped away.

"See how it's done, Ken?"

"I get the point, Bob, but I'm not riding with you again unless you drive no more than five miles an hour over the posted speed limit. The highs and lows with you are too extreme, increasing the risk of trouble for everyone around you. How many times have we crossed the border— thirty-five, forty? How many times have we been searched? Once. And it happened because it's zero distance from your head to your asshole."

"That's enough, Ken. We've had a great trip, so don't spoil it. Let's have lunch and ice down the fish."

I listened intently for seven more hours, mile after mile, as Bob laid out a litany of grievances laced with "I-told-you-so's" and placing blame on everyone except himself. Then he babbled about details of how I had screwed up the cable TV deal.

"I don't know what you're leading up to, Bob, but I'm warning you, there is considerable unrest in the firm. Mutiny is in the air."

"Don't worry about it, Ken. Remember, I always come out on top— the winner."

The Agony of Defeat

Bob charged into my office. "Ken, we have to talk."

"Settle down, Bob. What the hell is wrong?"

"We can't talk here. Let's go to the club."

On the way, the jury heard opening statements in the case of Jeffrey M. Morgan, plaintiff, hereinafter referred to as Morgan, versus Sheldon Spencer, defendant, hereinafter referred to as Spencer . The charges? Count one: Defendant Spencer 's absenteeism can no longer be tolerated. As to count one: Spencer, to the detriment of the firm, has spent time working for his wife's expanding clothing business while receiving full salary and share of profits from the firm.

"Hold on, hold on, Bob—forget the formalities. Remember, I'm not a lawyer. Just give me a narrative of the situation."

"OK, Ken, but I've had it with this guy ripping off the firm. He's in New York City two or three times a week, dealing with other business, whatever the hell that might be. Gloria gave me the cost of his non-firm-related phone calls. You won't believe the amount of money. Worse, now he's on another vacation at his Florida condo in West Palm Beach. On top of all that, he's doing monkey work. I can hire an attorney right out of law school at half the cost to handle workmen's comp and petitioners' cases. And while I'm at it, this business of the wives getting together at Fiddler's Elbow has to stop. The green-fee tickets name Clara Spencer, Betty Little"—she was the wife of a prominate insurance company claims manager Joe—"and Alice Crane. They're playing golf at the club at least once a week, but they never ask Peggy to join them. The Spencers are kissing ass with the Ellises to control our book of work from that insurance company. When we get back to the office, I'll lock Spencer 's door, call an emergency partnership meeting, and take back my law firm. Spencer is out. I want you to chair the meeting."

We sat for a moment, silent, my thoughts gathering while I observed sweat beads on his furrowed brow. His quivering lips shadowed his strange glare deep into another realm. Sympathy placed my hand on his shoulder and directed me to softly say, "Come on, Bob, let's stroll the back nine." Surprisingly, he agreed.

The weather was perfect, the path was paved, and our steps were casual. I spoke calmly, methodically, caringly, painfully slowly.

"Bob, I want you to listen carefully, without interruption, until I'm finished. Agreed?""Of course—go ahead."

"I will chair the meeting, but only if everyone attending votes for that motion. Also, I will try to control the meeting, knowing others may assert a charge of conflict of interest. I will not give advice, suggest a course of action, or support any motion, especially yours, for obvious reason. Do you understand and agree without reservation with what I have said so far?"

"You know I do. We're friends."

"Of course we are. But I want you to understand that every issue will rise and fall on its own merits, nothing else. I don't want another Curtis ordeal."

I continued: "Once you start the ball rolling, I will do my best to help everyone fully understand the ultimate consequences. But I will remain neutral at all times. Until then, heed my warnings. The venue for the validity and value of your complaints is a partnership meeting—not in the car, not in the boat, and certainly not on the golf course. You are positioning for a head-on collision with a train; the casualties may expand beyond just Spencer ."

"You may be right, Ken, but I don't think so. The attorneys have families and need the benefits of the firm. They need the money and can't earn as much elsewhere. Besides, we'll pay Spencer a fair price and divide his share equally. Also, don't forget: with your help, I control two-thirds of the gross income of the firm. They can't survive without me."

Time slipped by as I injected "what-ifs" until we reached the clubhouse. "Consider what I have said, Bob. Wait a few days to make the decision. Once you start the ball rolling, serious damage cannot be avoided."

"Thanks for your concern, Ken. I've been planning this a long time. The meeting will be in the conference room tomorrow after work, around five thirty."

Tension filled the air. A coalition was forming; battle lines became apparent, partners' billable hours dwindled as my office door became a revolving door. Questions without answers were the result. The meeting was adjourned one day, caused by Barry Hursh's emergency phone call to Spencer urging him to return immediately.

The meeting: Saturday, 9:00 a.m., behind locked doors. I began. "Gentlemen, because of the serious nature of our agenda, I have retained a certified public stenographer to record verbatim minutes of the meeting. All of you know T. C. Reporting Service and my daughter, Tammy. Our conflict of interest is obvious. We, of course, will recuse ourselves at your request. Do you want me to chair this meeting, yes or no? Let the record show the unanimous vote is yes. Do you want Tammy Crane to make a verbatim stenographic record of this meeting, yes or no? Let the record show the unanimous vote is yes.

"First, I want to tidy up necessary formalities, and then we will get right down to business. For the record, this is an emergency meeting of the full partnership known as Morgan, Spencer, Slagel, Hursh, et al. Partners present are Morgan, Spencer, Slagel, Hursh, Armanno, and Chismento. Again, for the record, you are here to decide the future of this law firm by ruling on Bob Morgan 's decision to expel Spencer from the firm.

"Loosely interpreted, I will intervene only when accusations fly, table pounding begins, and rage or anger drives the meeting out of control. We know it will happen, and you know I won't stay if it persists.

"Bob, you called for the meeting, so let's get started."

Confidently, he stood. Calmly, he began. Methodically, he presented his opening statement. Pathetically, his offense crumbled in minutes. Spencer was to stay.

Negotiations continued throughout the afternoon as private caucuses debated resolutions at reconvened meetings. The mood was solemn, the scene surreal. At stake was the financial well-being of thirteen attorneys, twenty employees, and their families. The consequences of each decision became more ominous if Bob did indeed control the firm's life-sustaining book of work. If the firm split, the majority of clients might follow him, here or elsewhere. But how can one divorce and still live in the same household, especially with personal liability for shared assets and living expenses? A daunting task indeed.

Incredibly, a stenographic agreement was recorded at 10:00 p.m. In summary: the firm name would not change. Morgan would remain in name only as sole practitioner. He would handle asbestos litigation exclusively. Liability and overhead would be apportioned and charged against each entity. In addition, he was to be paid one million dollars.

Everyone was completely exhausted; tension was the cause, especially for Morgan, who repeatedly tried phalanxes to isolate his prey, but each attack was quickly beaten off by Spencer 's unsolicited defenders. The meeting adjourned. I left quickly to avoid the obvious consequential apprehension all were feeling.

Alice listened intently as I applauded the power of coalition forces favoring integrity over the evil forces of money. Bob's partners refused to allow him to expel Spencer from the firm, yet once again, Bob had gained substantial money by expensing friends. Silently, I feared he had won and that the coalition had been too generous. Hindsight indicates that I should have recused myself. All parties should have hired independent counsel. But at least the forces capitulated.

It was 11:00 p.m. I quickly fell asleep, only to be awakened by ringing in my ear. The bell was at full volume for emergencies.

"Ken, I need your help. I'm calling off the deal. Fritz is here, and he wants to talk with you."

"Bob, it's after eleven. I'll deal with it in the morning."

"No way. Here, Fritz will explain."

"Ken, we have to talk. We should go to the farm together and straighten out Bob's deal. If not, the firm will be removed from our approved attorneys list, and our company files will be pulled immediately."

"OK, Fritz, I'll have a cup of black coffee and leave right away. Bob's house is about forty minutes from here."

As the firm had grown, marketing its expertise became a priority. Unknowingly, I had been involved with Bob's schmoozing important clients who controlled the lucrative defense files assigned only to preapproved law firms. The approval criteria were simple, as they are today: maintain a staff of qualified attorneys to defend against thousands of insurance claims, varying in complexity and potential monetary loss. For example, a million-dollar claim was filed for improper employee supervision. Employees harassed a meek fellow worker by kissing the air and goosing him. Each time, he would raise his elbows, hop forward, and burp. Whoops! He had developed a conditioned response, reacting the same way merely after an air kiss. As I recall, he was awarded $750,000. The case was called "The Golden Goose."

Years later, separate airplanes crashed into separate towers at separate times. That's right, the 9/11 incident. Barry Hursh was instrumental in saving the insurance company millions of dollars by successfully arguing that it was one incident, thus restricting the coverage limit to one insurance policy.

At Bob's home, Fritz espoused the virtues of his proposal. "Ken, I know about your association with claims managers and executives in the home office of various insurance companies, including mine. With your help, we can improve the deal for Bob and protect the law firm if the files are pulled and reassigned elsewhere."

While traveling to the farm from midnight till 3:00 a.m., Fritz laid out their plan. I labeled it a "scheme;" it always came with a caveat: Spencer must go.

Fritz delivered this ultimatum. "One, face the facts: it's Bob's law firm. His position there will not change. Two: Bob is to receive an employee contract with personal guarantees, negotiated and signed by all partners. Three: Peggy Morgan will be guaranteed a pension of one million dollars. Four: business will be as usual, except the firm title will include the name of every remaining partner.

"Details will come later, but basically, that's the deal. Take it or leave it. Take it, and everybody keeps their jobs. Leave it, and I'll have my files loaded on a truck the next day and reassigned to Bob's new firm, here or elsewhere. Either way, Spencer has to go."

"So why tell me?"

"We need your help to talk some sense into them. Also, as Bob's assistant, you will be highly paid to maintain a file count list of all cases assigned to each attorney."

"Fritz, I'm confident that all the important people I have fished with, including you, know me better than that. I have a professional responsibility to each of the partners, as well as to the firm. All are my friends and clients. Besides, I chaired the meetings, nothing more. My soul is not for sale."

Bob fell asleep as Fritz probed for an advantage. Birds were chirping, daylight was minutes away, and my patience had reached its limit. "Give it up, Fritz. I've had a lot of practice refusing bribes, but yours is the biggest and easiest of all. I'm going to walk to the farm."

"Good idea. I'll go with you, Ken."

"Sorry, Fritz, I want to go alone. I've heard enough."

An hour later, after breakfast at our local Bell's Pond restaurant and gas station near the farm, we headed south on the New York Thruway toward home, two and a half hours away. Traffic noise and car radio music muffled the front seat conversation, but now and then, I heard Fritz ask an innocuous question: "How's your wife doing? Where is your son these days? Is your lovely daughter still at the office?" My intended power nap remained impossible.

Suddenly, Bob came alive with renewed vigor. "That's it, Fritz, that's the answer!" Bob's surprise act was no surprise to me: here comes another deal.

After three cups of black coffee and a switch of drivers at a Thruway rest stop with Fritz in the passenger seat, quartered toward the rear, he made his final offer. "Ken, here it is in a nutshell. Bob gets everything we talked about. You get the big money we talked about. In addition, I will promote T. C. Reporting Service to become our exclusive court reporting agency in the state. Your daughter will have the largest stenographic company in the state of New Jersey. When we get back, tell her all about it and line up a staff of certified reporters."

"Fritz, you and Bob have gone off the deep end. Listen up for the last time, and get this straight. Tammy's dealings are none of my business. If you want to promote her business, go ahead—I won't. Bob's dealings with his partners are between them—it is none of my business. And frankly, Fritz, it's none of *your* business. You are way out on a limb— don't make me cut it off."

Clearly all shaken, we stopped, and once again drivers switched. Pale and deeply hurt, Bob gave a pitiful glance that explained it all. His father would not forgive him; his mother would not forgive him. And what about me? Silently, he stared straight ahead. I continued: "Get this straight, Bob. Before you started this mess, I offered you my opinions. You understood my warnings of a head-on collision bringing uncertain consequences. Also, everyone knows my involvement is conditioned upon a supreme caveat to remain neutral and unbiased. I intend to keep that promise. Besides, I phoned Hursh and told him the deal is off and that you and I were going to the farm. I mentioned Fritz's name.

"Now, here's what's going to happen next. When you're ready, I'll reconvene the meeting so you can start all over. For the time being, this business with Fritz shall remain confidential. If asked about this trip, I'll answer, 'No comment.'"

Still focused straight ahead, Bob softly but clearly said, "Thanks, Ken, I appreciate that."

• • •

The meeting reconvened at 1:00 p.m. and started with, "A few formalities, gentlemen. Let the record show by name that every partner is present. Also let the record show that the night of our last meeting at eleven p.m., I received a phone call at my home from Bob Morgan, at which time he declared the tentative stenographic agreement arrived at during that meeting is null and void. We will adjourn and reconvene this meeting at six p.m. Please bring your file count by client and the firm's estimated gross income per carrier."

Intense, frenzied activity continued that afternoon as attorneys, paralegals, secretaries, and staff compiled the data. It quickly became evident, if Morgan was correct, that the firm could not survive.

We dispensed with all formalities. Let the train crash begin! The issue: align with Morgan or go it alone.

The conference room was quiet, the partners solemn and pensive, each fully aware that their impending decision would start a landslide of events cascading their lives into the unknown. The coalition began to fracture as probing questions nudged each head closer to the chopping block. Severe consequences flooded their minds with agonizing thoughts that were quite different for each partner: some had mortgage payments, car payments, tuition payments, and family responsibilities. Some partners had children while others did not. Some of their wives received income, and others did not. Unresolved partnership responsibility questions screamed for answers. What would happen to our employees? Who would pay the long-term leases for cars, office equipment, and office space, each with a partner's signature and personal guarantee?

The crux: a Biblical thought—for the good of so many, one must be sacrificed. Spencer must go. I sat quietly as implications of the painful choice progressed around the table, beginning with the most vulnerable partners. Shortly, each partner would cast his vote, a simple yes or no. Spencer's future was bleak.

Suddenly, without indication, a middle-aged, fractional-interest junior partner stood and changed the momentum in seconds. In full control of his convictions, without gesticulations, he spoke. "What is wrong with you people? Morgan is about to divide and conquer. Look at his past; look at your future. Which one of you will be next?" There was no "sound and fury" in Arturo's calm, deliberate phrases carefully spaced with pauses. He continued: "I realize what is at stake is different for each of us. That is why I am speaking strictly for myself." Arturo faced Morgan, seated at the head of the long conference table, and emphatically declared, "I worked in the prosecutor's office many years, dealing with all sorts of low-life people, but what you are attempting now is one of the dirtiest, sneakiest, low-life maneuvers of all. For that reason, regardless of the others' decision, I will not be your partner, now or ever."

Arturo then faced the others. "Look, guys, I know what is at stake, so do what you have to do. I won't blame you for your decision, but I'm not staying in the same room with Morgan." Tired and disgusted, he simply said, "I'm out of here."

Spencer stood, interrupted Arturo's exit, and politely encouraged him to stay. Generally preferring to solve problems through negotiation, not confrontation, Spencer was well liked by all—an extreme opposite of Morgan. Obviously greatly inspired by Arturo's verbal assault against the senior partner, he surprised everyone, especially Morgan. Way out of character, Spencer swerved half the length of the conference table, poised six feet from Morgan, and discharged a volley of precise metaphors directly at him: "You're a snake, a viper, striking poison without care for the injured. I was on vacation, and you tried to stab me in the back. I don't know what my future holds, but I do know I won't be around for you to stab in the back again." Tense with anger, he leaned forward with hands on his hips, gasping for air as runners often do, and stormed from the room. Being a marathon runner, he continued to burn his adrenaline-driven frustration in the oversize parking lot.

I witnessed the crash. Negotiations ended; tomorrow we would search for survivors.

Thirty-six hours without sleep left me drained. The next day, well rested and intent on my mission of damage control, I drove slowly to meet Fritz Blow for a private lunch meeting close to his Bloomfield, New Jersey office. In fact, I signed the visitor's record and requested the security guard to initial the time and date of my presence. I was casually dressed, as our lunch was informal. My purpose here was made clear: "What are your intentions, Fritz?"

He began, "This is company business, and what I say here is strictly confidential. It goes no further."

"Sorry, Fritz, I won't agree to something I know nothing about. If you choose not to discuss your alignment with Bob, that's your choice. I'm here as a courtesy to you at your request and for no other reason."

"I appreciate your purpose, Ken, so here's where I stand. I've been good friends with Bob and Peggy for many years. As you know, we visit on a regular basis. But I also know that his primary purpose is to increase the defense files to his firm. My loyalty above all else is to the insurance company. That's my job; that's what I do. I asked you to meet here to tell you personally that insurance companies are concerned about their files when a law firm is in trouble. I haven't discussed this with Bob, but I'm telling you in strict confidence that I have removed myself from the evaluation process and, as events shape up, the ultimate resting place for our files will be decided by other executives. I will remain neutral."

"That's all I need to hear, Fritz. Thanks for being honest with me. When the dust settles, I'll teach you how to catch really big fish."

I insisted on paying the lunch ticket with my credit card, even though it was a modest charge. It was proof of our meeting—for tax purposes, of course. Ha, ha.

Black Wednesday

Morgan 's absence from the office since Monday was puzzling. His secretary also questioned his whereabouts. At 11:45 a.m., Barry Hursh entered my office, pale and shaken. "We've had it. The rat is carrying out his threats."

"What the hell are you talking about?"

"Our major client has removed our name from the approved attorneys list. We're finished."

I grabbed my phone and said, "Stay calm, Ken. Go directly to your office and wait there for a phone call." My phone call: "Hello, this is Mr. Crane calling for Mr. Blow. This is an emergency. Please put me through to him immediately."

"Ken, I'm in an important meeting. I'll call you later."

"Don't bother, Fritz. In ten minutes, tell Barry Hursh the firm is back on the approved attorneys list, or in fifteen minutes I'll be at the Somerset County prosecutor's office." My phone hit the cradle with a thud, punctuating the warning.

Seconds later, I entered Barry's office as he answered the phone and slumped back in his office chair with a look of absolute disbelief. He expelled an airy sigh of relief. "Fritz said someone made a mistake, but he took care of it. The firm is back on the approved list, and business will continue as usual."

Joe Ely, claims manager for two other major client, advised Spencer that his only concern was the quality of legal service rendered to his insurance company. He also preferred that Clara and Alice continue their golf outings with his wife, Fran.

• • •

Napoleon's offensive had been repelled. Defenders had coalesced. A counterattack was imminent. Thursday afternoon, all partners were present. Demoralized and stunned, Morgan slumped back in his chair as terms for his unconditional surrender were explained: the new firm would be called Spencer, Slagel, Hursh, Armanno, and Chismento.

I would calculate Bob's settlement the way I had for Cliff Curtis.

Bob and his secretary would vacate the building in one week, taking his book of work for asbestos litigation only.

The new firm would assume responsibility for all assets and liabilities except those related to asbestos litigation.

In other words: " Spencer will stay; you will leave."

Totally defeated, humiliated, and crushed, Morgan stared at nothing, talking irrationally to the glass surrounding my third-story, corner office. Impulsive hand movements exposed the paranoia of Captain Queeg, now of Morgan . When I entered the room, Morgan turned and pleaded. "Ken, what should I do? You have to help me. Please, please," he begged.

"I'm sorry, Bob, I can't undo a train wreck. All we can do is collect the pieces and survive the injuries. Of course, I will help everyone do that, but my mission remains the same: stay neutral and soldier an orderly transition of the files, carry out my professional responsibilities, and ensure an honest, equitable settlement for every partner's interest in the firm. I'll compile the financial data to determine your payoff, but I'm advising you and the other partners to have independent professionals verify the work."

"You're the only person I trust, Ken, so I don't need to involve anyone except you and Barbara Moffett."

"OK, but there will be formalities. Transfer authorizations will have to be signed before a file leaves this office. But no file is to be removed before a formal partnership dissolution agreement is properly executed. No file shall leave this office between five p.m. and nine a.m., during which time a Bridgewater police officer will be on duty and report directly to me until further notice.

"I will not mollify, placate, or show partiality toward anyone involved. I hope you understand. I have no choice in the matter if I continue my involvement as requested."

Bob, still quivering: "I understand. I know you'll be fair, Ken. I've never been beaten so low."

All legalities were completed in seven days, but to fulfill the provisions might take up to four years. The tentative document filled eight legal-size pages.

I played lawyer and suggested a simplified version of double-spaced paragraphs on less than two standard sheets of paper (see Appendix C: Exhibit XX). There is safety in brevity.

Morgan merged his book of work with that of Roland Winters, a single practitioner in Bloomfield twenty-five miles from our office. They named the firm Morgan and Winters. Shortly thereafter, still seething with indignation, Morgan began schmoozing insurance company executives and claims managers to increase his book of work, a clear violation of the noncompetition clauses above his signature in the settlement agreement with his former partners.

Our joint real estate investments and the law firm payments required monthly contact with Morgan, but our personal relationship became sorely tested, much like friendships trapped between rivals in a bitter divorce. Bob desperately wanted to continue our business deals. "It bonds our friendship." But I declined to represent the Morgan -Winters partnership and terminated my accountant-client relationship with him. I traded our joint-venture New Jersey real estate (sale pending) for Bob's appreciated interest in B-Jack Farms, thereby converting his equity share of jointly owned real estate into cash for him.

Shortly thereafter, by phone: "Hi, Bob, I have a check for you."

Sarcastically, he replied, "Fine, bring the check to my office. We have to talk."

Sarcastically, I replied, "Your wish is my command. I'll leave right now."

Bob never guessed how I had longed for this confrontation. He stepped from behind his desk to launch an offense. "I'm appalled by your conduct. As a trusted friend, you said you would protect my interests, but instead you cost me four hundred thousand dollars."

I had come prepared to counterattack. "Don't start your bullshit with me, Bob. My involvement was not to protect you, but to keep everyone honest, a quality you trashed for money. You breached the noncompetition agreement, and that's why the firm, not me, decided to stop further payments to you. I came here for one reason: to have it out with you, once and for all. I warned you not to screw around with that noncompetition clause, but as usual, you tried to outflank honesty. I now understand your father, your mother, Richard Clampton, Bart Bennuto, Benny Fernando, Cliff Curtis, Sheldon Spencer, and Alice—and many others too numerous to name—that you have injured by your greed, hate, and vengeance. You overlook my personal efforts that netted you a small fortune. But for you, that's not enough. Do you remember my warning? 'Unless you change your ways, Bob, you will have no friends, just money.' So be happy. After all, you said, 'I'll take it!' And now you are appalled by my conduct? A heavy burden has been lifted, because starting right now, you are out of my life forever. A person like you can't go to hell; you are already there. Appalled, you say. Well, stay appalled!"

A year later, Morgan and Winters parted company, bitter enemies after Roland Winters filed a lawsuit against Morgan charging grand larceny for misappropriating approximately $450,000 of partnership money to a secret personal account in Connecticut (see Appendix for the complaint filed).

I must confess that I enjoyed some great times with Bob. But he didn't abuse me to the extent he abused others. His unchangeable, life-long value was that any recognizable good to be found in his soul should be nullified by unspeakable, dastardly acts against the undeserving. Incredibly, it took twenty years of my dedicated effort to admit the obvious: I failed. I could not "change the spots on a leopard."

He would now be age eighty-eight, but there have been no Morgan sightings reported in five years.

Electrifying Experiences

The Bulb

My body is eighty-one years old, revealing scars from my early youth. A look back in time:

Fire in our wood-burning kitchen stove blazed throughout the day and early evening in Mom and Dad's home, "the big house." The water jacket on one side of the firebox received cold water from a galvanized, freestanding, thirty-gallon tank in the upstairs bathroom. Heated water flowed through a pipe connected to a water jacket on opposite sides of the firebox, causing it to return to the galvanized tank as super-heated water. Aunt Annie, Mom and Dad, plus ten siblings lived in the big house, causing hot water to be a luxury. A strict regimen based on age determined the lineup for use of the bathroom. Pop warned each member of the family to conserve the hot water by minimizing the amount used in the bathtub. Scheduled intervals between baths usually allowed sufficient time to replace the hot water. The schedule was strictly enforced.

I was tenth in line for the bath. As always, I felt the exposed return water pipe and then rubbed my palm up and down the tank to estimate the amount of hot water, warm water, or cold water that remained for my bath. We had no showers. As usual, my palm sensed cold metal, except at the top six inches of the five-foot tank. There was barely enough warm water left for me, so Ed and Dick would have to wash in cold water. Under such circumstances, we often sponge-bathed in a small wall sink further supported by two cast-iron legs. As usual at age seven, I climbed a chair and sat on the edge of the sink with my feet in the bowl of warm water.

Soon, my entire body sensed the cool air as I finished washing. I noticed an interesting, blue-grayish dead light bulb to the left of the medicine cabinet. Puzzled by this phenomenon, I reached for the bulb. In a flash, my legs stiffened straight out, propelling me up and out of the sink to crash onto the floor with a thud.

At the time, I only remember Pop saying that it had been difficult to pick me up because I was spinning in a circle with feet and arms flailing wildly in the air. I had screamed in pain as Dad had separated my three little fingers melted together by the electricity coursing through my body after my hand had touched the interesting light bulb.

Water had dropped from my hand, down the bulb, into the socket. With my entire body wet and my feet deep in a bowl of water, I became a high-tension electric line.

The scars are now faint, but the experience is vividly etched in my mind. Electricity became my nemesis from then on.

Downspout

Boldly, but often carelessly, I risked accidental electrocution. My body has been tranquilized twice by indirect lightning strikes during two fierce thunderstorms five years apart. Surprisingly, I enjoy violent thunderstorms to this day, intrigued by their immense power and uncertain lightning bolts from clouds to earth or the indistinguishable charges from earth to clouds.

A storm's path and distance from a reference point can be determined by converting the seconds to miles between observing the flash of light and hearing the clap of thunder. I saw the flash of lightning and began counting seconds: one thousand one, one thousand two, one thousand three, and so forth. The storm was six miles away. But then a flash of light came simultaneously with the crack of thunder! Instantly, I was paralyzed, locked against the aluminum downspout gushing water collected from the metal barn roof. Carelessly, I had been leaning against the downspout under an extended overhang of the roof protecting me from rain and hail.

Fortunately, most of the current followed the water and discharged into the ground. I retain little memory of the incident at age thirteen except for the lethargy and nausea that tied me to my brooder coop for a week, too ashamed of my stupidity to admit what had happened. But was it stupidity, ignorance, or carelessness that had caused that electrifying experience? Little had I known that one could be severely injured while in close proximity to an area supercharged with electricity. One thing is certain: I learned the smell of lightning.

The Brown House (Catskill Mountains, at our Hobart Dairy Farm)

I counted, "One thousand one, one thousand two, one thousand three." The storm was moving fast in a southerly direction, safely twelve miles away. *Wrong.*

It was 4:30 p.m. The cows, anxious to be milked, strolled ahead of me toward the barn. Moderate rain was falling, but just to the north was a cloudless, sunny, blue sky. The herd ambled on as I stepped out of the rain under a sprawling maple tree. Obviously, the storm would pass to the south in less than five minutes, and the sky would clear overhead. *Wrong.*

From the very fringe of a dark cloud and blue sky came that now-familiar, simultaneous flash of light and clap of thunder. Once again, my body froze rigid as a steel I-beam, only to crumple to the ground, barely conscious. Absentmindedly, I had just stepped under the leafy canopy when lightning struck the tree and burned a twelve-inch-wide path of bark the full length of the trunk to the ground. My survival was pure luck, but my carelessness was twofold: One, never be under a tree during a thunderstorm. Two, I had forgotten to divide the seconds between the lighting and the thunder by five. Ten second means two miles away. In less than a second, at age twenty-nine, I could have been a fried Crane.

• • •

Several years later, back at the Hobart Farm tenant house, an appalling saga unfolded. A two-story, three-bedroom, clapboard tenant house named "the brown house" needed extensive repairs. I enjoyed upgrading and restoring old houses.

In fact, over our fifty-nine years of marriage, my sweetheart and I completely remodeled seventeen homes in our spare time. Extensive repairs often included roof rafters, floor joists, windows, partitions, kitchens, and bathrooms; complete electrical wiring, including breaker boxes and GFI (ground-fault interceptor) outlets; and replacing old plumbing, including septic systems and connections to the underground "saddle" provided by a municipal sewer authority. What a challenge and pleasure to personally jack up a house, install a new foundation, lower it down, and apply new siding. When the above had been completed, my head majorette, junior prom queen, high school sweetheart—my wife—and I would paint the house, inside and out. But years ago, some homes required wallpaper in certain rooms. I did not hang wallpaper; Alice did. Even today, I hate the thought of gluey, wet wallpaper wrapped around my neck or carelessly dropped on my head over my ears. Regardless, I strongly believe that couples who play together, work together, pray together stay together.

We entered the brown house, shocked by the blended, putrid stench within. Rotting garbage was strewn throughout the kitchen. Two thawed, decaying dogs were on the sofa. Urine and feces were everywhere. Upstairs, a mother dog and several puppies were decaying, their body fluids soaked into an oversized mattress. Unbelievable, perhaps, but there is a lot more to explain. Clothes were hanging in the closets. Dressers were orderly, filled with the family's personal items. We discovered a refrigerator filled with food, including leftovers. The upper kitchen cabinets contained a huge supply of groceries. The dogs had scavenged the food in the lower cabinets. Questions raced through our minds: *How could this happen? Why hadn't Dick or Betty checked with the tenant for delinquent rent payments?*

Regardless, we loaded the salvageable contents into our farm dump truck and placed a canvas over it. Strangely, it included all of the family's personal belongings, including clothing, furniture, jewelry, and family picture albums, among other things. The next day brought a clear, spring morning with a gentle breeze, providing perfect conditions for an open fire. It burned all day as we fed the fire with garbage, carpets, mattresses, cushions, and dead dogs. We salvaged the refrigerator, but the electric stove was badly damaged by the dogs having chewed caked-on food from the oven and burners. It had to be removed and junked.

After cleaning, disinfecting, and fumigating the house, it was time to make repairs. But first, the electric stove had to go. Alice held a flashlight while I disconnected the electricity by removing every cartridge fuse from the fuse box, including the main fuse supplying power from the meter to the house. I disconnected three wires delivering 220 volts of electricity to the appliance and a safety ground wire. I forced the cable to the basement through a hole in the floor. In the damp, dark basement, Alice directed a flashlight as I continued to remove the high-voltage cable.

Bob Vila was not around, but "this old house" sure was. The loose rock foundation enclosed a dirt-floor basement and supported twelve-inch-square, axe-hewn beams put in place by early settlers. The modern, high-voltage cable was secured with two-inch metal staples every three feet driven deep into the solid oak beams. Not a problem, just a challenge. The extra-long claws of my leather-handled framing hammer drove deep under the cable between the points of the large staples, and with great effort, I pried out the first one. With the second staple came a big surprise. With a fierce thud, the hammer claws once again dug deep under the cable, but this time I was blinded by a blue-whitish flash of light as the claws of my hammer instantly melted away. I received no shock. Apparently, the hammer claws had simultaneously pierced the live wires and the ground wires, causing the short to cross through the hammer claws but not down the handle into my body.

But why was there current in the wires? I had removed every fuse, including the main cartridge, disconnected all the wires from the stove, and fearlessly pushed the wires back through the hole in the floor.

The secret was revealed an hour later, after I regained my eyesight. Cautiously, I discovered that the tenant had connected the high-voltage cable to the incoming lead above the meter, thereby stealing electricity directly from the power company's pole lines. Regardless, at age forty, I should have known not to work with electrical wires before attaching a voltmeter and making certain the wires were dead.

Betty and Dick, my in-laws operating the Hobart Farm, had been unaware that the tenants were fugitives from welfare fraud and had deserted the premises six weeks earlier, leaving everything behind, including the dogs. The parents, having been arrested and jailed without notice, had caused the children to be placed in foster homes.

After proper notice of my intentions, sadly, as the truck body rose, the family's personal possessions slowly slid off the truck into oblivion at the dumpsite. The undamaged furniture is still in use at our B-Jack Farms residence, including a kitchen table, china cabinet, and an antique cuckoo clock.

Our Driveway

My old Ford tractor with an attached Sherman backhoe bounced wildly as it cleared the ramps of the transport trailer. A Sherman hoe is made of hardened steel and is as strong as the World War II tank it was named after.

Our Neshanic, New Jersey, very modern, contemporary home needed no repairs. In fact, with vertical redwood siding and triple-pane, vinyl-clad Andersen windows, the all-electric home was virtually main-tenance free. Still, a paved driveway would be easier to maintain and also increase the value of the property.

While I planned my work, it became obvious that the driveway was lower than the lawn on each side, requiring a nine-inch-high retention curb to prevent erosion onto the new pavement. The solution: dig a three-foot-deep trench and properly frame it to accept reinforced concrete to form a ten-inch-wide foundation around the driveway. Rough-cut Belgian blocks were to be set on top of the foundation and mortised together, creating an attractive perimeter of white rock against green grass, outlining the blacktop driveway.

The backhoe labored throughout the day into the early evening. Suddenly, the blinding light and odor of electricity gone wild flooded the area as the teeth on the bucket of my backhoe melted away. With great care and finesse, through the smoke, fire, and fierce sound of a giant, electric welding machine, I instinctively touched the swing lever, causing the edge of the damaged bucket to separate the huge main cables supplying electricity to our development. I am perpetually amazed how the mind produces so many thoughts in nanoseconds when the body encounters emergencies that induce adrenaline-charged reactions. *Will the fuel tank explode? Should I leap from the backhoe?* No. The tractor wheels and stabilizer legs on the backhoe were insulated with thick rubber. If I landed on supercharged ground or close to the electrified steel, surely I would be electrocuted.

It is common knowledge that underground utilities are to be relocated and marked before excavating in a developed area. However, no chargeable offense could be filed against me, because the location of the supply cables did not conform to the development's engineering plans. In fact, the cables illegally encroached on the wrong side of the street, approximately four feet into our property. Two days later, a Monday, the power company relocated the cables, installed a covered, ground-level transformer, and restored the power for our development. Clearly, I had been lucky at age seven, lucky at age thirteen, lucky at age twenty-nine, and lucky once again at age forty. But was I running out of luck?

The Little House

Yes, once again I was working on the renovated chicken house where Tammy was born.

The upgrade was for Ken Jr., age twenty-nine, and his five-year-old daughter, Jessica. We were replacing the thirty-five-year-old hot-air furnace with a new boiler and a two-zone baseboard hot water heating system. Always mindful of my father's teachings—"plan your work and work your plan"—we proceeded according to a plan quickly sketched out. The plan: cut the wooden baseboards in each room to allow an enameled metal housing to be secured flush against the wall, install a heating element in each housing, and then solder all the copper piping together to complete a loop for the water to travel from the boiler through the heating elements and return to the boiler for reheating.

Throughout the day, step by step, we measured and cut three-quarter-inch copper pipe, shined each end with steel wool or emery cloth, polished the inside of every fitting—Ls, 45s, couplings, unions, and Ts—and applied soldering paste to each joint. The loop was completed by using a propane-gas plumber's torch to melt lead solder into every joint, making it airtight. As a precaution, I pressurized the system by installing a tire valve and waiting twenty-four hours to verify the air pressure had remained constant at fifty pounds per square inch. If it was, electrical connections would be completed, the system filled with water, and the boiler could be fired up.

This old house had no basement. Years ago, as a chicken house, I had jacked it up, dug a trench, and then lowered it down onto a concrete foundation of two parts sand, three parts stone, and one part cement blended together in a small, electric barrel cement mixer. The crawl space, averaging twenty inches high, was dark, damp, and extremely cold, where water pipes often froze in the winter. To correct that problem, we would simply install a heating element under the kitchen floor in the crawl space. After gaining access to the crawl space through a trap door, we intended to solder a ten-foot heating element to the system.

Ken Jr. maneuvered deep into the crawl space and positioned himself to push the short length of copper pipe through the hole drilled in the floor, allowing it to be connected to the boiler and completing the water circulation loop.

He shoved the pipe through the hole and held it against the return hot water pipe of the boiler. I was on my stomach, reaching through the trap hole, my head against the heating element previously installed. Then it happened. The instant I touched the final length of pipe, I became unconscious. Moments later, I heard Ken anxiously asking, "Are you OK?" Smoke from my nose and the nauseating stench of burned hair and flesh caused me to dry heave from time to time throughout the day.

Electricity had coursed through my head, burned the hair in my nose, burned the left side of my mouth, jumped through tooth fillings, and seared the right side of my tongue. It had discharged through my hand holding the last length of pipe. But why did this happen? Surprisingly, Ken had felt no electric shock because the pipe was grounded by the boiler. But a properly installed baseboard hot water heating system cannot be electrified. This system was properly installed, yet it was electrified.

I secured a TV antenna wire to the bathtub drain and by elimination discovered the source of the problem. At some time in the past, electric wires had been improperly installed through the wall studs, baseboard high. While I attached the metal heating element housing to the wall, a screw pierced the wire supplying current to the bedroom receptacles, thereby electrifying the entire heating system. I had simply become a jumper cable for the current.

I fully recovered from the injuries, although some people teasingly claim that I show signs of permanent brain damage. At age sixty, I guess I was lucky again. And so I continue to sing: "Lucky, lucky, lucky me, I'm a lucky son of a gun. I work eight hours, I sleep eight hours—that leaves eight hours for fun."

V. Retrospective

The Problem with the World Is Electricity

My wife charged from our Neshanic home, frantically yelling, "June is on the phone! Hurry, I think she's going crazy."

I rushed through the house to the kitchen phone, only to hear a panic-stricken voice screaming, "The Russians have attacked New York City!" Slowly, I recognized my sister-in-law's voice. "People are stuck in elevators, stranded in subways, and all traffic is shut down."

"Calm down. Calm down. Damn it, June, *calm down*!"

Frantically she said, "I have the car packed with clothes, canned goods, and food from the freezer. We're leaving right now. You should come with us." I declined to retreat without good cause. Still frazzled, but not hysterical, in a trembling voice, she said, "We're not waiting. There's no time to spare! Half the United States is knocked out! No radio, no television, and no electricity! I'm not risking my children by waiting for more information, so we're leaving for the cabin."

Our hunting cabin was about six hours away, high in the Catskill Mountains of upstate New York. The Cold War was in full swing. President Kennedy had demanded that Khrushchev remove all long-range missiles from Cuba. Apprehension and fear caused homeowners to equip their basement bomb shelters for extended life underground. The general public believed we were inexorably close to an atomic war with Russia. I was no exception.

• • •

The 1965 Northeast blackout was not, as feared, caused by a Soviet attack, but by a transmission failure in Ontario, Canada, which spread to New York City 11 minutes later. The root cause was our insatiable appetite for electricity, which in the decades since has overloaded most of the systems throughout the world. On a hot summer's night in 1977, New Yorkers experienced an infamous "night of terror" provoked by a blackout. During 1994–1996, the Northeastern U. S. experienced cascading power failures, which were followed by major blackouts in 1998. Another failure on August 14, 2003 left 50 million people without power. Moscow was hit by a severe blackout described as "Doomsday" on May 25, 2005. The southern, southeastern, and southwestern districts, including the central district of the city, were left without electricity. Within minutes, the power failure spread into the suburbs and the Tula, Kaluga, and Ryazan regions, leaving a total of six million people in the dark.

The risk of massive blackouts around the world is greater now than ever. The newest source of apprehension, fear, and potential hysteria is the threat of terrorist attacks against nuclear power plants and the electricity exchange grid system.

• • •

All these blackouts of the past came to mind as I switched off the electricity at home and embarked on our annual, well-planned fishing trip in northern Canada. Once again, I was excited with the anticipation of seeing my old friend and guide, Joseph Gray Feather.

Joseph Gray Feather was a full-blooded Indian of the Ojibwa tribe, a branch of the huge Canadian Algonquin Indian Nation. This tribe of approximately 125 men, women, and children live in the wilderness on the fringes of a tremendous lake system about three hundred miles northeast of Montreal. It is quite different from the Finger Lakes region of the United States. This expansive body of water is filled with thousands of small islands that create a huge puzzle, but no pieces connect in a recognizable pattern. Many long, narrow bodies of water join an aquifer stretching nearly a hundred miles, with shorelines totaling more than six thousand miles. Tall, thin pine trees are propagated across the area so densely that only animals follow the island trails. Most of the area must be reached by boat or pontoon plane.

Our annual trip included ten days at a fishing camp on the reservation. These Indian lands span thousands of acres. However, this tribe lives in a tight group of small cabins along a sandy bank approximately thirty feet above the shore. The setting allows a prominent view of a relatively large body of water about one mile in each direction. A one-room school, play yard, and ball field are at the north end of the village. A winding dirt path connects the homes to a small, white church with a low steeple that houses their treasured church bell. This particular and unique place of worship exemplifies absolute stark simplicity. No colored glass or other religious symbolism can be noted except for a cross over the entrance.

As we leave camp early each morning, the treeless area fades into the distance, but the church remains a vision even beyond sight. This scene casts a spell of peace, tranquility, and silence enhanced, but not transcended, by the echoes of black, white-spotted loons sounding their mating calls. It reminds me of the movie *On Golden Pond*.

While visiting this area for so many years, I have come to know and appreciate this natural beauty, so seductive that it causes people to fantasize about leaving behind the city, the shopping malls, and their complex electric bills in search of a simpler way of life. Only the hardiest of fools would dare venture deep into this vast wilderness of water and islands without a local guide, however, usually an Indian from the village. Each year, I retraced my path and extended the limits to familiarize myself again and again with features that at first appear much the same, mile after mile. After I carefully considered every detail, such as the shape of individual pine trees or slight dips in each island's landscape, the look-alike trees and islands formed a recognizable mosaic that gave me more and more confidence to venture farther and farther into this wilderness.

Upon returning to camp at the end of each day, we anxiously awaited the appearance of the white church steeple in the dim light of the setting sun. That is the way it has been, decade after decade. Fifty years later, as I traveled the same routes with Joseph Gray Feather's son, who prefers to be called simply "Gray Feather," I wondered why he concluded, "The problem with the world is electricity." To appreciate his viewpoint, it is helpful to understand the word *empathy*.

• • •

Although we traveled in half circles for hours through a maze of small islands to reach a favorite fishing spot, we were less than a direct mile from camp. Often it was necessary to slowly travel many miles south to find a water passage that allowed a course north. Speed invited disaster because boulders and water-soaked logs lay just below the surface. The nights were cool, but to most other than the natives, it felt downright cold in late June. The heat from the morning sun began to penetrate and offer its soothing warmth to our bodies and souls. We paused in a sunny, windless cove to savor a cup of hot coffee and enjoy its particular aroma wafting in the cold air. Now in our comfort zone, hugging hot cups of coffee, we became acutely aware of the natural beauty of this vast wilderness.

The stark silence was interrupted intermittently by the chatter of a squirrel, the call of loons, and the chirping of unfamiliar birds in the pine trees. Alice, my wife since 1955, stretched high and in a prayerful way said, "This is like a sunrise service." We heard the faint "ding-dong, ding-dong" of the church bell. The call to service interrupted all other sounds. When it stopped ringing, everything returned to normal. "It *is* Sunday," exclaimed Alice. "Gray Feather, do you go to church on Sundays?"

"I go to church every day of my life," said Gray Feather. "This is my church right here. I am twenty-four and have decided to live the traditional Indian way of life. My girlfriend, now my wife, also believes we should live the way of our forefathers. I thank God every day for the things around us that keep me free as the eagle now circling high above us."

"That's beautiful, Gray Feather, but your forefathers had no opportunity to enjoy the benefits of electricity."

"What benefits of electricity? Electricity is a curse!" This provocative statement led to a discussion...

• • •

"That is exactly the problem. You consider the benefit, but I consider the curse."

"Gray Feather, please explain."

He continued: "Our wedding plans included a formal ceremonial dress of pure, white ermine fur, which comes from the forest around us. I trapped them, skinned them, and cured the hides with tannic acid from the woods. My mother wove white fur in the braids of my bride's long, dark hair. She was beautiful. I gathered many wild things, including everything for an Indian-style, white birch-bark suite. Our wedding was a traditional ceremony in the way of our people. We spent our honeymoon deep in the forest. We were very happy. Two weeks later, everyone cheered as we walked to our cabin twenty-five minutes east of the village."

"I know that cabin, Gray Feather. You built it about a year ago. But why live there?"

"I have given it great thought, but our decision was very easy. You know the village now has a diesel generator. It makes loud noise for twenty hours every day. It drives everybody crazy, even though it's way back in the woods outside the village."

"I agree the sound is annoying, but it's good they now have electricity."

"It is not good. That's why I moved out of the village."

"I don't understand. Please explain."

"Those who live in the village need a refrigerator like everybody else. They have lights and a television. Some people want a telephone. They need a pump to draw water from the lake for a flush-type toilet. My wife may want an electric toaster or electric can opener. Her brother wants a gas furnace, but the furnace also needs electricity. Some have cars, trucks, and snowmobiles. My friend even has an electric knife to cut moose meat!"

"But Gray Feather, to me all those things seem good!"

"They are not good. That's why we don't live in the village. If we live there, I would need lots of money to buy all those things. I would have to travel many miles to find work so I could buy all those things. I would be away from my wife and family because it's too far to travel each day. My wife and children would miss me, and I would miss them. Once you have electricity, your hands are tied behind your back for the rest of your life.

"On the west side of the village is a big dump. The bears used to come there every day to eat our garbage. When needed we would kill a bear and eat him. Now we have to keep everything covered with dirt so the bears don't come there anymore. Life in the village looks better, but it isn't. The light bulbs don't last, refrigerators wear out, televisions break, toasters stick, and the snowmobiles won't start, so they buy new ones. The old ones end up as junk in the dump. They need more money to replace those things and again go away from their wife or go to church and thank God for their situation, but they are not happy. It will be that way until they die. They are not happy. They get money from the government every month if they live on the reservation. Their Indian identification cards let them buy cheap things at the government store. Many have lost self-respect and stay drunk all the time. The young girls have babies before getting married. Our council has lost control over the Indian way of life. Things in the village have changed too much."

"Things have been changing from the beginning of time, but I think it's better if we adjust to those changes and recognize our quality of life is much better now than ever. We should be grateful for the benefits of those changes."

"Better for you, but not for me! My people are not happy. They have lost their pride and self-respect. They are going in circles like a dog chasing its tail. Everyone is searching. They do this, they do that, always trying to put more fun in their life. They buy toasters, refrigerators, televisions, and then argue because the toast is burnt, or someone took the last cold beer. They argue over what to watch on television when they should be planning tomorrow's hunt for moose and gathering food for the village. Things are too complicated."

"Yes, things are more complicated now, but you have a nice village here, and a school with a nice playground. You have a simple, but impressive church in a picture-perfect setting, which should be the center of religious teaching. It is through the church that people are reminded that happiness can only be found through the grace of God. Religion puts the cornerstones of life in the right place and enlarges our conscience. That conscience gives people courage and strength, and in most cases, forces them to do the right thing. They will say no to the temptations to get drunk, steal, or have a baby before marriage. Those who follow religious teachings will find that elusive goal called happiness, and it will be with them even after death. But it can happen only through the grace of God."

"But that is *your* God. That is *your* religion. We are asked to go to that church and believe all those stories in that book you call a Bible. We are asked to celebrate Christmas and Easter, because those are your holy days. We are asked to believe that a long time ago, a baby was born in a barn. I think the mother's name was Mary. We are told she never slept with a man. That doesn't make sense to me. I think there was teepee creeping going on."

"I know those stories must seem strange to you and somewhat unbelievable. God is a spirit within us. Those who believe in him have a personal guide who will mark the right choices, no matter how blind or confused they may be. He will brighten your life and show the way when you get lost while traveling life's foggy swamps."

. . .

No one spoke for some time, and our thoughts returned to the natural setting and tranquil sounds of the wilderness. We drifted toward a small island with smooth, flat rocks on one end, where we could safely cook our shore lunch on an open fire. Gray Feather gingerly stepped ashore to secure the bowline around a stump. His confident sure-footedness gave proof of his being completely in tune with his way of life. Regardless, we were quite surprised when he slowly turned and squarely faced us. He stepped forward, put his right foot on the bow to steady the boat, and signaled us not to move. It was obvious he was deep in thought when he raised his fully extended left arm, as if to take an oath, spread the fingers on his giant right hand, and slowly placed it on his chest. We were momentarily transfixed by this perfect scene in front of us. I thought of politicians who reached for the crowd with one hand and placed the other over their hearts in an attempt to add credence to a profound statement that otherwise would be highly suspect. I felt a rush of shame for such a thought while facing this honest, decent man. He just stood there with no revealing expression.

"Gray Feather, are you OK?" I asked.

He replied, "Your God stays in his house, then asks people to come there and learn about *him*. That's good for some, but not for me! I want to stay a traditional Ojibwa Indian. My church is right here! My God is in the forest, in the lake, and on the mountains when the rain comes! *The problem with the world is electricity!*"

Lead Us Not into Temptation

"Lead us not into temptation." Yes, five intriguing words, but why do so many people, young or old, fail to heed the stop signs clearly visible along life's highways? Is our view ahead so fogged by greed, ignorance, or hedonism that it urges us to blow past signs reading "Warning: Danger Ahead"?

It is a curious characteristic we all possess. But ultimately, it is simply a matter of choices.

Please join us as we explore a desolate, oceanfront area in Marathon, Florida. It is a hike through a swamp choked with mangrove trees and roots up to the high-tide water's edge.

As we approached the mangrove swamp, I explained: "In fact, parts of the Florida Keys, from Key Largo to Key West, remain as dense today as when bloodthirsty pirates and buccaneers ruthlessly ruled these islands. Spanish treasure ships, wrecked and sunk by storms many years ago, lie buried just off shore. Mel Fisher, a professional treasure hunter, recently discovered the Spanish galleon *Atocha* and its scattered load of gold and silver, currently valued over millions of dollars. A violent storm wrecked the treasure ship on a reef near Key West in the year 1622."

But what would you do with such a find, or any other find—such as two thousand dollars in small bills in a purse near your car in a Shop-Rite parking lot, or a paper bag containing a pair of socks and two hundred dollars, or a container with no socks but containing a thousand or five thousand? And so on.

The history lesson was interrupted by Jessica, our twelve-year-old granddaughter. "Hey, Poppy, where are you taking us? It's like a jungle in here. I can't climb over all of these roots."

"Yes, you can!" encouraged her father, Ken Jr., age thirty-five.

I suggested that everyone follow closely behind me. "Do as I do and grab onto a branch before you step from root to root of the mangrove trees. Otherwise, you might be seriously injured by falling through the elevated maze of roots, tangled as if weaved together by an intoxicated monster."

We eased down two feet from the web of roots onto the sandy beach and discussed the array of interesting artifacts we had passed over on the way here. There were no keepers, just junk: plastic bags, party balloons, beer cans, and wine bottles—a collage of interesting but worthless dump-truck junk.

I further instructed, "OK, let's ease along the narrow beach and search for artifacts trapped within the web of mangrove roots at the water's edge. Make sure you examine everything of interest, especially debris deposited among the roots by the high tides, strong storms, and waterspouts. I have found lots of good stuff in such places: fishing lures, tackle boxes, boat cushions, and glass bottles that have crossed the ocean with messages sealed inside. Last week, I found a new chainsaw in the mangroves bordering Vaca Cut, four miles from here."

Minutes later, just ahead, Ken Jr. blurted out, "Hey, Dad, take a look at this!" There on the ground, barely inside the root system, lodged an item wrapped in black plastic and secured with gray duct tape. On the tape appeared mysterious codes and numbers apparently inscribed with indelible ink through a stencil.

"Don't touch it, Ken," I warned. "Use a stick to flip it over. There's no telling what's inside. It's unlikely anyone will find this, so let's get the hell out of here while we can."

On the way back to the car, I cautioned everyone not to disturb any unidentifiable item on or around the islands. I cautioned, "Last year, a man found a strange-looking clump of sargasso weed tangled on a heavy object encrusted with barnacles. The object had collected weed from the Sargasso Sea and traveled across the ocean to Marathon, hundreds of miles away. While the man was removing the sargasso and chipping away the barnacles, the object exploded, killing him instantly. He failed to recognize that it was a live World War II floating mine designed to sink ships."

Now at the Florida Highway Patrol station, a gruff, condescending police officer quipped, "Yes? What is your problem?" Perhaps the metal screen she spoke through caused her voice to sound harsh and raspy. I briefly resisted the temptation to retaliate in kind, but chose to respond politely. "I don't have a problem, but I want you to know that I believe we have found a large brick of cocaine."

Again in a terse voice and demeanor that defines public servants who treat people as pains in the ass, she demanded, "How do you know it's cocaine?"

By not making eye contact or giving a modicum of attention, she instigated my inclination to deliver a quick retort: "Look, lady, I don't know if it's cocaine, but I do know that if something acts like a duck, looks like a duck, and quacks like a duck, you can be fairly certain it's a damn duck."

Now she looked up. "OK, OK," she replied, "bring it on in."

"Lady, you can't be serious. Should I tell you another duck story?"

Arrogantly, she quipped, "Spare yourself the trouble. Where is the stuff? I'll send an officer there to investigate."

"It's deep in the mangrove swamp, four hundred yards behind the high school. I'll have to show them the location."

A big, burly officer and his average-looking sidekick followed closely behind with flashing lights on the police car. In the car on our way to the swamp, still agitated by the desk officer's attitude, I repeated the duck story but had a second duck story suppressed in my mind. *Yeah, lady, suppose I put that stuff in my car. Minutes later, as I get on Route 1, our car is rear-ended by a drunk driver. Then, in response to the investigating officer's questions, I explain, "We found the stuff in the bushes, and we're on our way to your highway patrol station to turn it in to the police." Now, folks, what do you suppose the officer would do?*

I parked the car as before, and the police car followed alongside. A good-cop, bad-cop relationship seemed to develop between the officers, a familiar ploy investigators use during interrogations. The situation deteriorated.

Bad cop: "OK, where's the stuff?"

"It's in the mangrove roots, about a thirty-five-minute hike on the other side of the swamp."

Good cop: "I hope you're not serious. Is there an easier way in from here?"

"I doubt it. As you know, it's a serious offense to disturb, molest, or destroy mangroves for any reason, including trimming access paths to the shoreline."

Following protocol, the bad cop questioned, "What were you doing out here? Why did you take your family through this tidal swamp? Any of you could have been accidentally trapped here to face an incoming tide. Also, many of these tidal swamps are infested with mosquitoes, no-see-ums, and dangerous snakes."

"It's no puzzle. I explore. You know, seek adventure."

We had been walking for some time. To everyone's relief, I exclaimed, "Yes! Here it is!"

The bad cop sliced a small opening in the package, and with a dab on his fingertip, tasted the contents. Through curled lips and clenched teeth, he declared, "Wow! That's the good stuff! " Once again, we searched up and down the shoreline while he continued demanding, "Did you find any more?" Periodically, they moved away from us and whispered to each other privately.

Their conduct aroused my suspicion, prompting me to ask, "How much is this stuff worth?"

The bad cop replied, "More money than you can imagine."

Finally, the good cop said, "Thank you for reporting this to the police. You may have saved the life of a high school student. You can leave now, but for safety, I will follow you back to your vehicle. Besides, I need a roll of film from the car so we can document the evidence."

"OK, but let's hurry. I want to check the *Marathon Lady* at four thirty and see the catch of the day. But first, take down my name, address, and telephone number for future reference."

"That won't be necessary, Mr. Crane. Besides, I lost my pen while climbing over these mangrove roots."

As the good cop lagged behind us, I revealed my suspicions to the others with me. "Those two cops are up to no good. They're going to deal that stuff."

Jessica insisted, "No way! They're police officers."

Ken injected, "I think you're right, Dad."

Alice sternly warned, "Leave it alone. You'll get us in a lot of trouble for nothing."

"No way," I snapped. "Trouble or no trouble, I'm not going to let a couple of dirty cops get away with it."

I retrieved a pen from our car as the good cop popped open the trunk of his police car, and while he talked on the radio, I quickly wrote my name, date, and time of day on a label inside his trunk.

We joined the crowd admiring the *Marathon Lady*'s catch of the day as the sheriff strolled by. "Hi, Sheriff!" Jokingly, I quipped, "It seems you guys are never around at the right time."

Alice nervously paced back and forth, warning, "Let's not get involved!" as I described the episode of that afternoon.

Instantly, the sheriff exploded in anger. "That unit is responsible for incidences along Route 1, nothing more. Why didn't they refer the matter to our dispatcher?"

"Sheriff, I asked them to do just that, but they insisted on handling the whole matter without further involvement."

"Well, there's going to be more involvement. That highway patrol unit is not supposed to do police work in our jurisdiction without notifying us. They have not followed an acceptable investigation protocol. Will you sign a police report detailing everything from start to finish?"

"Yes, of course!" I replied.

"I mean everything," demanded the sheriff, "including a description of the officers and a list of their statements, not having film for the camera with them, or a pen or pencil to fill out a police report for you to sign. That cocaine will never reach the evidence 'property room' without my intervention."

I naively signed the police report, but troubled thoughts formed in my mind as Alice chided, "What about Jessica and us? These islands are plagued with illegal aliens, bridge bums, and illegal drug dealers posing as fishermen, tour guides, or police officers. We are witnesses in this case and may be forced to testify in court against dangerous criminals."

Cautiously, the sheriff added, "Your wife is correct, but since you signed a police report, actually your risk of danger has been minimized." He continued: "The codes on the duct tape wrapped around the package reveal it is part of a large shipment of cocaine. In such cases, a full investigation is launched in cooperation with other law enforcement agencies, including the DEA's interdiction unit. Helicopters will scan the shallow reefs for underwater caches of cocaine bricks temporarily stored there waiting to be retrieved by drug dealers. It is then processed into narcotics such as amphetamines or crack cocaine. Since you disclosed the find to the authorities, criminal elements will not threaten any of you for information to secure the rest of their shipment."

Locals and out-of-staters expressed extremely different opinions regarding our chosen action. Their opinions ranged from "you did the right thing" to "few people here are that stupid."

A retired pharmacist from Michigan expressed his opinion as we did a walk-through of his house listed for sale. "Mr. Crane, you apparently found a large brick of pure, uncut cocaine paste. In its present form, you surrendered seven hundred and fifty thousand to a million dollars cash, no questions asked. Nobody in his right mind walks away from that kind of easy money. In fact, I would trade you my boat and this exclusive, all-furnished waterfront home for a package like that. Exactly where did you find it? The area should be searched at least once a day for a month. There is a good probability more bricks will be washed ashore by the incoming tides." He glorified the possibility of me owning his landscaped, manicured grounds, its beautiful home, and the new boat tied to his backyard private dock, all free of encumbrances. "This piece of heaven in paradise can be yours if you inform me of the location of similar packages instead of the police."

We cordially shook hands and said good-bye without further comment, but clearly he was mystified by my unexplained, efficacious choice not to capture the million dollars.

Back home, our precious granddaughter, Jessica, age twelve, listened intently as I offered the causes and effects of other temptations we had endured.

Mrs. Pearson, my Sunday school teacher, had predicted I would become a "man of the cloth" when I confidently recited the names of the books of the King James Bible. Even so, she never failed to soundly scold me for trivial wrongdoings.

At age six, I was a precocious "Dennis the Menace"-type boy, filled with insatiable urges to tease, torment, and play practical jokes on all living creatures. But Mrs. Pearson sealed her fate years ago by demanding that the New Jersey State Police arrest me if I ever again crossed her potholed driveway with our John Deere tractor. But that incident had jaded my respect for Sunday school, for church, and especially for Mrs. Pearson. But to this day, I realize her Biblical teachings unknowingly had profoundly influenced my entire life.

"So, Jess, tell me...what is the big deal about temptations? What is the seductive power of temptations that lure people into terrible predicaments? For a moment, put yourself in the shoes of the finder or the keeper, and consider the following authentic experiences:

"A few years ago, your Aunt Carolyn, Nanny's sister, rushed into our living room, excitedly exclaiming, 'You won't believe what happened! I stopped at the bank and picked up two thousand dollars, and then I bought a few groceries. When I got home, I realized I had left my purse in a shopping cart in the Hudson Shop-Rite parking lot. I raced back to the store, but my purse was gone. A Good Samaritan had turned it in to the store manager, cash included, but asked to remain anonymous.'

"Years earlier, Nanny and I checked into an Orlando, Florida motel. It was eleven p.m. when we discovered our vacation money was missing. The next morning at four, we attempted the nearly impossible return trip to a remote, desolate trailer park fifty-five miles southwest of Orlando. We retraced our journey street by street to a main highway and followed a series of paved roads through the countryside. Soon, dust and sand billowed behind as we wove our way along a maze of dirt roads through miles and miles of look-alike citrus groves. Throughout the cold, black morning, instinct alone was our guide. Futile effort was our challenge. Miraculously, our headlights reflected a small, side-road sign. Excitedly, Nanny blurted out, 'That's it, turn left! I remember the sign! Dead End— Fish Camp Four Miles.'

"The camp was silent except for a barking dog here and there. A horseshoe of poorly maintained trailer homes evidenced a pocket of destitute humans whose entertainment was fishing and drinking beer or 'white lighting' at the small, lakeside bar. We parked at the side of the building in front of the phone booth as early dawn stirred life in this desolate place. It was six a.m. Nervously, I was reminded of the movie *Deliverance*.

"I followed three haggard, old men into the bar when it opened at nine a.m. The bartender immediately asked, 'Are you here for something?' I thought, of course, that she must know our purpose here was to recover Alice's change purse containing seven hundred-dollar bills left in the outside phone booth around nine the night before. She continued: 'The owner has something for you, but she won't be available until about noon. A customer gave it to her this morning at closing time. She lives in the last trailer as you continue around the loop.'

"Three hours later, after a brief discussion, the owner handed Nanny the change purse. She refused to accept a hundred-dollar reward for the

Good Samaritan or herself, saying, 'No one here wants any extra money, but thank you just the same.'

"So, you see, Jess, it is simply a matter of choosing between good and bad, a matter of saying yes or no to a temptation. But remember, there is no such a thing as being 'a little bit pregnant.'"

The Power of Prayer vs. "Up Yours, Nurse Ratched!"

I heard the chatter of faulty wheels on a shopping cart. Bright lights, then dim, flashed overhead. Could I be traveling through the Holland Tunnel from New Jersey to New York City? Suddenly, I heard my wife's voice as she stepped from the going-up elevator: "That's my husband! Where are you taking him?"

The aides pushed my gurney into the going-down elevator and said, "Sorry, lady, no time to explain. We're on our way to the OR."

I felt no pain. My mind seemed clear. I was calm and completely relaxed, but puzzled.

• • •

A chilled glass of orange juice is a great way to start each morning just before daybreak. A slight headache, extremely rare for me, prompted me to pop two aspirins with the juice. Seconds later, stretched out on the kitchen floor, unable to breathe, I tried to relax. I knocked the cordless phone from its cradle and pressed the lighted 9-1-1 buttons. A voice said, "What is your emergency?"

Mind racing and unable to speak, I struggled to comprehend my plight. Could it be a heart attack? No, I had no pain; my pulse was normal, no cold sweat. I wondered if the orange juice had caused an esophageal spasm, forcing my epiglottis to block the air passages. Many years ago, a careless gulp of cough syrup had caused such a problem.

"Stay with me; stay with me," the voice chided. I could not speak and decided not to waste air by talking. Consequently, I held the phone close to my mouth so she could hear my vain attempt to suck in air. "Relax, relax! Help is on its way; you must relax!"

I wanted to say, "Lady, what the hell do you think I'm doing? I haven't fallen, pain level is zero, and I am completely comfortable except for a lack of breath." She had no way of knowing that biofeedback lessons had given me the ability to reduce my resting breathing rate from twelve to four breaths per minute. Fortunately, after drinking the large glass of juice, I had completely filled my lungs with fresh air by vigorously exhaling and inhaling twice in succession.

"Don't leave me; don't leave me!" she exclaimed. "They're almost there."Humoroulsy, my mind registered, *I'm on the floor and I can't breathe, so how the hell can I leave you?* I glanced at the wall clock and realized that time was running out for me. But now, by giving up fractions of precious air, I was able to secure minimum whiffs of air at the extremely high end of the breathing range. It is an unusual experience, and everyone should try this exercise: inhale to full capacity and hold as long as possible. When the urge to explosively exhale becomes overwhelming, breathe very slight whiffs of air while your lungs remain at nearly full capacity. I am certain this exercise prolonged my life.

• • •

It was now 5:30 a.m., and I had been on the floor about half an hour. Suddenly, normal breathing and speech returned, but I was completely exhausted. My first words: "What's happening?"

"They are there. They're in the driveway. Can you see the ambulance lights?"

"Nooo."

"The ambulance is at 274," the dispatcher said. "What is your address?"

Caller ID for 911 calls is standard for the system; however, unless corrective action is taken, it identifies the caller based on the billing address rather than the residence. Our failure to correct this problem had caused the ambulance to be dispatched to a mailing address nearly three-quarters of a mile from our home.

"Stay with me, stay with me!" insisted the dispatcher. "Help is on the way." Her anxious voice caused me concern but did not distract me from the effort to inhale slight bits of air in a short, relaxed rhythm. Slowly I began breathing comfortably.

"I'm at 375," I replied. "Go west about a mile, to the third house on your left. It's a big, two-story red brick house with a blacktop driveway. Drive to the rear, and a sensor light will come on."

"Stay with me! Can you hear them? Is the kitchen door locked?"

"Yes."

"Can you unlock it?"

Still prone, I inched myself around a counter cabinet, then ten feet to a double sliding glass door. "I'll try, but I'm really tired. OK, it's unlocked, but nobody is here."

"Are you breathing better?"

"Yes, a lot better."

"Well, you sound a lot better. Is the door unlocked?"

"Yes, but where are they? I called an hour ago."

"It's been thirty minutes, and they should be there any second."

"OK; they're here."

The EMS team expertly began the customary initial procedures of administering oxygen; the recording of vitals such as temperature, pulse, and blood pressure; and the start of IV solutions. While the young man busied himself with predetermined tasks, a young woman gingerly sat down on her feet and legs and gently placed my head on her lap. She grasped my wrist, stretched my right arm against her right shoulder, and held it in place with her chin while she inserted an IV port in a bulging artery of my arm. I was about to protest that the episode was over and that I felt OK. The only problem was that I was totally exhausted! My clear, unconcerned mind compelled me to let them do their job their way.

I could feel the usual burning sting as she forced the IV needle through the sensitive epidermis into the artery. She quickly loosened the restrictive band to again allow the normal flow of blood and IV solution. I could feel the release of tension as she completely relaxed with my head on her lap.

I'm a happy person with a strong sense of humor. Consequently, I enjoy engaging others with a provocative statement. My intention is to spark an unusual dialogue with an individual rather than tolerate impersonal, puppet responses such as "Have a nice day" or "Love ya!" My favorite, the late Will Rogers, prompted the right responses. For example, "I never met a person I didn't like; I just like some better than others," or "There's no such thing as a bad day; it's just that some are better than others."

When asked, "How are you?" my response is, "I'm so damn good I can't stand myself." (Some people can't stand me either, probably because I'm so modest, but I'm working on that.)

Most people smile, chuckle, or laugh and comment, "It's nice to hear a lighthearted, positive remark now and then." Occasionally, some just turn away without comment. Others have said, "Right, I think I'll puke!"

I found myself in a comfort zone with this wonderful, relaxed person soothing me. She adjusted the needle in my arm and I quipped, "Do you get paid by the hour for all of this, or are you paid by the number of people you stick it to?"

Smiling and chuckling, she calmly said, "We're rewarded in many different ways."

Suddenly, without warning, I tried to roll over. Painfully, the needle pulled sideways, causing blood and fluids to randomly splatter in all directions. Instantly, she tightened her hold on me. Still in the same position, this stout, gentle country girl stopped my roll and forced my head back to her lap. In nanoseconds, the orange juice and aspirin consumed earlier erupted from my stomach like the blow-off of a humpback whale. She held tight while this uncontrollable, peristaltic action spewed the acid-laden vomit all over her uniform and her lap.

I could not muster any humor. I begged for her forgiveness. "I'm so sorry; I don't believe this. So sorry."

"It's OK; don't worry about it. What are you feeling?"

"I feel fine, except for the puke on my face, in my hair, and all over you."

"It's OK; don't worry about that. We'll clean up all of this, but what about you?"

I insisted once again, "I'm fine; the episode is over."

"That's good," the young man said, "but we would like to take you to the hospital for a checkup."

I agreed, but I asked the uniformed officer, "Go upstairs, turn left, and wake my wife, who is sleeping in the first bedroom on the right. Please be gentle so you don't scare the hell out of her."

The organized chaos of this scene forced the sleeping beauty wide awake before dawn. "Honey, what is going on?"

"Don't start in; everything is fine. I've decided to go to the hospital for my annual checkup."

"Can I come with you?"

"No, that's not necessary. Just get dressed, have breakfast, and then I'll see you later. Stop worrying; everything is OK."

• • •

Several hours later, I awoke from a deep sleep while being examined by a physician. "How are you feeling?"

"I feel great, but I'm hungry."

"We can take care of that a little later, but first I want to ask you some questions." His examination revealed that I was in excellent health and had no recognizable serious, negative issues. He concluded, "I believe you have experienced a severe episode of vertigo, which can be controlled with proper medication. You can be released this morning, but I prefer someone fill the prescription before you go home." We shook hands, and he left.

I recall sitting up in bed checking the breakfast slip, when suddenly a ball-peen hammer hit the left side of my head just below and to the right of my ear. I toppled forward onto the bed but felt no pain. I could not distinguish up from down, but by keeping my eyes closed, I felt again that everything seemed normal. I blindly searched for the emergency button's cord alongside the bed rail. Each time I opened my eyes, I became disoriented, and everything appeared upside down and in the wrong place.

I humored myself with the thought of the shoulder operation I'd had a few years earlier to repair my rotator cuff. The staff had laughed to discover I had circled the area and marked it "Cut inside the dotted lines," but the surgeon had been upset. Today I thought of the joke: "Doctor, help me! Every time I raise my arm like this, I have excruciating pain!" The doctor says, "Then don't raise your arm like that!"

The thought convinced me not to open my eyes. Finally, I felt the icy-cold control settled in my palm. The call button was recessed in the casing. Unable to recognize the recessed button, I squeezed the entire control in my hand.

A voice came over the speaker. "Yes, can I help you?"

"I hope so. I believe I have just had a major stroke."

● ● ●

Specialists came and went in quick succession. Soon, I was speeded to Stratton Medical Center in Albany, New York, an hour away. It is a teaching hospital with a specialized stroke unit. Lights continued to shine, then dim, as I was rushed through the hallways, right, right, left, right, then into the operating room.

I fully realized my precarious situation, but failed to pray or ask for God's protection. I felt gentle, unemotional, and at peace, but I remained perplexed by my state of mind at that critical time.

Suddenly, a soft, female voice said, "Please start with ten and count backward." I thought of Doris Day singing "Que sera, sera. Whatever will be, will be. The future's not mine to see"—et cetera.

I became very tired and realized that sleep was just a few numbers away. Once again I heard soft, sweet voices in the distance. As they moved closer, I peeked to see if these people were upside down. I was elated to discover they were not; I had regained my equilibrium. I realized I was waking from one of those short, refreshing power naps that often create a ghostly realm of aberrations during the REM phase of deep sleep.

The peaceful atmosphere was abruptly interrupted by a harsh but polite voice. Now wide-awake with proper vision and a clear mind, I chuckled and then laughed at the scene around me. The voice did not match the person saying, "Mr. Crane, how are you feeling?"

My deep sense of humor inspired the following dialogue:

"I feel fine, so untie me."

"No, we can't do that."

"Where do you get that 'we' stuff? I'm asking *you* to untie me!"

"I can't do that."

"You can't, or you *won't*?"

"Have it your way. I won't."

During this exchange, I was able to manipulate my left arm and wrist to untie my right arm. With lightning speed, a huge black man pounced directly on top of me. Instinctively, I fought back. He yelled, "This guy is strong as an ox! Help me!" The ugly nurse with the harsh voice grabbed my outstretched left arm. Others came at me like killer bees signaled by pheromones to attack. I was now being hog-tied like a steer ready for branding.

As the ugly nurse tried to bend my arm toward the tie-down, I said, "Before you tie me again, please let me pull back on the throttle."

"The throttle?"

"Yes. I can't hear you over the noise."

"Do you know where you are?"

"Of course I do. I'm trying to slow my Bobcat so I can hear your lovely voice."

"You ride bobcats? I suppose you also ride wild lions and polar bears?"

"Oh, you're very funny. Any idiot can see this Bobcat is a modern skid loader with a four-cylinder gas engine, but obviously you can't handle an intelligent situation, so you have your goons tie me down."

She did not respond, but her lockstep demeanor was arrogant and condescending, just the kind of challenge I enjoy. I quipped, "You're probably one of those women's libbers, but no, it's obvious with those two fried eggs you couldn't participate in any bra-burning demonstrations. Are you married?"

"That's none of your business."

Silently, I was overjoyed at my success. I had pushed the right buttons that had exposed her true character. Annoyed, I said, "Don't be so serious; I'm only teasing," but she would not accept my apology. Instead, she renewed her attack, which caused me to respond accordingly. "I know… you're divorced, probably one of those women who received a free ticket on the gravy train by getting married. The guy works hard, brings home the money so you can have a free joyride through life. When the trip gets boring, you simply cash in the ticket for alimony and get back on the gravy train with a new ticket from another loving, unsuspecting, hardworking, innocent man."

"That's ridiculous!"

"Of course it is. I'm only teasing, and don't believe a word of it. Now untie me and let's be friends."

"I told you, no. You might hurt yourself if I untie you."

"Why would I hurt myself? I feel fine. I have a good wife, a good family, and lots of money in the bank. So please untie me!"

"For the last time, the answer is no. I don't trust you."

"You don't trust me? God does, but then, God loves men more than women; that's why there were no women at the Last Supper. He kept them in the kitchen where they belong. God doesn't trust you, and I don't trust you apple-eaters, either."

My last comment really got to her. She looked at me and snarled, "I don't have to take any more of this!" And she began to walk away.

A strong urge to have the last word compelled me to say, "Wait!" I raised my tethered forearm, curled my wrist, and exposed the middle finger on my right hand. "You don't want to take any more of that? Well, then, take *this*: up yours, Nurse Ratched!"

• • •

I felt happy with my victory over this ignorant stranger who had decided to engage in battle over such ridiculous comments. Now alone, I wondered, *Why did she do this? Why did she have her goons tie me down?*

I like people, even those who are too serious and express a shallow sense of humor. Still, I felt deeply saddened that Nurse Ratched hadn't realized I was only joking throughout the verbal exchange and never accepted my apologies.

Suddenly, a loud, foreign voice exclaimed, "That was great; she needed that. You really put her in her place." He swung my gurney around and excitedly critiqued the whole incident. "What you said to her was really great. You would do very well in my country. Men in *this* country are afraid of women; they think it's OK for a woman to tell a man what to do. Men do the food shopping and woman's work in the home. The women are allowed in the same room while men are discussing business or politics. In *my* country, women keep their mouth shut about such things and do not wear pants like men. They keep their faces covered and do what they are told by the men. In my country, men are in complete control of the women. You would do very well in my country." I believe he was from the Middle East.

I listened in silence as he wheeled me from the OR to the ICU while continuing to ridicule American manhood. My satisfaction, glory, and pleasure evaporated as I became overburdened with shame and regret over my earlier conduct.

• • •

I was placed in the second position of a semicircle of approximately eight beds separated by half-drawn curtains. The nurses' stations seemed to be at the foot of each bed. Caregivers, doctors, nurses, and aides were darting here and there as they rushed to deal with an alarm, warning light, or a patient begging for relief. I fully realized now that my condition was not critical, and I suggested that any special attention be given to those who needed help more than me. A line from a Shakespeare play flashed before me: "All the world's a stage, and all the men and women merely players."

The night passed ever so slowly. Each time I sparingly entered the realm of sleep, an aide rushed in and asked, "Are you OK? How are you feeling? What is your name? What day is it?"

"I'm very tired and frustrated, so I prefer you leave me alone."

The response was consistent: "I'm sorry; we can't do that."

• • •

At last, morning arrived. Early morning is my favorite time of day. I always feel great in the morning, and I'm anxious to get involved so that as night approaches, I will be satisfied that nothing has been wasted. As the cliché explains, "Remember, this is the first day of the rest of your life."

Alice and her younger sister, Carolyn, entered my area. Carolyn stiffened with anguish at the sight of me. Her scared look gave me the impression that they knew much more about my condition than I. To lighten the scene, once more my humor kicked in. I said, "I'm OK! Stop worrying; we can still have sex." Carolyn laughed and delivered her usual response. "Why, you damned fool!"

Alice looked very worried but maintained her self-control. "Everything is a joke to you, but it has been a nightmare for us."

"Well, it doesn't have to be that way. We've had many discussions about the idea of self-flagellation and people who beat up on themselves. So stop worrying."

Clearly annoyed, she gently touched my hand and said, "I don't think you understand. Before dawn, a uniformed stranger came into our bedroom. I rushed downstairs to a scene with you on the floor hooked up to bottles and wires, blood splatters on the wall, and vomit all over the girl. I was not allowed to go with you as they hurried you into the ambulance and left for the hospital without me. I was later told you were OK and that it was just an inner ear problem called 'vertigo.' The next day, Carolyn frantically rushed into the beauty parlor and said, 'Ken has just had a bad stroke. They're taking him to a specialist in Albany.' Everything was now happening lightning fast. Ken Jr., Judy and I raced north on the New York Thruway at high speed, following the ambulance around Albany through heavy traffic to the hospital. Finally, we caught up to you and spent all day at the hospital. I wanted to be at your side for the night but you would have no part of it. We received a phone call at five the next morning 'Urgent! Bring my estate files to me as soon as possible.' Ken Jr., Judy and I rushed to the hospital and as we stepped off the elevator just in time to see you with your eyes closed on your way for surgery. The operation took more than five and a half hours. All brain surgery is very dangerous. Now we are here. A path has been shaved through your hair from your neck to your forehead. Your scalp is stitched, covered with bandages, and tubes are sticking out of the front of your skull."

With tears flowing, she explained, "They said you had a huge blockage that was removed through the back of your head. The surgeon explained that he removed a massive cerebellar infarction and the damaged tissue killed by the impaired flow of blood." She gently held my arm down as I responded to a twinge of pain on my neck and halfway up the back of my head. "Don't touch it!" she exclaimed. "If you bump those tubes, you may severely hurt yourself." Tortured by her concern for me, she asked, "Do you still think there's something funny about all of this?"

"Not exactly. I should be more considerate of the feelings of others when faced with extreme situations. I should remember you're much more sensitive than me. Do you remember years ago, how different passengers reacted when Flight 851 from New York to Puerto Rico caught on fire and we made an emergency landing? Shortly after takeoff, about a thousand feet in the air, suddenly the cabin filled with putrid smoke. If you recall, the stewardess tossed pillows and blankets from the overhead bins to the passengers as she moved to the rear of the plane. About halfway down, where we were sitting, she suddenly turned around, ran forward to her safety seat, and strapped herself in. The plane turned to make a loop for an emergency landing. You might recall as the plane banked left, we could see fire engines, rescue squads, and the entire emergency equipment racing to their assigned positions along the runway. The captain made no announcement except, 'Fasten your seat belts; we are returning to Newark Airport.' People were praying aloud. Tourists were totally hysterical with fear. The two college girls alongside us were joking while observing the rescue equipment and said, 'Oh, look...we're going to get a tow job.' The man in front of us grabbed the top of his head with both hands and literally pulled out two clumps of hair while screaming, 'I don't want to die! I don't want to die!' You were softly weeping but maintained self-control while saying, 'What about the children? What about the children?' Do you remember? I gave you a quick shot in the ribs with my elbow and said, 'We have no control here, so get ahold of yourself.' We landed safely, nobody was injured, and we scheduled the same flight for the following day—we hopped on a different airplane."

I continued: "The point is, different people may react differently to the same situation. That does not make one better or worse than the other. It doesn't make someone a hero, a tough guy, or a coward; it just means that they're different. But you already know how I am. Death is no big deal to me, because it's in the natural order of things; it is the consequence of living. Regardless, I'll try to be more considerate of your feelings."

I remembered another story that demonstrated my point. "You remember the fish fry we attended last year in the Florida Keys? Nearly fifty-five people were having a great time. Good food, lots of beer, and wine were provided in a large room beside a screened-in swimming pool. A soothing, warm breeze caressed palm fronds that shaded the pool area from the hot afternoon sun. Tom jumped into the swimming pool with Louise, Pat, and Sharon. The three women were bobbing around in the water, wearing flowered tropical bathing suits. Tom exclaimed, 'Isn't this great? It's like being in a beautiful flower garden.' My humor prompted a quick retort. 'You're right, Tom, three beautiful flowers and one wilting pansy.' Everyone clapped and laughed except Tom, who said, 'I owe you one, Ken.'"

"I remember that," said Alice.

"Well, then, do you also remember an hour later when everyone was laughing, joking, and having a good time? Tom tapped a heavy, glass pitcher with a spoon and said, 'Can I have your attention? Attention please! Would someone like to give thanks?' The party was casual and jovial, so I stood up and responded, 'Here's to Eve, mother of our race; she wore a fig leaf in the proper place. Here's to Adam, father of us all; he was in the right place when the leaves began to fall.' Everyone laughed and applauded this short interlude, except Tom. Tom said, 'Now that Ken is finished, let's bow our heads and say a prayer to give thanks to the Lord.' Thereafter, the jovial good time converted to serious discussions about children, grandchildren, and family members. I suppressed the urge to leave, realizing it would compound my error. I had failed to consider the feelings of people in a mixed group and didn't know our host was a devout Jehovah's Witness. I certainly didn't want to disrespect our host or hurt anyone's feelings. My problem is that I find humor where others don't. Occasionally I make a huge mistake by advancing humor at the wrong time."

I thought of a third example and continued: "Do you remember that black doctor who said, 'Mrs. Crane, you look very pale.' Smiling, I instantly remarked, 'Compared to you, Doc, what the hell do you expect?' He smiled but did not laugh."

• • •

The day passed quickly, but as evening approached, I recognized the staff becoming more concerned about me. The morning hustle-bustle in the ICU was relaxing compared to the excruciating, sleepless night now ended. Throughout the night and next day, staff members rushed to my side in response to the incessant alarms triggered as my condition deteriorated. I slowly accepted the realization that the end was not far off.

During the next several hours, my condition worsened as my heart raced out of control at critical limits. Nurse Wanda, assigned to the ICU, instructed me to forcefully inhale through a plastic gadget with a gauge that measured the vertical lift of a weight in an upright cylinder. I easily forced it to the very top. I received no prize as I usually did at the county fair by driving the puck to the top bell with one swing of a heavy, wooden mallet.

Craig, also assigned to the ICU, was dashing in and out, injecting me with liquid Lopressor. The injections briefly lowered my blood pressure about five points, but minutes later, it would surge an additional ten points higher. This went on hour after hour. I asked Nurse Wanda to have Alice bring me our estate file, which contained my living will. It was comforting to know our estate matters were in complete order, as intended, to avoid complicated legal problems when the time came.

Ken Jr. handed me the thick, red folder of legal documents as Alice positioned a bedside chair. Visibly shaken and distraught, with considerable effort she held her composure, a daunting task indeed when faced with the obvious, which belied my protests. "Stop driving yourself crazy with worry. I'll be OK."

"Your name has been added to the prayer list of many churches, and we are all praying for you."

"That's nice, but which way are they praying for?"

"There you go again with the jokes. Your friends and family are worried sick, but you seem to be making fun of our feelings."

"We've been through this before. I'm not making fun of their feelings. It's just that this is no big deal. We have no control over the outcome, so why take everything so seriously?"

I reviewed the estate file to ensure nothing was missing. "It's boring here, so I figured I could get a little work done instead of wasting time. Remember, today is the first day of the rest of my life. Lighten up and stop worrying; I'll be OK. It's getting late, so go home and get some sleep."

"But I want to stay here with you!"

Sternly, I said, "That's not necessary. I prefer you leave. Ken, take your mom home and calm her down. I'll be all right." Wounded, she rubbed my hand as she kissed me, and with tear-filled eyes, she slowly disappeared down the hallway.

• • •

There are times when I wish I were kinder and gentler, but occasionally circumstances do not allow me that luxury. At such times, I often think of Popeye the Sailor Man: "I am what I am, because that's what I am." Besides, I didn't want Alice to see my suffering or interfere with the urgent business at hand.

An expert estate attorney from Princeton had prepared my living will and medical directives in great detail. Regardless, state laws determine when and how injunctive relief may be applied, even when a living will clearly stipulates: "If at any time I should have a severe and irreversible or incurable illness, disease, or condition, which in the opinion of my physician is a terminal condition, or if I am permanently unconscious, and such determination is confirmed by a second physician, I direct my attending physician to withhold or withdraw life-sustaining treatment. I specifically include in the treatment I wish to be withheld: cardiopulmonary resuscitation, mechanical respiration, and mechanically administered nutrition and hydration. I want treatment limited to measures to provide comfort and to relieve pain, and authorize the administration of pain-relieving drugs, even if the administration may hasten the moment of my death."

As my condition worsened, my clear, conscious mind feared living, but not death. I realized a major stroke might not be "terminal." The provisions of a living will cannot be carried out if the victim is conscious and able to eat, drink, and breathe but is otherwise totally paralyzed. In these circumstances, many people would be grateful to still be alive. I would not.

Euphemisms, metaphors, and clichés abound when we attempt to define life or death. When does life begin? When does life end? Neither can be defined without first defining the other. The thesaurus says that *death* is an antonym of *life*. Also, death is well defined by state and federal laws and by physicians. Death may be defined as "the ending of being alive" or "the cessation of all vital functions or processes in an organism or cell."

What is life? The general public and modern and ancient pantheons of physicians, theologians, and attorneys-at-law advanced often significantly different opinions. Until recently, stem-cell research was illegal based on the theory that it involved the taking of life, even when conception occurred in a test tube. Abortion laws differ significantly from state to state because there is no uniform definition of life. Consequently, well-intentioned professionals perpetuate life as *they* choose rather than honor the individual's declaration for death as he or she chooses.

My understanding that a severe stroke might not be life-threatening elevated my fear of living. I feared no one would honor my preference to die when my "life" ended. I defined life as a broad spectrum, physical and mental, requiring consideration of humanity's six senses: sight, hearing, smell, taste, touch, and paranormal. Life is more than the chemical action inside a living cell. For example, a few of the very obvious physical functions of life include walking, talking, working, seeing, hugging, kissing, protecting, defecating, fishing, and propagation; the list goes on and on. Mental functions of life are equally obvious, including a brain's cognitive ability to record and react to our six senses. All too often, these wonderful things are taken for granted until the functions are lost or significantly impaired. When faced with the loss of some or all of their senses, or if they are wracked with untreatable, excruciating pain, many people would conclude their lives had ended. But clinically, they are not dead. Most people will face the dilemma and ponder the dichotomies: "What is life? What is death? When should one surrender life and accept death?" Clearly, one fact is absolute: everything that has ever lived has died or will die. There are no exceptions.

• • •

Nurse Wanda stood near the foot of my bed in the ICU and with tear-filled eyes said, "I'm sorry, I'm so sorry. We're doing everything we can." Alarms were sounding and warning lights were flashing as my blood pressure soared out of control to a killing level. Craig was reading Bible verses to a dying patient behind the adjoining curtain. Nurse Wanda anxiously insisted, again and again, "Craig, hurry, please hurry!"

My head, like a balloon stretched to its limit, began throbbing with every heartbeat. Clearly, I was at the threshold of a blowout that could end my life. But would I die?

Craig appeared at my bedside as life-support sounds faded and stopped for my ICU neighbor.

With Bible in hand, this pious, solemn stranger asked, "Mr. Crane, do you want me to read any special verses for you?"

"Absolutely not," I replied. "I have taken care of business every day of my life. I don't have many feelings of 'I wish I had done' or 'I wish I had not done,' but thank you anyway."

Craig politely replied, "We want to do all we can for you, so is there anything else you would like?"

"Yes, there is. What you are doing obviously is not working, and you may be prolonging my death, but not my life. Here is my living will. I want you to unhook these machines and stop the alarms. I want you to turn off those flashing warning lights, put out the overhead lights, close my curtain, and leave me alone. I don't want you to come in here every five minutes to ask me how I'm doing."

"We're doing what we think is best for you, Mr. Crane. We want you to stay awake and continue answering our questions."

"My blood pressure is now 281 over 132, my head is pounding with the rhythm of a boom box, and I'm exhausted from giving you the same information hour after hour: 'What is your name? Do you know where you are? What day is it? What month? What is your age? When were you born?' I know what *you* want, Craig, but do you know what *I* want?"

"Yes, I do. You have the right to refuse further treatment. But do you understand what you are doing?"

"Hell, no, I don't! You had me sign all sorts of papers to absolve you and the hospital of certain liabilities. Did I understand them? Hell, no! But I signed them anyway. Clearly, the treatment I am receiving is not working, so now I want to do it my way. I believe I will heal in my sleep. So close the curtain, and I'll rely on a little divine intervention."

• • •

After ten hours of uninterrupted sleep, I carefully checked the range of motion for my physical functions. My five natural senses seemed OK, so I pressed a call button attached to my bed rail. I expected to give Nurse Wanda and assistant Craig a look of "I told you so," but much to my disappointment, the ICU was now charged with a completely new staff of professionals. A young surgeon entered my area and said, "Good morning, Mr. Crane. How do you feel?"A young surgeon stood close to my bed and asked, "How do you feel?"

"I feel great! My headache is gone, but I do have a little pain. On a scale from one to ten, I would say about a three. I'm really starving. Can I have something to eat?"

"I think so, but first I want to take your blood pressure and ask you a few questions...Your blood pressure is a little better. Do you know what day and month it is?"

Agitated and annoyed, I whined, "Please, don't start in again with all those questions."

"OK, Mr. Crane, I'll bring you a painkiller and ask the kitchen to send up a special order as soon as possible."

"You had a big stroke. You're going to be OK. I saved your life."

His expression seemed to belie his statement. So I said, "Sorry, Doc, I gave at the office," implying that he was looking for a tip. He smiled and without comment eased toward the next patient.

Pursuant to my requests, no medication was administered except Lortab for pain and various anticoagulants to fight blood clotting. Within three weeks, my blood pressure stabilized at 130/90. Postoperative cardiologists suggested a daily intake of natural supplements such as fish oil, garlic, and oats, with mild blood pressure medication.

Four years later, at age seventy-five, my average pressure stabilized at 117/75. My life was pleasant and completely normal, except for a slight loss of short-term memory. I still feel tinges of guilt, but I was not perplexed by these past events. My conduct was consistent with my belief in nature and the natural course of events. I can only hope that the well-intentioned professionals could distinguish clearly the difference between extending my *life* and extending my *death*.

I remain pensive and uncertain while contemplating how I will be treated when I again face life or death. Regardless, under the same set of circumstances, I predict I would do nothing different, including my gesture: "*Up yours, Nurse Ratched!*"

Alice & Ken-Fiftieth Anniversary

Are We Married?

Like most mornings, I awoke at dawn this sixth day of August 2005. Inspired to share every moment of this special day with my spouse, I gently caressed her and eased her awake by humming our favorite songs. Again, I challenged her to "guess that tune," but this time, she snuggled close and offered a stimulating, warming kiss. Suddenly, the "guess this tune" game became less important.

Later, calm and fully relaxed, we reminisced about our days in high school, the rendezvous on summer evenings between two buffalo hides stretched out beneath a cherry tree. My first true love, I was age seventeen, she was age sixteen. We talked about being apart while I was back in high school in New Jersey, she in New York, and my refusal to exchange class rings. We discussed the current high divorce rate and the wisdom of testing a relationship prior to marriage, as we had done for five years. Soon, the conversation drifted back in time, and I humorously remarked, "Perhaps we have been living in sin. Maybe an old geezer at the church will recall what happened that day, fifty years ago. Afterward, we can visit our old stomping grounds."

The forty-minute drive from Hudson, west on Route 23, provides an exhilarating view of the Catskill Mountains, especially at Point Lookout. On a clear day, for 180 miles, the fringe of five states can be sighted beyond the valley below. We marveled at the panoramic view, and with great anticipation, continued on to Prattsville. The small church in

Prattsville, New York was unchanged. It was still the same as when my high school sweetheart and I walked down the aisle precisely fifty years earlier.

The pastor and congregation of ten people warmly greeted us, questioned our presence, and did not applaud my brief testimonial. My voice echoed through this hallowed place of worship with guarded compassion. "Ladies and gentlemen, fifty years ago today, we walked down this aisle to be joined together in holy matrimony. We were poor as church mice; therefore, our wedding reception was held outdoors at my brother Howard's "airport farm" in South Gilboa, twelve miles from here. Fortunately, it was a perfect day that August sixth, 1955, allowing thirty friends and relatives to celebrate this glorious event. After 'you may kiss the bride,' I invited the pastor to join the festivities at the farm. I paid him five dollars for his services. We had no more money after paying for essentials such as the wedding gown, rings, and food for the reception. Our honeymoon was to be one night at Niagara Falls, but that didn't happen, thanks to your former pastor, who disappeared, taking our money with him."

Everyone froze with an expression of disbelief that thawed as I continued: "Here are the facts: my brother Don, best man, had spread the word that we had no money for gas or the one-night honeymoon at Niagara Falls. Unbeknown to me, my father-in-law passed his hat around and badgered everyone at the reception to contribute cash for our honeymoon. Late that afternoon, when asked, 'How much money did you get?' I simply replied, 'What are you talking about?' My father-in-law had his hat, but I had no money. The only person missing was the pastor. He was not just missing from the reception, but also missing from your town. I often wondered if he made an honest mistake. Did he steal our money, or was it the fault of our alcoholic fathers, who 'art' not in heaven?

"But folks, whichever the case may be, it's fine with us. It simply doesn't matter. The pastor signed our wedding license according to the law. He officiated at a marriage made in heaven that gave us the love to forgive each other's transgressions and cause us to be married fifty years ago today and never separated a night in anger."

Everyone was intrigued by the story, prompting their need for more information as we lingered after the service. An elderly church member remembered the pastor from when she was a young girl and the gossip at that time. She mused about his surprise departure from the town, never to be heard from again. She insisted that he did not steal our money. With a quick retort, I reminded her, "It doesn't matter to us."

She continued: "Will you come back? Everyone is wondering about your honeymoon."

"We probably won't be back, but this is what happened…Our gas tank was half full, not half empty. We drove fifteen miles to a trout stream where, years ago, we had spent days and late evenings together. It is across the road from a cave called 'the Devil's Kitchen.' It could be reached only through a hole in the ground, descending to a pool constantly churning cold mountain water from a falls seventy-five feet above. Secluded and unknown to the public, we often cooked hot dogs and marshmallows and swam in the deep, cold pool during the summer.

"We parked the car by the stream above the falls, being afraid to enter the cave at night, and built a campfire. Inspired by the gentle, babbling brook, the steady hum of the waterfalls, and the flickering campfire, I retrieved my guitar from the car and sang love songs to my wife. Cigarettes, drugs, and alcohol were not in our lives, except via our fathers (who may be in heaven). Late that night, the flameless fire glowed bright red and died out when doused with water. Totally at peace with the world, we retired to the familiar backseat of our car, cocooned ourselves in a Marine Corps woolen blanket, and welcomed dreamland like two snuggling puppies.

"The next morning, we shared a breakfast of corn bread, fresh-caught trout, and coffee. I sang a couple of songs but did not risk playing the game 'guess that tune.' So, spread the word throughout the congregation: your former pastor must have had a direct line to heaven. By virtue of the authority vested in him, through the grace of God, our honeymoon was fantastic."

Epilogue

A Wonderful One-Way Journey That Ends in Death

I often talk with my family and friends about the journey to death, a journey every living thing has made or will make. There are no exceptions. Is it morbid, negative thinking? Or positive thinking, a search for the ultimate answer to the ultimate question: "What is the meaning of life"? But why have so many, for so long, pondered and searched for the answer to a mystery that is not a mystery? It need not be a search, but a simple recognition of life.

The search began when humanity first recognized spirits, hallucinations, paranormal images, and, of course, religions. Millions of books have addressed the question, but only a few religious texts comfortably offer plausible answers—for example (not in order of importance), the Qur'an, the Torah, the King James Bible, and the philosophical texts of Buddhism (although it is perhaps not a religion).

Around 632 BCE, a prince named Gautama was searching for the true meaning of life. Traveling the countryside, he saw a sick man, an old man, and a dying man. "What is the purpose of life except to be born, suffer, and die?" For six years, he searched for the answer but never found it until a Hindu explained, "It is in your consciousness." At that moment, the philosophy of Buddhism was born

Jesus lived in the desert for forty days and forty nights until experiencing the divine intervention of God, the Supreme Being. The true meaning of life is to serve God. No matter how religious methods or approaches may differ, they have one concept in common: to guide people. Through such guidance, most people discover "the meaning of life." But not me.

The ultimate answer to the ultimate question is before us every day: to seek and hold that elusive treasure called "happiness." Metaphorically, happiness is the Holy Grail, whether found in the cosmos or here on earth; it is faith, wherever it can be found—in religion, nature, or compatibility with incompatibles. Everyone seeks happiness, but at what intensity or degree of satisfaction? That is our journey. Knowingly or unknowingly, that is our quest; there are no exceptions.

What has made my life so prodigiously interesting is that I've toiled away from the supernatural world; this left me in one world—the natural world—that engendered satisfaction and tranquility in one life, the one I have lived every moment of my existence. "I am what I am, because that's what I am." So says Popeye the Sailor Man; so say I. I have no last wishes and few feelings of "I wish I had done" or "I wish I had not done." You recall what I said after my brain surgery: "If this night I am to die, that is my destiny. Unhook all of these machines, turn off the lights, and don't check on me until morning. I'll rely on a little divine intervention." The year was 2001.

Like most people in their fourth quarter of life, I look back on the degree of happiness bestowed on me. The chapters of my memoirs reveal a plethora of interests fused together by events that constitute my life. My unusual experiences and unbounded interest in all things, I suspect, many people would have avoided, and certainly some experiences would not have been tolerated. Regardless, those were my choices, the alchemy of my own Holy Grail, explained in part by my spirituality, but mostly by leaning toward nature, a simple cause and effect: environment versus heredity, challenges versus problems. Unknowingly, perhaps, I am a Buddhist who found happiness, not by searching for it, but by recognizing the amalgamation of my identities as a self-reliant boy, taxidermist, dog trainer, hunter, fisherman, trapper, US marine, college student, farmer, landlord, electrician, plumber, carpenter, public accountant, and, as I approach the apex of my life, an aspiring entomologist. I am a wealthy man, but as for money, I am merely a pimple on a whale's ass. I am rich in many other ways. The key to my success—happiness—is in my consciousness, unlocked by my conviction to always do my very best with what I have to work with. I have no answers for others but include in the appendix position letters on matters of the heart.

I am writing this final chapter of my life in advance, guided by biblical lessons from Ecclesiastes, written by Solomon, son of David, king of Jerusalem. Ecclesiastes is the book of a man "under the sun" reasoning about life. His theme: all is vanity. "The same fate to all, to the righteous and the wicked; as are the good so is the sinner. The same fate comes to everyone." The message here is that of a bacchanalian: "eat, drink, and be merry, for tomorrow you may die." All living things have died or will die; there are no exceptions, and that's the end of the story. *But is it?* Ask Solomon the teacher. See the Old Testament's Ecclesiastes.

Family history indicates my life expectancy is to age eighty; I am now eighgty-one. Perhaps I will be granted time to continue my journey and complete the unwritten chapters of my life, during which time, hopefully, I will finish building my coffin. A fitting end for the lumber I have milled from trees that sheltered thousands of deer, descendants of those I hunted for much-needed food in the days of my youth.

Paul Tournier epitomizes the journey in *The Seasons of Life*, 1974, paraphrased below:

"When does old age set in? I didn't know until I recognized the success of the upward journey must inevitably give way as I learn to go back downhill. To do otherwise would be to dwell in the past, perhaps with some despair that would impinge upon the happiness to be afforded as I grow old."

My happiness includes compatibility with the successes and failures of our children, grandchildren, and great-grandchildren.

Consider the saying, "The saddest words from mind or pen is to dwell too long on what might have been." Tournier wrote, "Thus the hour for revision of values comes for whoever does not die prematurely." I recognized that hour on December 20, 2000, the date of my last will and testament. While "working my plan" in cooperation with my sweetheart, we gifted away substantial assets to our adult children. In so doing, and against legal advice, we opted for the present good at the risk of future despair if the value is carelessly lost.

My radical and authentic reevaluation of old age came about by accepting that "all in my life is not of equal value" (Tournier). Surrendering the past for true, intrinsic values in the future, such as deep appreciation of friends and family, is simply a matter of choosing. Choices, choices, choices—good or bad, life is a supreme vocation of choices. I choose to continue the journey as long as possible, acknowledging that the end is not far off. It is precisely that self-understanding of the moments in my life when, turned in a new direction, I would see ahead the dim glow of the Holy Grail that morphed problems into challenges, and I had fun.

My final challenge is to secure a happy death, but not knowing the manner of my demise, I may need your help.

To Whom It May Concern

What is life? What is death? Who controls them?

Any attempt to answer "issue" questions like these involves a plethora of definitions that may cause my death to be extended, not my life. For example, when I am deaf, blind, and aphasic, and I have lost the sense of touch, I consider my life ended. But because this condition is not terminal, I would not be clinically dead. I implore all who may read this to safeguard all resources for a purpose greater than extending my death. Do not leave me trapped in a pestilential prison with no way out except death that may be denied by well-intentioned professionals.

Will my plea be granted as my journey ends? Will my representative make all health-care decisions on my behalf and direct that all medical, surgical, or death-prolonging treatment be withdrawn, including food and water I can ingest if it is placed in my mouth? In addition, will he or she engage all legal means to hasten my death, believing my active mind is in great pain and requiring large doses of morphine? If this is done, I shall have completed a happy journey ending in death.

I must adjourn for now, but I offer one last thought:

Keep your *faith*, dear reader. It's the *only sure thing* you will ever have!

Kenneth V. Crane

Bibliography

Berger, Betty. *Heaven to Earth*. Bloomington, IN: AuthorHouse, 2009.

Deen, Edith. *All the Bible's Men of Hope*. Garden City, NY: Doubleday, 1974.

Ehrman, Bart D. *God's Problem: How the Bible Fails to Answer Our Most Important Question*. New York: Harper Collins, 1982.

Feinberg, Margaret. *Scouting the Divine: My Search for God in Wine, Wool, and Wild Honey*. Grand Rapids, MI: Zondervan, 2009.

Johnston, Mini J. *Identity: An Adventure in Zest-Filled Living*. Grand Rapids, MI: Zondervan, 1973.

Jones, Timothy P. *Conspiracies and the Cross: How to Intelligently Counter the Ten Most Popular Arguments against the Gospel of Jesus*. Lake Mary, FL: Frontline, 2008.

Lupton, J. Daniel. *I Like Church, But...* Shippensburg, PA: Destiny Image, 1996.

Saul, John. *The God Project*. New York: Bantam Books, 1983.

Silbert, Gerald, Henry W. Enberg, and Practising Law Institute. *Tax Sheltered Investments*. New York: Practising Law Institute, 1973.

Smith, Joseph Jr. *The Book of Mormon*. Reprint, Salt Lake City: Church of Jesus Christ of Latter-Day Saints, 1982.

Tournier, Paul. *The Seasons of Life*: Ninth printing, United States, 1974.

Watch Tower Bible and Tract Society of Pennsylvania. *Is the Bible Really the Word of God? The Truth That Leads to Eternal Life*. New York: 1968.

Appendix

Dear Diary ----------------- I DON'T UNDERSTAND ----------- December 24, 2009

Dear Mommy and Daddy

I just don't understand ! I can't quite figure out where to start, because I can only guess about the beginning. Vibes tell the beginning is a feeling like GOD, HEAVEN, and TRUE LOVE - Something no one can touch. It must touch You. --- Perhaps YOU don't understand ! !

I'm very happy and content even while not knowing how all my troubles began. Why do I have to suffer? I suppose that's what life is all about. Right now I'm warm and cozy, well protected, with a roof over my head and plenty of food and drink. The best part is that I don't even have to work for it. I enjoy my seclusion, but lately well intentioned friends and family infringe on my privacy. Also, you are becoming increasingly unpredictable and irritable each day. Extra pounds have changed your personality and my environment. You and Daddy keep bugging me. -- Why! ---- I just don't understand. ---

With fingers spread wide, Daddy rested both hands around my world, as if positioning a basketball for a three pointer from center court. You and Daddy are fooling around and laughing at me. I moved just a bit to signal my displeasure, but Daddy wouldn't leave me alone. He pressed his ear tightly overhead while gibbering strange unmanly sounds as your silly, childish voice urged him to be careful. My space has already been invaded and squeezed by your overeating. Lately, everything seems to be closing in on me. My world is coming apart and right now, I don't need more pressure in my life. But, Daddy wouldn't stop; I just don't understand ! Annoyed, I lashed out with a swift kick to his ear. You groaned a little as he tried again, but you warmly insisted, enough for now. One by one, we drifted into dream land. ---At last ---, peace and quiet -- ah --deep sleep.

Abruptly, I'm forced wide awake. Hour after hour I'm pushed, poked and shoved, as sleeping accommodations are constantly being rearranged. I've been robbed of sleep, rest, and comfort, the entire night. Suddenly, at 8:33 am. Saturday, March 28th, 2009, my comfort zone is torn apart. I'm struggling violently as a frigid, new environment, surrounds my body. Bright lights everywhere cause a foggy haze to register in an unknowing mind, as it frantically seeks that first breath of life. In pawed hands raised high, my arms and legs flailing wildly, through quivering lips desperate with fear, I scream out; Waaaaaaaaaa! Why have I been thrown out in the cold. No more privacy in which to suck my thumb. No automatic food or water. I even have to work just for air .

WHY-O -WHY did MOMMY and DADDY force me out of my comfort zone?

Maybe, I shouldn't have kicked Daddy in the ear.

I JUST DON'T UNDERSTAND !

Allison M. Demarest

Written by Great Grandfather

4/12/01

Dear Nanny and Poppy, How are you doing? I'm doing great! How is it in Florida? Here, it is about .34°F Anyway, here is what you've been waiting for,

CONTRACT

#1 Don't turn the t.v. up to loud,
#2 Don't sit close,
#3 No watching t.v. until homework is done,
#4 turn it off when mom tells you to.

Consequences

If we don't follow the rules we don't get to watch T.V. for the rest of the day and the whole next day.

By signing below we agree to the above promises

AGE	From	4/12/01
		DATE
8 yr	Shawna	
8 yr	Dana	
	9 Doug	
	yr	

John and Jane Doe
Last Known Address
Every Farm, Suburb, Town, & City   October 8, 2007

Dear Teenagers;

  Enclosed is a trended outline of the past, present and future life of John and Jane Doe. Their
lives, once properly controlled are now in shambles. The list s not complete and specific events
may be out of chronological order. Regardless, dangerous habits and misconduct cause serious
emotional trouble and waist large sums of money. Most teenagers are fully aware of this , so
why do adults aggravate them by continuously telling them things they already know.
The answers may seem obvious, but careful thought provokes much more. Why do people of all
ages repeat or perpetuate bad choices knowing that nasty consequences are sure to follow?

  The attached outline suggests a respectful dialogue of the How's & Why's is essential.
Confrontation is inevitable for all who want a life better than that of a bridge bum. Emotions
run high and tempers may flare; but that is the price for caring. Regardless parents, counselors,
teachers, and all others who care, have a legal moral responsibility to test your skills as you
approach life's dangerous cross roads. It is the test of your life..

  The outline is intended to expose and deal with issues that perpetuate anxiety , distrust and
unhappiness within a family. Alienation or criticism is not intended. Although that may be a side
effect if you fail to make proper adjustment along the way. The specific purpose of this outline is
to highlight certain life altering choices that wash away opportunities essential for a happy,
healthy life. Deal with it as you choose, after all, it is YOUR life. But, recognize people usually
get what they deserve! I am confident you will too.

  I extend my warm personal regards to the entire Doe family and wish the very best, especially
for you and Jane as teenagers.. If you require assistance in any way, please, please, don't hesitate
to ask for help..

Respectfully submitted,

Caring Adults Every Where

Encl.
KVC/kvc

K. V. CRANE

Teenagers and Their Life Altering Choices

All teenagers experience significant physical and emotional changes that usually stabilize during maturation. As one becomes solely responsible for their choices it is imperative to know that some choices are habit forming while others may simply be an impulsive mistake. Regardless, good choices made during this growing-up stage of life will promote a happy, satisfying life. On the other hand, bad choices may over whelm parents, as they try in vain to help their teens avoid depression, guilt and anxiety. Most teens initially make the right choices and those who don't, usually correct their mistakes as they mature. The remaining group of teenagers may be classified as ignorant, (uneducated, unaware, not knowing), stupid, (one who knowingly makes the same mistakes over and over again), and those who just don't care. This group seems to follow a familiar path. step by step as they descend to the depths of "hell on earth".

Choices - Choices - Choices; Good or Bad, Endless Choices will deliver the life YOU choose. Of course there are exceptions, but you will get what you deserve.

ALL CAN BE STOPPED — MANY CAN BE REVERSED— SOME ARE PERMANENT
1. Smoking alcohol   2. Lack of Education   3. Tattoos - pregnancy issue's
   Laziness   Conflicts with parents   aids, unforgiven hateful words

Trends: Once self discipline is compromised erosion weakens resistance. SO! Please, please, don't be so naïve as to think one step cannot lead to the next, even if the order may be different.

1. Sleep late - sloppy clothes
2. Disciplinary problems at school, grades decline
3. Wide mood swings, funky hair styles
4. Lazy, Bored, Hang out at shopping malls, and/or with wrong people
5. Start smoking cigs, then pot, try alcohol. Demand total freedom of choice. Complain that "you are always on my ass," "Stop telling me what to do"
6. Eye brow rings, ear rings, tongue knobs, nipple rings, navel rings
7. Deceive or lie to conceal bad choices or to avoid someone "on your ass all the time"
8. Steal, first cigs, then money to support addictions, usually from friends or family
9. Constant conflicts with parents, voluntary or forced to quit school, more tattoos
10. Plagued with anger, hopelessness, and depression, except with those involved in the same situations
11. Minor encounters with the law, followed by serious charges requiring court action.
12. Unwanted pregnancy
13. Good jobs available, but not for this young adult. Even the military doesn't want him
14. Won't keep any job. Depression deepens, Does nothing to improve his situation
15. Ignores court ordered support payments. Arrested or jailed.
16 Moves in with bastard child's grand parents; NOW, fill in the rest of this person's life..

Questions: Are you in this trend? If Not, Why & How - If Yes, How and Why?
   Will you stop or reverse this trend?   HOW - HOW - HOW ----- WOW ! !.

Religious Faith Trust + affectation

EXHIBIT-2

LAW OFFICES

WESTLING, LIME & WELCHMAN
71 ROUTE 206 SOUTH
P.O. BOX 636
SOMERVILLE, N.J. 08876

WILLIAM R WESTLING
DANIEL A. LIME II *
THOMAS J. WELCHMAN

* MEMBER OF NJ AND NY BARS

TELEPHONE 722-0770
AREA CODE 201

May 12, 1984.

Mr. Kenneth V. Crane
1011 Route 22
PO Box 897
Somerville, New Jersey 08876

Dear Ken,

It is 8 days since Friday, May 4.

When you called me at about 11:00 A.M. that morning, I was about at the end of my tether. Among other things, I was working under some very severe time constraints; I did not know where to turn; and I was not feeling very well. As I say, I was about at the end of my tether.

Your phone call turned it around for me. You gave hope, and gave me so much more. Now, more than a week later, I am still unable to describe how much those few seconds meant to me. Maybe, though, you will tell from this: when I went home that night I picked up a hitchiker for the first time in years. I always used to do this, but no longer. But I felt so good that evening I had to share. This guy was in his 40s and all he had was a big cardboard box. Maybe you remember, Friday evening was rain threatening, dark. I offered this guy a choice where to go: shelter or food. And when I let him out I gave him some money to get him the rest of the way. His look to me paid me back more than money ever could. But he really didn't know it was Ken Crane's kindness that had reached him by the side of the road that evening.

None of this makes much sense, but I need to tell you how I feel.

Bill Westling   *Died 7/15/84*

[handwritten notes: "✓ Okay Appendix 'Legal'" "Exhibit-A-1" "Copy to al chim 1/16/83"]

AGREEMENT

BETWEEN ████████████████████████

and

████████████████████████████████

AGREEMENT dated April 30th, 1983, ("Agreement"), by and between ████████████████████████████████ ██████████████████████████████ ████████████████████ hereinafter sometimes referred to collectively as "Partners" and individually by name;

W I T N E S S E T H:

WHEREAS, the parties hereto are joined together in a Partnership known as ████████████████████████, and have entered into agreements in the form of written memos and understandings over the years with respect to their activities in the practice of law; and

WHEREAS, ▮▮▮▮▮▮▮▮▮ desires to withdraw from the
Partnership and receive his fair share as herein provided; and

WHEREAS, the parties hereto have negotiated at great
length to arrive at this settlement, therefore, it is
understood that this Agreement supercedes in all respects any
other Agreements, memos or understandings, whether oral or
written, express or implied, anything to the contrary notwith-
standing;

NOW, THEREFORE, in consideration of the mutual covenants
and Agreements herein contained, the parties hereto hereby
agree as follows, for themselves and their respective successors,
heirs and assigns:

1. ▮▮▮▮▮▮▮▮▮ hereby withdraws from the partnership for and in consideration of the sum of ▮▮▮▮▮▮▮▮▮
▮▮▮▮▮▮▮▮▮▮▮▮▮▮▮▮▮▮▮▮▮▮▮▮▮
and hereby relinquishes all right, title and
interest is said Partnership;

2. The settlement shall be paid to ▮▮▮▮▮ as quickly
as economically possible, but, in any event, full settlement
must be made within five (5) years;

3. All parties hereby waive their rights to a full
accounting of the Partnership assets and liabilities in consideration of this negotiated settlement;

- 2 -

4. ██████████ hereby agrees to assist in an orderly transfer of professional responsibility to the remaining partners, and further agrees to give his full cooperation to the remaining partners with their efforts to retain the present clientele and maintain the level of income to the remaining Partnership; and

5. It is further understood and agreed that for tax purposes only said Partnership shall continue until further notice from the Partnership's accountant.

IN WITNESS WHEREOF, the parties hereto have hereunto set their hands and seals on the day and year first above written.

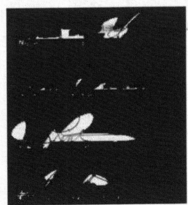

_____
WITNESS

ORIGINAL FILED WITH ~~~~

EXHIBIT A-2

FILED ~~~~ ~~1985~~
Chambers of
JOHN E. KEEFE, J.S.C.

GREENBAUM, ROWE, SMITH, RAVIN, DAVIS & BERGSTEIN
COUNSELLORS AT LAW

☐ GATEWAY ONE	☒ ENGELHARD BUILDING	☐ PARKWAY TOWERS
SUITE 500	P. O. BOX 5600	P. O. BOX 5600
NEWARK, N. J. 07102	WOODBRIDGE, N. J. 07095	WOODBRIDGE, N. J. 07095
(201) 623-5600	(201) 549-5600	(201) 750-0100
ATTORNEYS FOR	ATTORNEYS FOR	ATTORNEYS FOR

Plaintiff

Plaintiff
████████████

vs.

Defendant
████████████

SUPERIOR COURT OF
NEW JERSEY
CHANCERY DIVISION
MIDDLESEX COUNTY

Docket No.

CIVIL ACTION

CERTIFICATION

██████████████, being of full age, hereby certifies
that:

1. I am the plaintiff in the above-entitled action,
and am fully familiar with all of the facts of this case. I
submit this certification in support of my application for an
order to show cause with temporary restraints.

2. I am an attorney at law in the State of New
Jersey. My practice is an active general civil practice and I

had practiced law with my uncle, █████████████, from the
date of my admission to the bar, 1951, until ████████████
death in 1982.

   3. The defendant ████████████████████ is also
a New Jersey attorney admitted to the bar in 1957 who speciali-
zes in insurance defense cases.

   4. I first met the defendant ████ approximately
seven years ago on an alumni trip together, and we became
friends at that time.

   5. Approximately three and a half years ago, I
received a call from ████████ wife asking me to come over to
console ████. When I arrived at ████ house, he told me
that he was then leaving his former firm over a dispute about
clients. ████ further stated then that he did not know in
what manner he would be able to continue to practice law actively.

   6. At that time, I invited ████ to share office
space, the library, and secretaries with me (my uncle, ██
████ had recently passed away), so that ████ could continue actively to practice law. ████ accepted my invitation
in May 1983 and shared my office space at ████████████ in
Edison, Middlesex County, New Jersey.

   7. In the latter part of May 1983, ████ asked me
to form a partnership with him to allow him to attract legal
business from major insurance carriers. ████ urged that the
partnership name have his name first to attract insurance

carrier business. I agreed to allow the partnership name to be ████ and ████. I also allowed ████ to assume control over the day to day management of the firm, including control over the books and records of the partnership.

8. From the outset of our partnership, ████ and I agreed that all income and expenses would be shared equally. We filed federal partnership income tax returns reflecting this equal division.

9. However, ████ paid no money to me for all existing library, furnishings and office equipment when the partnership was first formed, despite his agreement to do so.

10. Shortly after the formation of the partnership, on or about September 14, 1983, ████ insisted that an additional capital outlay was necessary to upgrade office equipment and to purchase office supplies. At ████ request, each of us contributed fifteen thousand ($15,000.00) dollars for that purpose.

11. In mid-1984, ████ sought and obtained my agreement to allow ████ a higher weekly partnership draw, which was not to affect our equal share of partnership profits. We agreed that an adjustment in my favor would be made out of the partnership's profits at the end of the year.

12. On December 18, 1985, ████ presented me with an announcement to clients which he had drafted and signed and wanted me to sign. I signed this announcement on December 18,

-3-

1985, which stated that as of November 30, 1985, the law partnership of ███ and ███ was dissolved.

13. On this same date, unbeknownst to me, ███ sent
out notices to former clients of the partnership asking that
payment for legal services performed by the partnership be made
to ███████████ A copy of one such notice is annexed
hereto as Exhibit A.

14. ███ had done a considerable amount of legal
work in the asbestos defense area extending back for a period
of more than two years, a substantial amount for which,
unbeknownst to me, he did not bill the partnership's clients.
Approximately six months ago the insurance companies in New
Jersey notified New Jersey law firms involved in asbestos litigation that virtually all asbestos defense work would be done
by the firm of McCarter and English, and that all arears in
billings from other law firms had to be submitted for payment
by November, 1985. At that time, ███ engaged in a crash
program to have the partnership process and send out these
large amounts of bills. It should be noted that these bills
include also services which I, and an associate of the partnership, rendered for these clients originated by ███
Payment for these bills recently sent out has been arriving at
the former partnership's offices over the past month.

15. I have recently discovered numerous facts which
indicate that ███ did not in the past, and was not planning

-4-

to share partnership assets equally with me in the future, as
evidenced by the following:

  (a) On or about December 18, 1985, ██████ asked
me to endorse a stack of checks totalling approximately
$200,000 payable to ████ and ████ for legal services per-
formed by the partnership between 1983 and September, 1985.
████ asked me to endorse these checks as a favor to him
because the "new" bank was now requiring two endorsements and
he was planning to leave for a vacation in England. When I
examined more carefully the reverse sides of these checks, I
saw that they all bore the endorsement "Payable to ████
████" As a result, I refused to endorse these checks.

  (b) Subsequent to my refusal to endorse these
checks, I found a deposit slip in the name of ████████,
██., in the amount of ten thousand ($10,000) dollars, which I
believe to be partnership funds deposited by ████ into his
own account.

  (c) On December 20, 1985, the defendant opened a
pension trust account in his own name with ████, ████,
████ and ████ in Concord, New Hampshire. This account was
opened with a deposit of $190,000, which I believe to be part-
nership funds taken by ████. A copy of ████ letter
opening the account and transmitting the $190,000 is annexed
hereto as Exhibit B.

  (d) On or about December 22, 1985 I saw an envelope containing checks being opened by ████ secretary, Ann

██████, and I asked her about any instructions she had
received about these checks because ████████ did not usually
handle checks. She advised me that before ████ departed on
his vacation, ██████ said that only she should open the mail
addressed to ████ and that she was to place in ██████ desk
for safekeeping all checks received. According to ██ Burdasz,
Graham further instructed her that nothing else was to be done
with these checks until ████████ return on January 2, 1986.
These checks total in excess of two hundred thousand
($200,000.00) dollars.

16. On December 21, 1985, ██████ left this country
for the United Kingdom, and is scheduled to return on January
2, 1986.

17. Recognizing that vast amounts of partnership
checks were arriving at the firm subsequent to the partnership's dissolution date, I determined that I had to deposit
these funds. I opened a ██████ and ████ Partnership
Dissolution Account at the First Fidelity Bank, Account Number
██████████. This account expressly requires two signatures
before funds can be withdrawn. I deposited into this account
the checks described above which were to be put in ████████
desk drawer, after photocopying and inventorying these checks
and placing these photocopies and the inventory in ████████
desk. I also deposited into this account checks which I have
received from the former partnership's clients addressed to me,
after I deducted money to cover my overhead expenses.

-6-

319

18. Inasmuch as ▓▓▓ exercised full control over the firm's billings, to this day I do not know how much in receivables is due and owing to the partnership. Additionally, I do not know how much ▓▓▓ previously withdrew from partnership assets. Therefore, an accounting is necessary so that an equal division of all partnership assets and liabilities can be made.

19. Unless restrained, the defendant ▓▓▓ will continue to misappropriate partnership funds and convert them to his own use. Moreover, there is a substantial likelihood that ▓▓▓ will dissipate or conceal the partnership assets. The extent of this misappropriation and the amounts previously misappropriated by ▓▓▓ will be unknown unless the defendant is enjoined and made to provide a complete accounting.

I hereby certify that the foregoing statements made by me are true. I am aware that I am subject to punishment if any of the foregoing statements made by me are willfully false.

DATED: December 30, 1985

March 3, 2006

Dear Ken;

O' GREAT GARUE', that you think your are, I have a problem but don't know what to do! After filling the feeders the little birds gather until they are full. They love it and it's such a pleasure to watch them.

BUT, the hawks are now waiting. They attack without warning and kill the little birds.

So -- what shall I do?

Love;

Estell
"Trust in God"

June 10, 2007

Dear Estelle,

A wise Guru such as I, deals mainly with matters of the mind and heart. Although your inquiry deals with neither, as usual, I know exactly where to start.

- You must start at the end-

By feeding the birds, you have caused them to congregate.
You have interfered with God's work.
You are responsible for the murderous attack upon those sweet, innocent birds.
The bloody carnage; the death of history's treasured symbol of love and peace; God's special creature -- The Dove! —— Their blood is on your hands.

—— NOW ——

You ask this humble Guru- What can I do?
As usual, I have a precise answer for you.

- You must start at the end —

Shakespear said, "The fault lies not in the stars, Dear Brutus, but in ourselves."

You are luring those precious birds to their death. for a fleeting moment of your pleasure, while observing their frenzied last supper. Your misguided passion is sending the birds to their execution.

YOU MUST !
Stop preparing the table before the hawk!.

You sealed your letter -- "TRUST In God" —

SO --- To save your birds, you must start at the end!

...The foregoing parables were siphoned from the mind of the ancient one:

Monk Crane

August 24, 2007

Dear Monk Crane;
I have given your letter lots of thought, however it has all come to naught.
God made the flowers and God made the trees, He also made the birds and the bees, The hawk fall under the category of birds, He also provided food for all, some times a nicer bird must fall.
Hawks do some good they eat the field mice, and that's nice it helps keep some from coming in the house.
I still say in "IN GOD WE TRUST" Say what you will, Do as you must.

God Bless,
Estelle

Dear Estelle,   January 29, 2008

    Each of the short stories in your Feb. '05 "Guide Post" is quite interesting. They're similar to those in Alice's "Daily Bread" which provides amusing, casual reading. It's comforting to read nice inspirational stories that are fairy tales or wishful thinking. The story "Three Women, Three Faiths, One Dream, is such a story. The author, Hinch, is perplexed that a "Muslim, a Jew, and a Protestant had achieved what the rest of the world could only dream of." Why should he be perplexed? The women developed a friendship out of a common need for the benefit of their teenagers. He postulates, the rest of the world may dream of this. I don't think so. In fact, I believe the true answers come from an understanding of nature and not from religions.

    The stuff that would allow all people to satisfactorily co-exist is quite obvious, but it's no mystery why most people choose not to pursue that laudable, (not of this world) goal. The answer is much the same everywhere and can be observed everyday, in every home, city, or town, and in every back yard, field, or forest. All earthly things are different. That difference distinctly separates each thing, including every person, fish, flower, animal, and snow flake. Although some mutation is expected, it appears that environment and heredity will perpetuate those differences.

Charles Darwin advanced the theory, that life evolved through natural selection of a species. DNA science, proved the point. In fact, experts claim we are one DNA molecule removed from monkeys. Honest contemplation forces the conclusion that prejudice and discrimination are endemic to all living things, including every person on earth. Inherited traits have caused all wars, the 911 attack, and personal aggression toward other people or things. There are no exceptions. We look for and protect our comfort zones. That is why we mark of our property, record a deed, and fight anyone who threatens our space. I call it the pissing dog syndrome. That also, is why you prefer the company of your church people, rather then the general public. All living things seek out and protect their comfort zones. Discrimination and prejudice is perfectly natural and will always be with us until "Armagedon".

In the famous Scopes, Monkey trial, attorney Clarence Daryl eloquently defended the right to teach Darwinism in predominantly Southern Baptist public schools. The harsh reality is that we have descended from animals and carry inherited traits that provoke people who believe GOD created all humans, and the Anti-Christ corrupted those who believe otherwise. The worldly benefit would be much greater if the author's of "Guide Post" and "Daily Bread" stopped promoting secular fairy tales and strongly urge everyone to live according to the Ten Commandments, regardless of their race, color, or creed

    Alice and I donated a dollar to a homeless man in Key West Florida carrying a sign that read, "If they can get along, why can't we. He was leading a dog on a leash. On the dog was a cat. On the cat was a mouse. The police arrested the man for pan handling.

    The Book of Revelation, as I recall, informs us that after Armageddon God shall gather all the living or dead and separate those who have been his loyal followers. For a millennium there will be world peace. Love and happiness will prevail. The lion shall lie down with the lamb. All others shall be left to the Anti Christ. The Devil.

    Through the miracles of " Bernadette " we are told "those who believe, no explanation is necessary" Those who don't believe, no explanation is possible.

You asked for my opinion, so there you have it.

Love to all

Ken and Alice

I am a stroke victim & my memory fails me some time. So check out the details.

February 29.2008

Dear Ken;

I've read your letter many times. When I first read it there was just a twinge of anger, but that turned to sadness. Now I'll try to answer.

We obviously have very different opinions on the subject, so for peace in the family I think we should agree to disagree. And each keep our own view point.

I do have a couple of questions, If by some unlikely chance Darwin is right where did the creatures and bugs come from? How could we follow the ten commandants, there wouldn't be any since they came in Biblical time. And let's just say for the sake of communication , supposing there really is a Heaven and Hell, which place do you want to go. I have made my choice.

WE hope you and Alice are enjoying Florida, Alice would be freezing up here, Spring is almost here and I can't wait.

Don is working on some more of our kitchen cabinet doors, when he gets them all done it will really look nice and the kitchen will be much brighter.

God has been good to us ,He gave Don the wisdom to know how to do many things that most people have to call some one else in to do.

Have a good day, God Bless, Love Estelle

Dear Estelle;   March 14, 2008

Admittedly, my letter of JAN, 25, is quite provocative. My intention is to provoke a recognition that all flesh and blood beings, including homo-sapiens, are "created with certain unalienable rights" regardless of their genesis, race, color, or creed. I am hopeful that our knowledge and beliefs will expand to a point in time, when there will be no "tinge of anger" "that turns to sympathy, because one may not fit the preconceived mold of others. To "agree", "disagree", or "agree to disagree", is not my concern, although a different view point on politics or religion often offends people who prefer a narrow comfort zone of their own . Religion is, and always has been a double edged tool. It cuts both ways. - - -good and evil - - - -But most certainly, I am not qualified, or even want to, disturb anyone's religious beliefs. The subject motivates me to provoke thinking people to contemplate a bigger picture of life, rather than the tunnel vision many have acquired, through blind faith in segments of a segmented Bible. I believe, to understand life and death, heaven and hell, one must also understand nature. Even limited knowledge and understanding of nature can provide most answers to life's problems, great or small. Whereas, all religions prompt more questions then provide answers, except for those with blind faith in God. My favorite segment of the King James Bible is the book "Ecclesiastes". Its insight into life comes not from dreams, or some kind of divine revelation of Prophets, but from a deep understanding of the world and how it works. My interpretation, - - - NATURE - - - - - Please correct me if I am wrong, but I understand, the theme presented by the author of that Book, Son of David, King of Jerusalem, "Teacher" is simple. "There is nothing better then to eat, drink, and find enjoyment in their toil". Eccles: 2:24. Try Eccles: 7:5, 8:14. and 9:1-3 "The same fate to all, to the righteous and the wicked". "as are the good, so are the sinners" - - - - the same fate comes to everyone" The message here, as I understand it, is to "eat, drink, and be merry, for tomorrow we my die". All living things have died or will die and that's the end of the story. "There are no rewards or punishments after death! Life is all there is so it should be cherished while we have it" " A living dog is better then a dead lion". Eccles:9.4.

"Not intended to change your mind, but should expand our knowledge" Life 101

I'm tired of fitting houses, so instead, I'm trying to fit my mind!

MONK CRANE

ENCL: "DON'T SNAP YOUR FINGERS"
"The PROBLEM WITH THE WORLD IS ELECTRICITY".
LTR. "To JOHN & JANE DOE"

March 19,2013

Dear Kenny;
Every once in awhile I get the feeling God wants me share something. So I will try, please don't take offence. When I get these feelings I usually wait a couple of days and if I still feel I should send it I do.
I have been praying for you, and I'm sure Alice is praying too plus many others.
A long time ago I asked you if you believed in God> You gave me a one word answer. ABSOLUTELY.
Now you say you don't because of the bad things that happen to children.
You know the bible quite well, much better than I do. I don't know where to find certain verses, and they may be mis-quoted but the meaning is the same. They are.

Your ways are not my ways. He treats everyone the same the just and the unjust.
I think God is telling you HE will take you back into the fold when you are ready, you are His child and He loves you,

Enjoy the Florida weather we're still getting snow up here, right in this area, not a whole lot just enough to make things messy.
Thank you for the nice visit we had with you, I enjoy ed playing cards even when we lost .
Alice I had a dream about the four of us, we were all in your kitchen up here in NY, I don't remember all of it but we were having fun, in my dream you fixed yourself a sandwich on a Kieser roll sat at the table and said "if you want anything fix it yourself" And we all laughed again, it was silly but better than the nightmares I used to get.

Take care and stay until it gets nicer up here. God Bless, Estelle

The foregoing is a reproduction of letters between Ken Crane , in Fl. and his sister-in-law

,in up-state N. Y The originals are held by the National Historical Document Museum

located in the woods, east of Newman and Hiscox Road, Hudson N. Y..

Replicas are conveniently displayed at eye -level , in front of the north hole of

a wooden, two seater, outside toilet.

The donor felt the greatest appreciation for these historical documents could *be*

realized while relaxing during those hugely pleasing moments of defecation.

✓ Old Testament + New 7/15/10

Howdy Ken!
    You must be back from FL by now. Hope you and the family enjoyed the 4th and all its festivities. ☺ I was thinking about you the other day and thought I would drop you a line. Yes that's right Ken, I do think about you. Don't let that go to your head! It's probably difficult enough to get your hunting cap on as it is....lol *(that means laughing out loud for the texting illiterate and is the extent of my vernacular as far as texting is concerned).*
    If am not mistaken you have been doing personal research concerning being called by God. Another question you posed was, "Why is it that people who are Christians and that have come to God, all share having gone through some traumatic, stressful or for lack of better words difficult time in their life?" My thoughts are that the two questions are interrelated.
    The answer to these questions is trust. We need to learn to trust. The Bible consists of <u>66</u> books and letters are the <u>OT</u>, The Prophets and the <u>NT</u>. All share the common thread of humanity developing a relationship with God by being able to trust God.
    God to those who have not initiated a relationship is essentially something they cannot entertain as real. We usually use the five senses to interact with other people and our surroundings. When we interact, we use our senses to evaluate, judge and essentially decide what is real to us. Our physical senses tell us people are real. A person is a physical reality that we can interact with in a multitude of ways.
    God does not appear real to us, because He doesn't fit our criteria for what is real. In this, God is seen as an inanimate object or perhaps a delusional concept to lean upon when we encounter great distress. God in this respect is like radiation or even gravity. These are forces that cannot be seen, felt, heard, smelled or tasted yet we know they exist because we are able to detect their presence by their effect on us and our surrounding environment. Until that point, radiation and gravity were unknown to us and therefore in our limited concept of what is real did not exist. God to those who have not recognized His presence therefore does not exist. If He does not exist to us then He is a delusional concept for those that claim He does exist. We have difficulty trusting in others to say the least.
    So what necessitates the drama to get to know God exists? It isn't always that way. Again it is a means of initiating trust. A child raised in the Lord inherently trusts God because He has always trusted God. There was never any reason not to trust God. They have been taught as such and God has shown them that He can be trusted. The nonbeliever would call this brainwashing because, and as previously stated, to them God does not exist. Therefore, Christians are the blind leading the blind, i.e. blindly trusting what their parents or schooling has taught them...when in fact it is quite the opposite. It is because they see that they believe. But before they could see they had to believe and believing begins with trust.
    The act of asking for assistance is in itself an act of trust. To cry out to anyone in our distress is to place trust in that person(s) or thing. We trust that they will help us even if we are unsure of their ability to help. We make a decision that we cannot continue in the state that we are in and can no longer rely on ourselves to get out of the situation. In this we must extend trust, even to a stranger or that which does not appear to be real like the glass walkway over a canyon that doesn't seem to be there until we step out onto it. It can be very difficult and is always a challenge. One key that I have gleaned in all of this is that we must overcome fear first and foremost by recognizing what it is that we fear and why it has gripped us so. It is only in this recognition that we can move past the fear and into trust.
    If we decide to develop a relationship with the one who has helped us also involves trust. We begin to question their motives. Did they help us? Did they do so without stipulation? Did

they have an ulterior motive in helping us? Was it coincidence or did they come in response to our cry for help? If I continue to trust them in the future, will they betray me? These and many more are all questions each individual asks themselves before placing additional trust.

So, I would say that God uses these situations in order to give us an opportunity to accept Him as a part of our reality. Trauma and distress are not the only ways He interacts with us. There are times when He comes to us personally and physically or through messengers, i.e. angels, His creation, other Christians, secular individuals a book or even Christ Himself manifest in the flesh. God is not limited in His accessibility or His means of access. We, however, place limits on ourselves in our ability to trust or accept what is not always readily seen as we choose to see it.

What does it mean to be called by God? Sometimes this phrase is used to describe an individual who has shifted their understanding and now accepts that Gravity does exist. They may not understand much about it, but there is no doubt in their mind that it exists. It is the desire to develop a relationship of trust with the One who is most trustworthy.

Another meaning is where an individual has developed such a relationship with God that they know implicitly that God is asking them to enter into a deeper relationship with Him and pastor His people on His behalf. It is a difficult thing to know the difference between the desire to tell everyone about God because of your own relationship with him and knowing that God is asking you to pastor His flock. Most people that are called by God would not normally venture into that arena knowing what it entails. Again, it is in Trust that they are obedient to God and in His behalf welcome being a servant to His people.

Does this mean that those that are called to the clergy are unable to fail? They are still human with all the characteristics that go with that. And, it is because of this that they will undoubtedly fail to the degree of their humanity. We cannot escape our humanness and in that can only trust in God's grace.

I hope my long winded Response helped to answer some of your questions.

RANDY PIKE God's cowboy
270 COUNTY Rt. 17
VALATIE, N.Y. 12184
518-935-8451

K. V. CRANE

Dandy Randy,   August 1, 2010

What a pleasant surprise to have received your dissertation of "trust". Politics and religions evoke extreme provocative reactions with most people, causing them to avoid meaningful unbiased discussion of the subjects; but not me! The more provocative the more I like it. It stimulates a deeper understanding of people and things. How many people care enough or take the time to learn about the endless mysteries around us, every day, here and beyond? For example: Do Ants Have Assholes?

Since I am interested in all things, here and beyond, it should be no surprise, therefore, that I am compelled to respond to your explanation of the force, "trust" may exert on people choosing to become an apostle for God. "So what necessitates the drama to get to know God exist"? Can it simply be a lofty choice of profession? Is it man's attempt to ponder the imponderables, explore the unknown, or is it nature at work, at its finest? So here it comes, from the testicles of knowledge, balls and all.

"Trust" isolated, is easy to explain. It requires endless effort to attain, but can be lost in a heart beat. However, when "trust" is linked with religion it invades the very fiber of every living animal, except humans without a conscience. You postulate, one cannot have religion without "trust"; I agree. But, one can have "trust" without religion, however it must be learned, inherited, or perhaps both. The 23rd Proverb teaches us to "trust in God with all your heart and not lean on your own understanding"; on the other hand, *but are within the species. they cannot be tame.* wolves, cottontail rabbits, and a few others inherit "trust". Regardless, most well trained animals, including humans, mitigate fear with "trust". It is the unresolved, age old, conundrum - Heredity vs. Environment as explained by Sigmund Freud's experiments with "conditioned responses" such as Pavlov's dog.

The central question to be answered is, why do so many people throughout the world seek religion. What prompts the "calling" to be a Priest, Pastor, Rabbi, Monk, Shaman, or witch doctor; a BrigamYoung, Charles T. Russell, or Mahatma Gondi; a Jim Jones, Harry Krishna, or the wacko from Waco? Did each experience an epiphany or is it a means to become an alpha male or matriarch? Is it self- aggrandizement? It appears to be another age old conundrum - Nature vs. Religion, as juxtaposed by Clarence Darrow in the Scopes/Monkey trial of 1925. Ultimately the answer to such questions is simply an opinion.

Opinions, opinions, opinions, wonderful opinions, we all have them! But the credibility of an opinion is measured by trusting the accuracy of the information supporting the opinion. To do that requires more than faith, more than "Trust", we must think, even if it is contrary to the 23 Proverb.

When asked, "DO YOU BELIEVE EVERY WORD IN THE BIBLE", a true believer must answer-YES, because the Bible is the word of God. But many theologians, seminary scholars, and a host of others, try in vain to answer the question, "Is The Bible Really The Word of God". Volumes have been written expressing secular opinions formed by trust in God and the Bible. But which God? Which Bible? To most people the answer is obvious, but is it? The battle within the general religious population of the world has raged on since 2000, BCE, still there is no answer, scientifically or otherwise. Check out the following:

1) "The Sumerian King List" reports eight Gods of Babylonia:

    1st   "A-Luim" ruled for 28,800 years
    2nd "Alalgar" ruled for 36,000 years
             2 Kings ruled for 64,800 years
    3rd   et.al. 8 Kings, as Gods, ruled for 241,000. Years.

2) Belief in an immortal soul can be traced from Babylonian myths through Egyptian, Greek, and Roman MYTHOLOGY to Christendom.

3) Some historians say that Hinduism had its roots around 3500 BCE in a mass migration of people into a valley located mainly in Pakistan. It is claimed that Hinduism has 330 million Gods, yet it is said Hinduism is polytheistic. How can that be? Then came the reform religions, lets consider a few simply for example.

MEMOIRS

Dandy Randy, Aug. 1, 2010, pg. 2

Sikhism, with treaties written about 600-300 BCE that set out the reason for all thought and action according to Hindu philosophy. They "worship an elephant head, God of good fortune". "Phallic symbols are venerated by Hindus as God of fertility". Jainism, "Jains worship a 57 foot high image of a saint" whose karma sparked Buddhism". This stuff is happening even today, in the year of our Lord 2010.

4) A majority of the writings from Egypt, Assyria, Persia and Babylon were devoted to the king or national Gods. This begs the question, are those writings (scriptures) honest. Should we "Trust" without thought of creditability? Histories at that time were compiled by priestly scribes whom vigorously opposed the religion of the Jews. By favoring their king, (God) accuracy and honesty may have been compromised. At the very least, they exaggerated their views, cuneiform inscriptions prove it.

5) Exodus, reports Jews are Gods chosen people. He spoke to millions through Moses who received the Ten Commandments at Mt. Sinai around 1513 BCE, written on a stone by God with his finger.

6) Around 632 BCE. "Gautama", inspired by Buddhism while searching for "Truth", saw a sick man, an old man, and a dieing man. "What is the purpose for life except to be born, suffer, and die"? For six years he searched for the answer, but never found it until a Hindu explained, "It is your conscience".

7) Much of the foregoing is based on dreams, superstitions, hallucinations, fears, and down-rite fabrications to gain control over the pack. -- Mythology -- Christianity, on the other hand, was first written in Greek 100 BCE. But what is the basis for Christianity, myth or fact? What shall we TRUST? The 27 books comprising the New Testament, Paul's 14 letters, followed by "Revelations" written by John, all convincingly declaring Jesus is the Messiah? Should we TRUST The 39 books of the Old Testament, denying Jesus is the Son of God? Should we TRUST the Bible, the Koran, or Buddhism. It takes more than TRUST. Each has suffered a shipwreck on the rocks of faithlessness, greed, and self-indulgence. "Believers" have fostered wars, enslaved nations, tortured and killed millions upon millions of people, all in the name of religion, whose catalyst was Mythology or otherwise.. There is little difference between the churched and the unchurched largely because of a lack of knowledge and faith in the common thread that connects all the Bibles, religions, and Myths for one purpose; the pursuit of happiness now or everlasting. I suggest that is the only reason we have holey people such as Priests, Pastors, Rabies, etc. No matter what gender, race, color, or creed, "Believers" cannot survive without hope for that elusive part of life called happiness. Who can find it without serving God?

"Glory, Glory, Hallelujah His Trueth Is Marching On" Thus, it goes on and on throughout the world; each sect placing their trust in their God, their way; but WHY. The plethora of reasons is as varied as the peoples of the world. Regardless, The answer can be found in "The Miracles of Bernedet" "Those who believe no explanation is necessary. Those who don't believe, no explanation is possible"

Keep The Faith Brother, it's the only sure thing you will ever have.

Monk Crane

P.S. Please remember, this is the progeny of a brain damaged by a nearly fatal cerebella infarction, surgically removed through curved holes in the back of my head. Who knows what other crap impregnated in the hemispheres of my brain remains or was sucked out along with the mass of dead dural tissue?

Ha, Ha. Please spare me your answer!

332

9 - Dec · 2013

Rev. DR. Randall Pike
PO Box 412
Larimore, ND 5?-51-0412

582.51

Felix dies Nativitatis!
And thank God for Latin translations on Google.
Merry Christmas Everyone.

Certainly for me, 2013 has been a Blessed year. I have had the opportunity to gather with friends and family that I have not seen in many years. In as much as it has brought joy, there has also been loss. It pains me to see loved ones suffer, yet, it is also a blessing to be able to offer prayers and comfort to those in need. Believe me when I say I walk this path beside you in prayer and empathy. You are not alone. The Christ, Our Lord, does not look down from above as if seated upon a lofty perch, but walks with you in this season of remembrance. I use the word season, because these times of remorse shall pass and transition into a new Spring. Not that we shall forget our loved ones and friends, or even the pain of their passing, but that we remember all the more the joy they brought while sharing their time here with us.

There are those among you who have fallen and raised yourselves up again. I say, *"Drive on, my friend! May the Lord strengthen your girth in truth and shod your feet with the readiness that comes from the Gospel of Peace. Raise the shield of Faith to quench the fiery arrows of thine enemies, donning the helmet of your salvation in thought word and deed, and forget not the Sword of the Spirit, which is the Word of God, The Christ, sharp enough to cleave soul and spirit. Above all, protect your heart with the breast plate of righteousness in that we are not righteous of our own accord, but in the sacrifice that Christ has made on our behalf. Know that there is no greater love than this - that a man lay down his life for that of another. For not only has Christ laid down His life on your behalf, but was given authority to pick it up again in triumph over death. You have not fallen my friend, only growing in understanding.*

There are those among us that hold to an understanding that their salvation rests in that they are the seed of Abraham. I say to you, this has never been so. The relationships between Isaac and Ishmael, Jacob and Esau share kinship through Abraham with one God, but they do not share in the same promise. That promise of salvation is and always has been in the Christ. This is the reason we celebrate. It is through Christmas that we celebrate Mass in honor of the birth of our salvation, the Christ, Jesus of Nazareth, who lives and continues to remind us of our place within His fold as brothers and sisters, sons and daughters, and saints glorified in His Love for those who believe and place their faith in Him. This is the promise that we celebrate. A promise that was born to be freely given for all too freely accept. Let this be a time that we call upon the promise and become one in Christ, rightly accepting His sacrifice in our behalf, and placing our trust and faith in Him.

Hear the Word of God to all who truly turn to him.
Almighty God have mercy on you, forgive you all your sins through our Lord Jesus Christ, strengthen you in all goodness, and by the power of the Holy Spirit keep you in eternal life. --Amen.
The peace of the Lord be always with you, and with thy spirit.

-randy +

Christi crux est mea lux.

Rev. Dr. Randall Pike
Canon, Abbot, North and South Dakota, Diocese of Saint Alcuin

Theological Seminary
Order of Saint Alcuin of York

Rev. Dr. Randall Pike   January 9, 2014
P O Box 412
Larimore, N. D. 58251-414

A BIG HELLO FROM HUDSON, NEW YORK

It was great to receive your professional update letter. With every Merry Christmas and Happy New Year inspired people everywhere ponder "The Seasons of Life."

> "Spring - A Time to Be Born
> Summer -A Time to Plant
> Autumn - A Time to Pluck
> Winter - A Time to Die"

_____Ecc. 3:1 & 3:2 _____

Your letter seemed to acknowledge those seasons by informing us of yet another phase of your life and another step toward the laudable pursuit of happiness. It warms my heart to know another person has found their niche in life. Keep up the good work.

We haven't communicated for some time so here is our family update. Seasons come and go so fast, at least it seems that way with Alice (79) and Me (80), as we prove the old cliché' "time flies when your having fun," married 59 yrs. and never separated a night in anger. But - - - - ALAS - - - - Winter is upon us! Regardless of our season we are very fortunate to be healthy in body and spirit, except for my stage three prostate cancer. Regardless, we continue spending four months in Florida during NY's coldest weather and enthusiastically look forward to each trip that enhances our winter, invites an early spring and lengthens our summer.

While enjoying past successes we are learning to go back down hill, but don't allow our aches and pains to impinge upon the benefits of growing old. Alice reads incessantly, mostly about castles, knights, and medieval drama. She reads a chapter, toils with exquisite quilting, reads another chapter, settles in a new location for tedious art work on her paintings, then back to the book.

My life at the farm is that of a caretaker, maintaining 18 buildings, 5 homes and 300 acres of land, but here in FL things are less demanding. I relax in our backyard under a grapefruit tree and interact with the abundant wildlife drawn to the Withlacoochee River flowing into the Gulf of Mexico three miles downstream. Otters twist and dive scattering water birds as pods of manatees pass by, occasionally guiding a suckling calf safely away from our resident alligator sunning on the bank. These natural interludes provide a needed pause for mind and pen as I continue writing my memoirs.

Our favorite time of year, of course, is Thanksgiving and Christmas, a time for family and friends. As usual 25 happy souls joined hands around a dinner table spanning two-thirds of our huge, but modest living room. (You have been there). Random seating included our three children, now in their 50's, 9 grandchildren, and their friends, ages 15 to 32, and a 4 yr old great-granddaughter. Of course, like most people, they are challenged by their ever-changing "Seasons." Next came Xmas and New Year's that we combined with Alice's birthday, Dec. 30th, as a compromise for everyone concerned.

Once again the room filled, but this time everyone gathered around a fat Christmas tree partially obscured by the huge pile of gifts, all inexpensive. For three days the noise level was inspiring, invigorating, and downright exciting. The get-togethers are fantastic and fill potential voids in the lives of our family: BUT! - BUT! - BUT!

But, like fish and houseguests, there is high risk of spoilage after three days.

1. Dishwasher is overloaded
2. Ice maker is always empty
3. Washing machine & clothes drier -running nonstop
4. Toilet paper is at a premium, so we posted a NOTICE:
- - - - -USE BOTH SIDES - - - - - - -

A happy, successful future is our heartfelt wish for you. Please send us a personal letter to let us know if our wish came true. You know, one of those letters that answers the concern "I wonder how Randy is doing."

Ken and Alice Crane
274 Fingar Road, Hudson N. Y. 12534 518-828-4558
P O Box 928, Inglis, Fl., 34449   353-447- 2918
P. S.

I have enclosed copies of our prior letters touching on religious matters. Also enclosed are draft copies of the Prologue and Epilogue to be edited and included in my memoirs. I would be grateful if you would critique the information and grant permission for its inclusion in the appendix of my book, "Memoirs." It is nearly ready to be edited and published in color book form, and is intended for family, friends, and colleagues.

Keep the faith, brother, it's the only sure thing we will ever have.

Married fifty-nine years, never separated a night in anger

Made in the USA
Lexington, KY
28 February 2016